P9-AQG-673

Information Productivity

INFORMATION PRODUCTIVITY

OTHER PUBLICATIONS BY PAUL A. STRASSMANN:

Information Payoff–The Transformation of Work in the Electronic Age–1985
The Business Value of Computers–1990
The Politics of Information Management–1994
Irreverent Dictionary of Information Politics–1995
The Squandered Computer–1997
1986-1999 Journal and magazine articles on http://www.strassmann.com

INFORMATION PRODUCTIVITY

Assessing the Information Management Costs of U.S. Industrial Corporations

Paul A. Strassmann

THE INFORMATION ECONOMICS PRESS
1999

Graphics and Composition: Paul A. Strassmann
Printing: The Information Economics Press
Design and Production Coordination: Enoch Sherman

Order Directly from Publisher:
THE INFORMATION ECONOMICS PRESS
P.O. Box 264 or Fax: 203-966-5506
E-mail: Publisher@infoeconomics.com; Web page: <www.infoeconomics.com>
New Canaan, Connecticut 06840-0264
Printed in the United States of America
Printing number 2 3 4 5 6 7 8 9 10

Strassmann, Paul A.
Information Productivity–Assessing the Information Management Costs of U.S. Industrial Corporations
1. Strategic Planning. 2. Information Technology
3. Business Management I. Title
1999 658.4
Library of Congress Catalog Card Number 99-094582

ISBN 0-9620413-8-6

Table of Contents

FIGURES

INTRODUCTION

The U.S. has achieved its current economic pre-eminence by leading in the transformation from the reliance on the productivity of land, labor and capital to an economy based on information as its most important resource. The U.S. workplace now finds 55% of employees devoted to information creation, information distribution and information consumption.

The information-based economy has now surpassed the capital-based economy. For an U.S. industrial corporation the costs of management of information far exceeds the costs of ownership of capital. The U.S. industrial corporation now devotes more of its discretionary spending to information management than to owning its capital assets.

Returns on capital have hitherto been the primary focus of attention by shareholders and corporate executives, as attested by the emphasis found in all financial reporting. It is the purpose of this book to add to the existing repertoire of capital-based measures of productivity (such as Return-on-Assets, Return-on-Investment and Return-on-Equity) an additional measure that focuses on the productivity of corporate resources that are devoted to the management of information.

Though one can find an enormous number of studies about the productivity of land, labor and capital, very little has been done so far to communicate about the productivity of corporate information-creating and information-consuming resources in ways that are useful to business executives. In view of the enormous share of corporate spending on information resources it would be useful in planning, budgeting, as well as in performance evaluation to measure how information resources are used in creating Economic Value-Added.

The effectiveness in deploying information resources has potentially a greater effect on corporate financial performance than any other economic influence. That is because corporate executives have greater discretion in directing what their information management staffs will do than in setting the terms for materials purchases, employee compensation, taxes or interest rates. The expenses for information are mostly in the form of overhead costs. Because expenses for information are mostly overhead costs and not for costs of goods, the prudent decision-maker should have a wide array of discretionary options available for allocating this resource. Unfortunately, such a great number of options is not readily apparent in the absence of generally accepted measures of productivity.

Until recently almost all of the efforts on measuring effectiveness have been concentrated on assessing the productivity of every occupation except that of managers and professionals. The managers evaluate everybody else. The owners of firms have now realized that it is the managers and the professionals who make the critical difference in the fortunes of a firm. Managerial and professional wages and salaries now consume over forty percent of all compensation expenses. With recognition of these facts comes the urgency to treat information management as if it were any other resource. It is the purpose of this book to show how that can be done by concentrating on measuring the productivity of information.

Whether productivity growth is positive or negative is not a purely academic question. It is the subject of the most important economic debate at the highest levels of U.S. government, as this book is written.[1] This issue is central to the concerns whether corporate America is becoming sufficiently productive to sustain the economic boom of the 1990's without having to raise prices, induce inflation or sacrifice profits. Ultimately, U.S. national wellbeing and even national security depend on a continuation of historical productivity gains. This book presents evidence that there has been a steady rise in Information Productivity since 1990. However, these gains can be fully explained by favorable financial circumstances. The "computer paradox" remains. We can see computers everywhere except in economic statistics. Moore's Law, that has been widely cited as the foundation of a new stage in historical progress, remains a phenomenon of physics, not of economics.

1 Uchitelle, L., "U.S. Data May Understate Productivity Gains," *The New York Times*, March 31, 1999

It is the objective of this book to illustrate how to calculate and analyze the Information Productivity® of a corporation.[2] In Chapter 5 (Applying Information Productivity) we will illustrate how business executives can benchmark the productivity of their information resources to find out if they are deploying their information management resources effectively as compared with their peers and competitors. Included in the Appendix C is the ranking of the productivity of 1,586 U.S. industrial corporations. Appendix D features a list of 400 high productivity firms.

The primary audience for this book are corporate planners and budget analysts who are still searching for quantitative methods that would allow them to benchmark their organization's performance in terms that relate to business process improvement programs as well as to investments in information technologies. The methods outlined in this book and supported by the Information Productivity ratios for listed firms should be helpful not only as diagnostic measures but also as performance tracking metrics.

Appendix B (Importance of U.S. Firms and Women in Information Management) may appear as a digression from the chapters preceding it. It is included to illustrate that productivity is not only a financial matter but also a reflection of changes in the underlying global and social influences on productivity. This book is the second volume in a series that was announced in 1997.[3] It has a different format than what has been published so far. I trust that the inclusion of company-specific indicators and examples how to apply a new methodology will be welcomed by the readers.

Paul A. Strassmann, New Canaan, Connecticut

2 The registered Trademark for Information Productivity® was granted by the Commissioner of Patents and Trademarks, U.S. Department of Commerce in March, 1996 to Strassmann, Inc.

3 P.A. Strassmann, *The Squandered Computer*, The Information Economics Press, 1997. A follow-on volume will analyze the information productivity of the financial and services sectors of the U.S. economy. The Knowledge Capital® ranking of U.S. firms will appear shortly afterwards.

SUMMARY OF FINDINGS

The line items reported by U.S. industrial corporations as Sales, General, Administrative and Research & Development expenses offer the most reliable public estimates of what it costs to manage and coordinate a business internally and to communicate with suppliers and customers. This expense, normally identified as "overhead," is as good a representation of the costs of information management as is available from public sources.[4] It includes not only the payroll for the people engaged in information tasks but also expenses for advertising, promotion, consultants and information technology.

An examination of how the costs of information management relate to all other costs of doing business offer not only valuable insights into the "information economy but also the only verifiable measures of corporate information productivity that is available at present."[5] During the last ten years U.S. industrial corporations:

- Lowered the costs of information management required to deliver goods and services to customers;
- Increased per employee information management costs faster than employee compensation;
- Lowered information management costs in support of revenues;
- Lowered the ratio of information management costs to operating profits;
- Lowered the ratio of information management costs to net assets in place;

4 A more comprehensive analysis of detailed cost records is done when examining company-specific data. Strassmann, Inc. research shows that the audited data reported as public information understate the actual costs of information management. Generally, corporations tend to classify many of the information-based coordination activities of direct labor as cost-of-goods sold.

5 Government statisticians now acknowledge that they are unable to adequately measure the productivity of information-related work. See Dean, E.R., "The accuracy of the BLS productivity measures," *Monthly Labor Review*, February 1999 and Gullickson, W., and Harper, M.J., "Possible measurement bias in aggregate productivity growth," *Monthly Labor Review*, February 1999.

- Improved Information Productivity, but only on account of more favorable interest rates and not as the consequence of information technology investments.[6]

While these changes were taking place the U.S. industrial corporations also showed the following characteristics:

- Ninety-two percent of firms incurred higher expenses for information management than for the costs of ownership of their net capital assets. This makes the utility of asset-based productivity ratios (such as ROA, ROI or ROE) questionable as a measure of performance;
- Forty-two percent of firms delivered negative economic value-added (EVA[7]). This makes accounting profits inconclusive as a measure of operating results.
- There was no relationship between the costs of information management and profitability;
- There was no relationship between the estimated costs of information technology and profitability;
- Information management costs were concentrated in a few large corporations;

Although U.S. industrial corporations have recently improved information management performance, the record of actual accomplishment still falls far short of its potential. When one examines the enormous disparity between the top ranking U.S. industrial firms (in terms of Information Productivity) and the bottom laggards one finds that a large percentage of organizations are not productive. The bottom ranking firms spend huge sums on information management that does not deliver economic value-added. That acts as drag on further progress of the entire economy.

The U.S. industrial corporations are not even close to achieving what is possible by getting information resources managed with

6 D.S.Oliner and W.L.Washer, "Is a Productivity Revolution Under Way in the United States?," *Challenge*, Novermber-December 1995. Olliner and Washer are economists with the Board of Governors of the Federal Reserve System and have not been able to attribute productivity gains to new investments in information technologies. Idential conclusions are also found in D.S. Oliner and Sichel, D.E, "Computers and Output Growth Revisited: How Big Is the Puzzle?," *Brookings Papers on Economic Activity*, 2:1994.

7 EVA® is a registered trademark of Stern Stewart & Co.

greater effectiveness. It now becomes the task of corporate management to establish the improvement in Information Productivity as one of the key objectives for corporate planning and budgeting.

1.

INFORMATION MANAGEMENT INDICATORS

Information management costs now consume the equivalent of about a third of the cost of goods and about a fifth of the revenues of U.S. industrial firms. The ratio of the information management costs to the cost of goods and to revenue have been improving cyclically. The information management costs–the corporate overhead–has been rising faster than wages and salaries. There is no evidence that corporations have applied information technologies as a substitute for wages and salary costs. Information management costs are, however, a large multiple of corporate profits and remain completely unrelated to shareholder returns. The ratios of information management costs to profits and assets under management have continued to show a remarkable decline.

The Costs of Information Management

The purpose of this chapter is to display the characteristics of corporate information management costs in U.S. industrial corporations.[8] For the purposes of my analyses the costs of information management are defined as the sum of sales, general, administrative (SG&A) plus research & development (R&D) expenses. Industrial firms incur these expenses in the process of managing, planning, promoting and coordinating their organizations for the purpose of effective delivery of goods and services to customers.

Insofar as information costs may be classified elsewhere as production overhead (and included in the costs of goods) and as depreciation of assets (such as computers and office furniture), the

8 It should be understood that all dollar values, including data about individual corporations, come from the November 1998 Worldscope Data base and represent Fiscal Year 1997 annual totals.

reported information management costs are likely to be understated.[9] There is also a strong incentive by local management in decentralized firms to understate overhead costs as these attract the attention of budget analysts.[10] The motive to reclassify overhead expenses as direct cost is particularly strong for firms that engage in cost-plus contracting for the public sector where up to two thirds of information management expenses are loaded directly to the cost-of-goods sold instead of appearing as a general administrative cost.

INFORMATION MANAGEMENT AND THE COST OF GOODS

The ratio of the cost-of-goods sold to the cost of information management is an important indicator for assessing the productivity of information resources. It takes information to produce and deliver goods. That much is obvious. What few analysts realize is that the

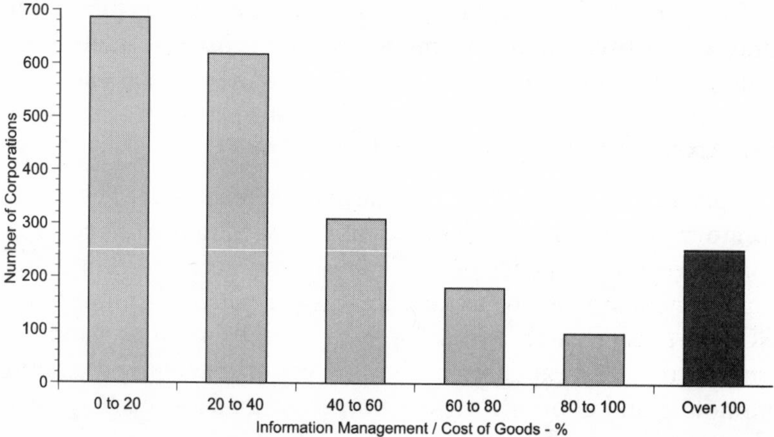

Figure 1-1–Information Management Can Be a Multiple of the Cost of Goods

9 This bias, understating information management costs in favor of their inclusion as costs of production and services was discovered in a number of consulting engagements where detailed cost reporting information was available. Inter-divisional pricing practices and the accounting for purchases will mask the recognition of the full costs of information management. For instance, in the case of outsourcing of information services, the purchases will be often classified as "cost of goods" thus reducing the reported levels of overhead.

10 S.L.Mintz, "The Fifth Annual SG&A Survey," *CFO Magazine*, December, 1998

median value of the information management/cost of goods ratio is 31.4% and could be much higher than that.[11] To produce a dollar's worth of the goods in 1997 for over half of U.S. industrial corporations required over 31.3 cents worth of information management

Out of 2,151 industrial corporations there were 254 corporations (12% of the total number) that spent more than twice the dollars on information management than on the direct costs of goods and services. In 36.3% of corporations information management costs exceeded the cost of goods. These were firms that incurred high marketing and product development expenses in producing high-value products, such as in the pharmaceutical industry. There were a small number of firms–mostly high technology start-up firms–that spent up to nine dollars for information management for every dollar's worth of cost of goods.

It Takes Less Information to Deliver Goods Now

Over an extended time period the relationship between Information Management and the Cost of Goods is a telling indicator of the effectiveness of how individual firms manage their coordination of employees, suppliers and customers. In fact, the ways in which the information resources are organized and how they are deployed offer the greatest leverage for improving corporate profitability. The marketplace largely determines the costs of raw material, rent expense, capital and labor. Management can affect them with less choice than when they direct their own operations.

One of the most useful ways of examining Information Management trends is to measure the amount of information required to produce a dollar's worth of goods over a ten year period. If firms succeed in lowering their costs of information (by lowering their

11 Median value for 2,151 US industrial corporations in 1997. Throughout this chapter the "median" is used as the measure of the center of the widely varying distribution of values, ratios and other indicators. "Median" is the middle value. That is, half of the values in a data set are less than the median value and half are greater than it. The computation of the median may be more difficult than other measures of the center of a distribution, such as averages, if calculated by manual methods. Because of the enormous range of corporate data, median is the preferred indicator because it is not affected by occasional extraordinary data values.

overhead ratios) and at the same time enhance their ability to sell goods to customers at attractive prices, their economic viability improves.

Figure 1-2 shows the data how much information U.S. industrial firms required in producing their goods and supporting services. The ratio of how many dollars of the cost of goods were supported by a dollar's worth of information management shows a period of decline from 1987 to 1990. That was followed by an increase in 1990 and again from 1995 to 1997.

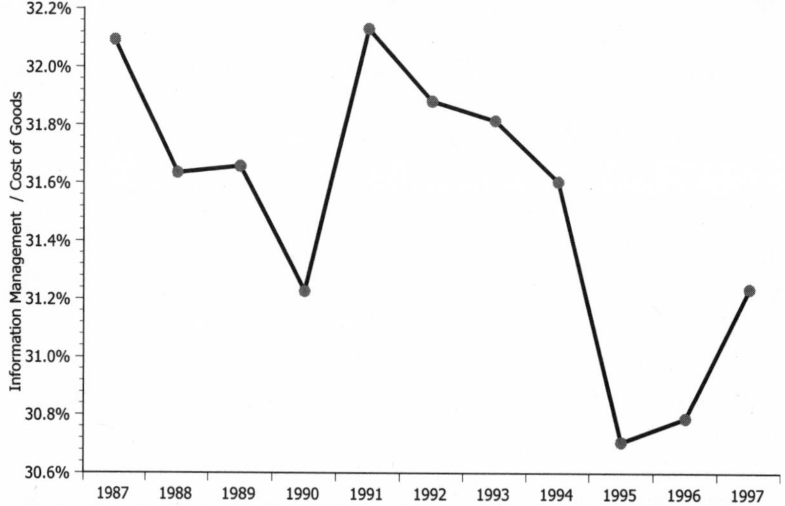

Figure 1-2–Information Management/Cost of Goods Ratio Improved [12]

Since 1987 the amount of information required to produce a dollar's worth of goods has shown a downward trend in two cycles. These cycles most likely reflect the prevailing five-year waves of adoption of new information technologies. The important observation is that the overall trend is favorable. Judging from this one ratio alone one could tentatively conclude that the "productivity paradox" could be disappearing. For U.S. industrial corporations it now takes less information to produce goods than was the case ten years ago.

12 Medians of value for 1,213 firms. Because of start-ups, mergers and changes in reporting practices ten years of financial data were available only for that number of firms.

The long-claimed – but never conclusively demonstrated – favorable effect of information technologies on the amounts of information required to manage corporations is finally making an appearance in corporate financial data. However, the cyclical characteristic of this ratio suggests – coinciding with a period of unusually favorable raw materials and labor costs – that we may have to wait for at least another ten years before safely concluding that U.S. industrial corporations have succeeded in permanently lowering their costs of information management.[13] Meanwhile, the best a corporation can do is to add the Information Management/Cost of Goods ratio into its portfolio of critical indicators that must be monitored for planning, budgeting and performance evaluation purposes.

General Electric – An Example of Contributions to Excellence

According to Fortune magazine the General Electric Corporation (GE) is one of the most successful U.S. corporations as measured in terms of its increase in shareholder value over the last decade.[14]

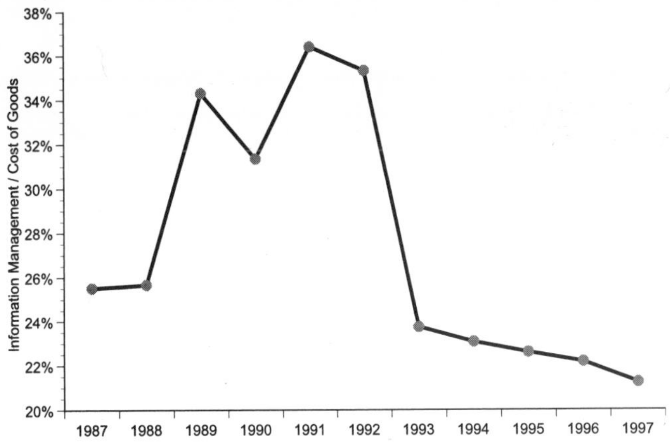

Figure 1-3 – GE's Ratios Have Improved Recently

13 The Commodity Research Bureau Index of all commodity prices shows a decline from 255 in 1996 to 198 in 1998 – a 22% reduction according to *The New York Times*, February 17, 1999, p. A8

14 Gains in shareholder value are measured as annual changes in market capitalization (e.g. share price x number of shares outstanding).

To illustrate the utility of the Information Management/Cost of Goods ratio as one of the planning, budgeting and effectiveness evaluation indicators, Figure 1-3 displays the ten-year ratios for the General Electric Corporation:

The General Electric data show that in the ten-year period from 1987 through 1997 their Information Management/Cost of Goods ratio improved from 25.5% to 21.2%. It is also interesting to note that the General Electric corporation shows a similar jump in this ratio around 1990 as was found for the medians of all U.S. industrial corporations. It seems that the "back-to-customer quality" focus that shows up in the financial results delivered since 1993 reflects the abandonment of management's preoccupation with other management theories and return to business fundamentals.

While the General Electric's Information Management/Cost of ratio was deteriorating from 1988 until 1992, the gains in the firm's market capitalization was only moderate and not superior to comparable industrial corporations.

Subsequent to 1993 General Electric was able to reverse years of declining information management/cost ratios and begins an era of sustained improvement. To further test the proposition that share-

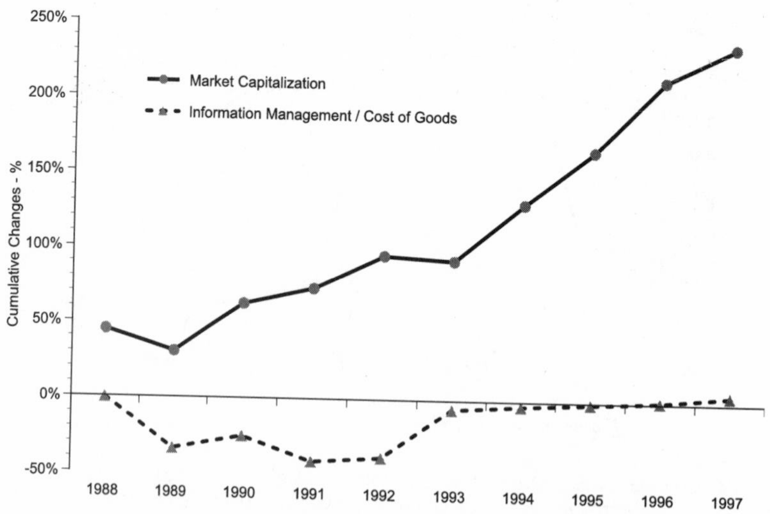

Figure 1-4–GE's Improvements Track Shareholder Value

holders react favorably to the improvement in GE's financial results, the above Figure shows a graph that compares improvements in the information management/cost of goods ratio as compared with the gains in market capitalization of the General Electric Corporation.

Certainly, the shareholders must have recognized this as a favorable development. The remarkable gains in General Electric's market capitalization since 1993 also coincide with its drive to improve its overhead cost ratios.

The purpose of the General Electric case study was not to prove that the information management/cost ratio is directly related to stock prices. Nevertheless, executives ought to consider that shareholders are likely to view with favor any such improvements as a sign of superior corporate management.[15]

INFORMATION MANAGEMENT PER EMPLOYEE

The cost of information management per employee is another measure of the complexity of businesses. A high level of SG&A plus R&D expense per employee is a telltale indicator of a firm's information intensity.

Our corporate database shows that the median value of information management expenditures per employee for U.S. industrial corporations was $38,304 per year, which is materially greater than the average wages and salaries in industrial firms as reported by the U.S. Bureau of Census.[16]

Since employees engaged in production generally receive lower compensation that those who are engaged in information occupations, each dollar's worth of wages included in the cost of

15 The GE case is not an isolated instance. Several of my corporate consulting studies showed similar relationships.

16 Based on a sample of 2,115 US industrial corporations in 1997. The compensation of full-time wage and salary workers in the same period was $32,983, per U.S. Bureau of the Census, *Statistical Abstract of the United States: 1997*, Washington, DC, 1998, "Table 666–Annual Total Compensation" and "Table 668–Annual Percent Changes in Earnings".

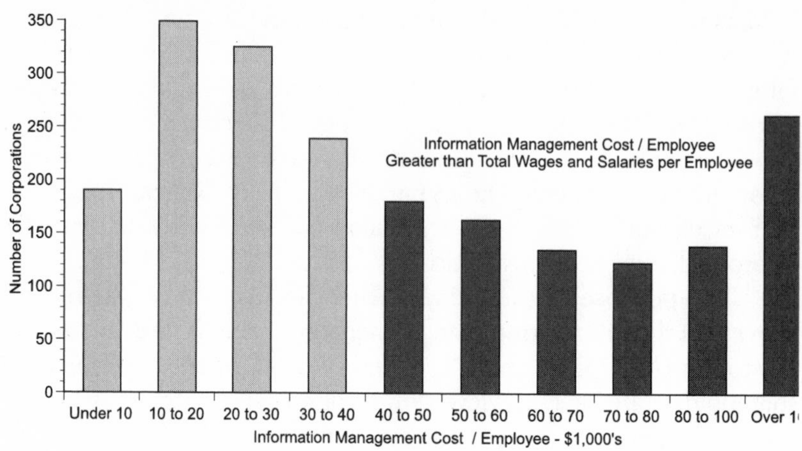

Figure 1-5–In 55% of Corporations Information Management Costs Exceed Salaries

goods must be burdened by a substantial allocation for salaries incurred in supervision, coordination and administration.

The above Figure shows that the information management costs per employee for about half of the U.S. industrial corporations are equal or greater than average compensation. That explains why in a number of corporations the direct labor cost of goods and services is often burdened by an add-on for overhead costs that may range anywhere from 50% to over 100%.

Information Costs Rising Faster than Wages and Salaries

Figure 1-6 shows that the costs of coordination for a firm, as measured by the information management per employee ratio, have been rising steadily.

17 This dramatic decline, below the cost of living increases, is coincident with the spurt in corporate re-engineering that must have inhibited salary increases. If that hypothesis is correct then the effect of re-engineering was not to reduce the total costs of information management, but only temporarily lower the compensation of the intimidated managers and administrators.

In the 1987-1997 period this amounted to a cumulative increase of 58%: The peak year for increases in information management costs was in 1991, followed by a sharp drop in 1992.[17] After 1994 the annual cost increases resumed their trend of inflating faster than the cost of living index. On a cumulative basis, the costs of management per employee have risen faster than employee compensation levels. This rise in costs was not only a matter of wage gains, but also an

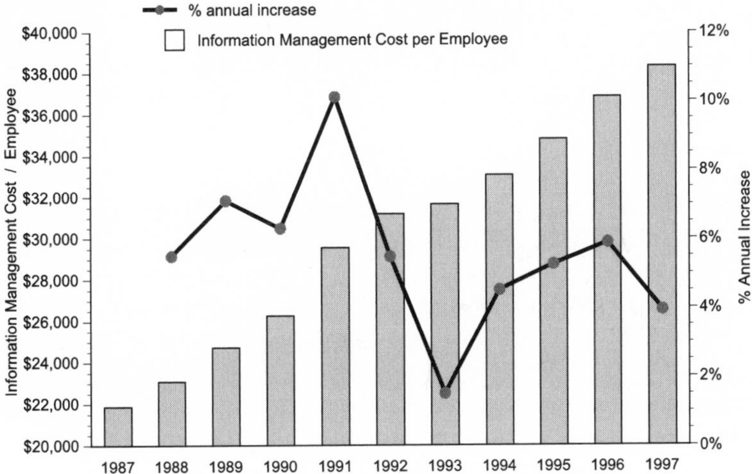

Figure 1-6–Information Management Costs Show Large Increases

increase in the overall levels of spending for information management. These increases have consistently exceeded the annual percent changes in earnings and compensation of employees.[18]

In the ten-year period from 1988 through 1997 the cumulative increase in the Information Management Cost per Employee was 57.9% as compared with reported gains in employee wages and salaries of only 40.5%.

The most likely explanation for this difference in these rates is the change in the composition of the workforce. Corporate bud-

18 U.S. Bureau of the Census, *Statistical Abstract of the United States: 1997*, Washington, DC, 1998, "Table 668 Annual Percent Changes in Earnings".

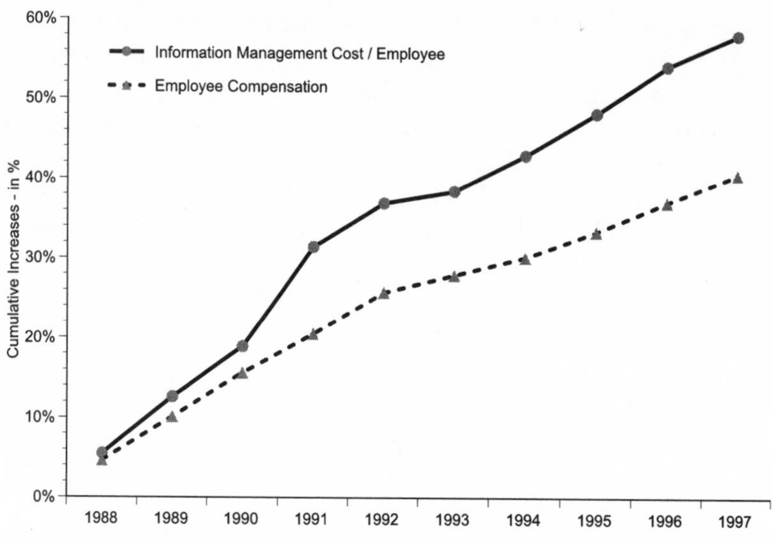

Figure 1-7–Information Management Costs Increased Faster than Compensation

getary practices that emphasize headcount controls offered a strong inducement to operating managers to shift the mix of their staff from lower-priced administrative personnel to higher cost professionals, consultants and outsourcing contracts. This disparity would have been even greater had it not been for rapid additions of lower-seniority (and lower wage) women to the workforce.

Personnel in higher cost occupations are working longer hours than people in non-managerial jobs.[19] If they were fully compensation for the additional time, at overhead rates, the information management cost ratios would be even more unfavorable than shown in our analyses. One of the presumed benefits of information technologies–reduction in the amounts of information work–is not

19 Koretz, G., "Who's Stressed Out at Work–Higher Skills mean longer hours," *Business Week*, April 12, 1999. According to a study by Jacobs, J.A. and Gerson, K., reported in the *Review of Social Economy*, more than 33% of professional men and 17% of professional women now put in 50+ hour weeks, as compared with a smaller number of excess hours by all others. College graduates spend about four time more hours in excess of a 50 hour week than those with less than a high school degree.

apparent from the available data. The number of information workers has increased relative to everyone else in the workforce while they are working longer hours.

Effects of Information Technology on the Costs of Information Management

If information technologies, with rapidly declining prices, were as effective as is generally claimed, then cheap computers would be substituted for expensive information labor at an accelerating rate. If that were so, then information management costs per employee would have increased at a slower rate than the labor cost index of wages and salaries. That is not the case. In fact, we have here an indication that the presumed favorable effects of computer investments on trading of technology for labor costs may not be valid.

Perhaps the best way to show how rapidly decreasing information technology costs did not substitute for gradually increasing information management labor is to examine how the Federal government accounts for the assumed contributions of computers to the growth in national wealth.

In a recent report on the emerging "digital economy" government statisticians produced a table of deflationary indexes for calculating the "real" value of the I.T. industries' contributions to U.S. economic prosperity.[20] Accordingly, a dollar's worth of I.T. spent for a computer was actually worth $3.24 in 1996, when compared with what a dollar purchased in 1990:

	1990	1991	1992	1993	1994	1995	1996
Actual Spending	$1.00	$1.00	$1.00	$1.00	$1.00	$1.00	$1.00
Deflation-Adjusted Worth of IT	$1.00	$1.12	$1.35	$1.61	$1.80	$2.28	$3.24

Figure 1-8 – Computer Spending Assumed to be More Valuable

20 "The Emerging Digital Economy," *Secretariat for Electronic Commerce*, U.S. Department of Commerce, April1998. http://www.ecommerce.gov/emerging.htm. The deflation index averages 17.5% per year.

If the presumed labor-substitution benefits of computers were, as represented by the U.S. Department of Commerce, actual rather than hypothetically "real", the corporations would be replacing expensive and inflating (e.g. wage) dollars with cheap and deflating (e.g. computer) dollars at a rapid pace, thus lowering labor costs.

However, the financial results of U.S. industrial corporations do not show that such improvement is taking place. The effects of the presumably cost-effective computing investments do not show up in labor wage indicators. Though corporations now employ less workers than before to produce the equivalent amount of revenue, they have offset any efficiency savings by hiring more expensive labor. The only plausible explanation for this pattern is that computers are not seen any more as the means for automating labor reducing employment by hiring a lesser numbers of less expensive employees. Instead, computers seem to be emerging primarily as a tool for transforming corporate operations through business process improvement.

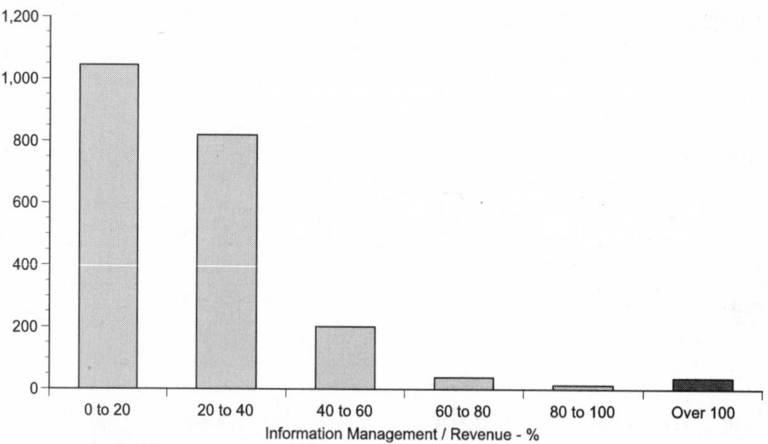

Figure 1-9–Information Management/Revenue Shows Importance of Overhead

INFORMATION MANAGEMENT AND REVENUE

Information management costs draw on a large share of revenues of a corporation. They consume resources that otherwise could be expended either on increasing the intrinsic value of goods and services or be passed on to shareholders as added profits.

In our study the median value of the information management to revenue ratio was 20.4%. Thirty-seven firms incurred information management costs in excess of revenue–a financial profile one is likely to find mostly with new corporate ventures. In our sample there were 158 firms where the expenditures for information management were equal or greater than 50% of the corporate revenues. In those cases information management costs dwarfed all other resources. Therefore, the ratio of information management (e.g., SG&A) to revenue is increasingly receiving attention in many corporations.

It Takes Less Information Management to Support Revenue

The Figure below shows how much information U.S. industrial firms required in producing their revenues.

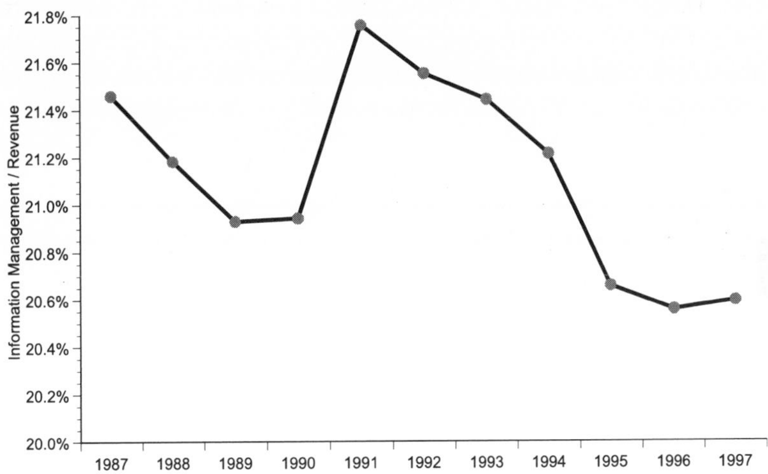

Figure 1-10–Information Management/Revenue Ratio Has Declined [21]

One of the most useful ways of examining the relative importance of information management costs is to find how much infor-

21 Medians for 1,240 corporations with a full set of published financial data for ten years.

mation was required to produce a dollar's worth of revenue over an extended time period. If a firm succeeds in lowering its costs of information (e.g. lower its overhead), while increasing its ability to boost revenues and/or prices, its economic viability should improve.

From a historic perspective it is interesting to note that the dollars of revenue supported by a dollar worth of information management reveals a period of decline for 1987 to 1990. It is followed by an increase in the period from 1990 only to resume a decline to 1997. Since 1987 the amount of information required to produce a dollar's worth of revenue has been declining cyclically, and remains below the average levels earlier in the decade. The anticipated favorable effect of information technologies on how much information is required to generate corporate revenues shows an improvement over the last decade.

The attention given by financial executives to this ratio may be misplaced. The financial spread between the reported revenues and the reported values of SG&A are influenced by many unrelated factors and therefore may introduce excessive statistical variability into any comparisons. The principal sources of such variability would be fluctuations in profit, tax, debt and depreciation amounts.

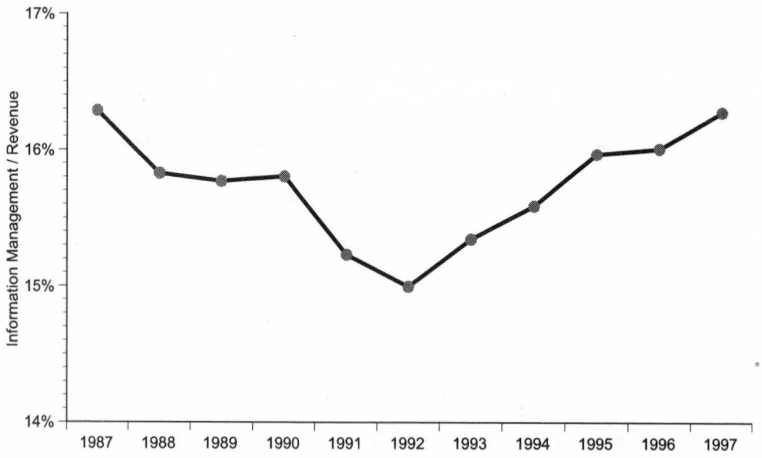

Figure 1-11 – Wal-Mart Did Not Reduce its Information Management/ Revenue Ratio

Relating information management costs to cost of goods, profits, to Economic Value-Added and to the cost of capital yield more reliable insights.

Wal-Mart–A Study of Presumed Excellence

Over the past few years a number of computer magazines have consistently rated the Wal-Mart Corporation as one of the best as well as most advanced user of information technologies in the U.S. To study this paragon of computing the following shows Wal-Mart's ten-year history of their overhead to revenue ratios:

Wal-Mart's information management/revenue ratio of 16.28% in 1997 was essentially equal to its 1987 ratio of 16.29%. In the case of retailing, with its small profit-to-revenue ratios, tracking of the information management/revenue ratio will have considerable merit as a management control indicator. In the case of Wal-Mart their inability to lower this ratio during the decade should raise questions. This does not speak well of its information management practices at a time when the median U.S. industrial corporation showed contrary trends.

Notwithstanding the journalistic acclaim of Wal-Mart for innovative information management practices, its rising information management/revenue ratio since 1992 deserves attention. At the very least, the chief information executive of Wal-Mart may have to reassess the deployment of the company's systems and reexamine the strategic directions for its huge information technology expenditures.

INFORMATION MANAGEMENT AND PROFITS

One of the most revealing ratios that would focus the attention of corporate executives on information management costs at budget time relates to their comparison with corporate profits. Figure 1-12 gives a graphical representation of this ratio.

The 1997 median value of the information management to profit ratio was 225% for 2,161 U.S. corporations. To extract one dollar of profits, more than 50% of U.S. industrial corporations had to spend over $2.25 for coordination, administration and management.

Losers Spend More Money on Information Management

In the sample of U.S. industrial corporations shown in the Figure below there are 446 companies that lost money (e.g. reported negative profits). These firms nevertheless spent $2.57 on information management for every dollar lost. Curiously, the losing firms were spending more on information management per dollar of losses than most moneymaking firms were spending per dollar's worth of profits. Executives of the losers were compensated to manage enterprises that were spending large sums on information management while their shareholders were losing money.

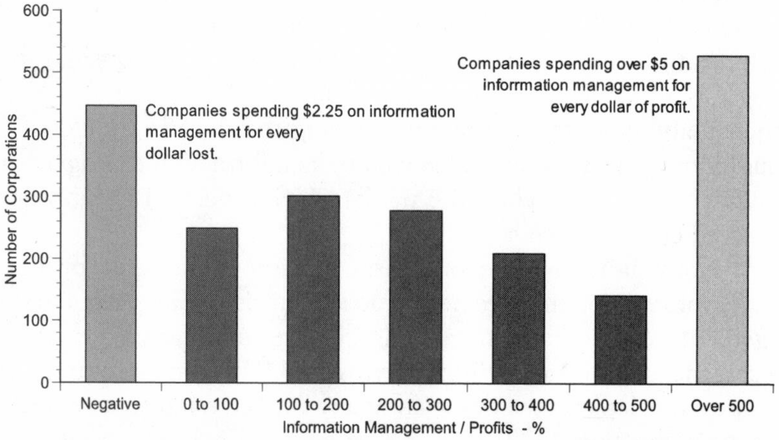

Figure 1-12–Information Management is a Large Multiple of Corporate Profits

This state of affairs shows that spending above the median rate for information management does not protect against losses. Information management can be entirely constructive when it produces profits or can be totally wasted when mismanagement prevails. It is not how much you spend, but how you spend it that tells what is the value of information.

These characteristics should be recognized by those computer magazines that for many years equated increased spending on information technologies as an index of corporate information "excellence." In annual praise-heaping announcements these magazines ranked corporations according the firms' presumed superiority in information management largely on the basis of the size of their I.T budget. It is a fact that there is no correlation whatsoever between I.T. budgets and any measure of profitability. The same lack for correspondence also applies to the relationship between information management costs per employee and Return-on-Shareholder Equity (ROE).

Information Management Unrelated to Return-on-Shareholder Equity

Since 1984, I have been plotting in several books and magazine articles a scatter diagram showing the relation between information management per employee and return-on-shareholder equity.[22] The random pattern indicating no correlation between these variables has not changed except that each iteration has added more data demonstrating the persistence of this lack of a correlation. The following Figure represents 1997 data for 2,017 U.S. industrial corporations:

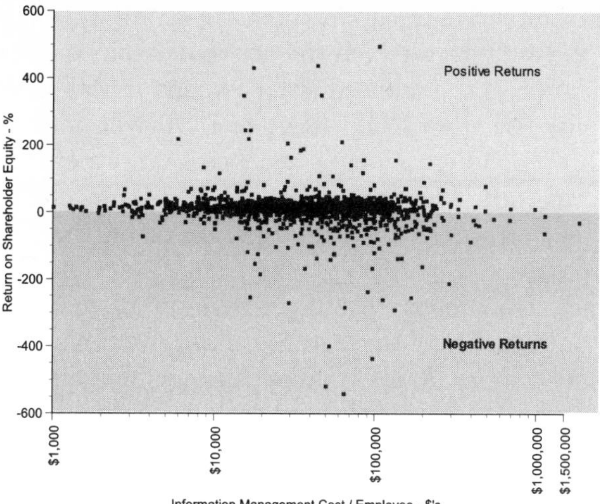

Figure 1-13 – Higher Spending on Information Management Unrelated to Profitability

22 Plotting information management spending per employee or information technology spending per employee against Return-on-Equity (ROE), Return-on-Assets (ROA) or Return-on-Investment (ROI) display similar unrelated patterns.

The 1997 median value of ROE for U.S. industrial corporations was 12.8%, with 375 corporations (20% of the total) delivering negative shareholder returns. A particularly bleak view of performance comes from observing that 623 (32% of the total) corporations showed ROE results below 7.6% which is below the average cost of corporate capital. These are firms that reported operating profits to their shareholders, even though the investors would have been better off investing in less risky corporate bonds or fairly safe mortgages.

The corporations with negative returns reported a median value of information management cost per employee of $50,168. The corporations with positive returns on shareholder equity were able to function well with median information management costs per employee of only $36,405. The reduced costs by the successful firms suggests that the moneymaking firms were able to take some of their reduced overhead expenses and pass them on to the shareholders as increased profits.

Those who argue that an information-based economy is superior to a labor-intensive or capital-intensive economy will find little comfort in the data from which the above diagram is constructed. As will be shown in the tables that follow, any traditional measure of productivity (whether ROE, ROA or ROI) will not rank information-rich companies as being necessarily more effective than those who are not. Moreover, profitability is unrelated to the amounts spent on the costs of information or on the quantity of capital invested.

Appendix D includes a list of 400 high productivity firms. The financial characteristics of these firms do not discriminate between firms that spend more on information management and those that own more assets. An asset-rich firm, such as can be found in steel manufacturing, may display a comparable level of profitability as an information-rich organization such as a computer software firm.[23]

23 What matters is how effectively a firm deploys its information management resources.

It Takes Less Information Management to Deliver Profits

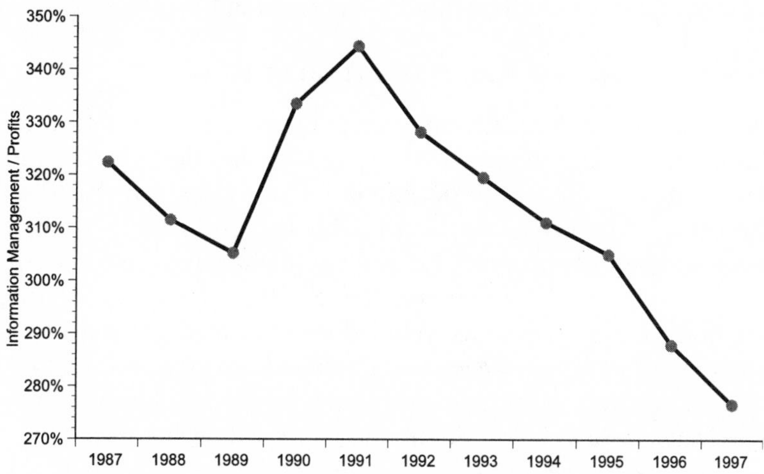

Figure 1-14–The Information Management/Profit Ratio Shows a Remarkable Decline [24]

According to the above Figure the median values of information management/profits have declined during the past ten years by 14.2%. What accounts for this decline? Is it due to a decline in information management costs or is it derived from the remarkable rise in corporate profitability of U.S. industrial corporations on coming from other efficiencies?

As previously shown, information management costs have risen faster than labor costs. Therefore, much of the source of the improvements in this index should be attributed to the remarkable increases in the profitability of U.S. corporations since 1990. These recent gains have their origin in favorable wages, reduced raw material costs and lower interest rates. Corporate management cannot take entirely credit for these profit-enhancement contributions. Both

24 Medians for 1,243 corporations with a full set of financial data for ten years. The 1997 median value for this group was 276%, which was higher than the median of 225% recorded for the 2,161 corporations analyzed in the Figure above. The difference in these two ratio can be explained by the fact that the ten year history reflects the performance of well established firms, whereas the much larger 1997 sample also includes start-ups and recently restructured firms that do not have a long financial record.

lower interest rates as well as lower commodity prices are the results of a confluence of unusually favorable geo-political and national policy developments that may not be replicated in the future.

The Influence of Reduced Interest Rates

Profits in the last decade have benefited from national political conditions that were favorable to the U.S. dollar. Perhaps the most important was the steady decline in interest rates, which reduced the costs of carrying corporate debt. In 1989 and in 1990 the median values of corporate interest payments were 2.0% and 2.1% of total corporate revenues respectively. By 1996 and 1997 these corporate interest payments were reduced to a median value of 1.4% and 1.5% of corporate revenues. These reductions accounted for a 29% reduction of corporate interest payments, and became immediately available as a contribution to increased profits.

One must also consider that the median 1997 profits for U.S. industrial corporations were 4.38% of revenues. Thus the reduction in interest payments by 0.50% will by itself account for almost all of the gains in the reported profits.

It was the actions of the Federal Reserve and the increased readiness of the rest of world to loan money to the U.S. debtors–and not necessarily actions taken by corporate executives–which should get much of the credit for the observed improvements in the information management/profit ratios. Should the geo-politically favorable conditions cease, U.S. corporate management should be ready to compensate for their deteriorating profit margins by taking actions that rely on internal productivity improvements to counter unfavorable external developments. When that condition occurs, the need for improving the productivity of information resources will become paramount because these may offer the only material and discretionary cost-cutting options.

The Influence of Lowered Commodity Prices[25]

An influence equally important as the lowered costs of capital has been the remarkable decrease in the costs of imported raw materials. The most noteworthy of these has been the 41% drop in the price of petroleum. That explains another 13% gain in potential profitability since the costs of energy, transportation and a few key raw material sources are coupled to the global prices of petroleum.[26] Thanks to the deflation in the prices of petroleum and of a few key metals that made it possible for U.S. industrial firms to enjoy increased gross profit margins without requiring added investments.

Certainly, the deflation in raw materials prices over the last decade has been an unprecedented economic bonus. It should not lead anyone to place an undue attribution on the improved profitability of U.S. industrial corporations to the increased uses of information technologies, to the conversion to a digital economy or to an increasingly computerized workforce. It cannot be denied that information technologies have had a pervasive influence in how work is done in U.S. industrial corporations. The problem is that so far we have been able to measure only the tangible effects, such as the lower cost of capital and the favorable cost of raw materials to explain why the U.S. industrial corporations are now more profitable.

INFORMATION MANAGEMENT AND NET ASSETS

For the fullest understanding of the role of information management in corporate economics we will now devote particular attention to the relationships between capital and information resources.

25 In a large sample of sole proprietorships, 32% of revenues were allocated to the cost of purchases, materials and supplies and only 10% to wages and salaries. In the absence of other available data it is fair to assume that regardless of size of business the price of purchases will have an enormous effect on the profit margins.

26 Crude oil prices per barrel of oil declined from $24.10 in 1985 to $13.20 in 1994, $14.60 in 1995 and $18.50 in 1996 while all other corporate prices were rising. (See *Statistical Abstract of the United States: 1997*, "Table 932"). US energy expenditures, significantly dependent on oil, now account for 13% of the inputs of the Gross National Product, with 64.6% of those expenditures concentrated in industry and transportation. (See *Statistical Abstract of the United States: 1997*, "Table 927").

The next Figure shows that in 1997 U.S. industrial firms were spending large amounts on information management relative to every dollar's worth of net assets employed.[27]:

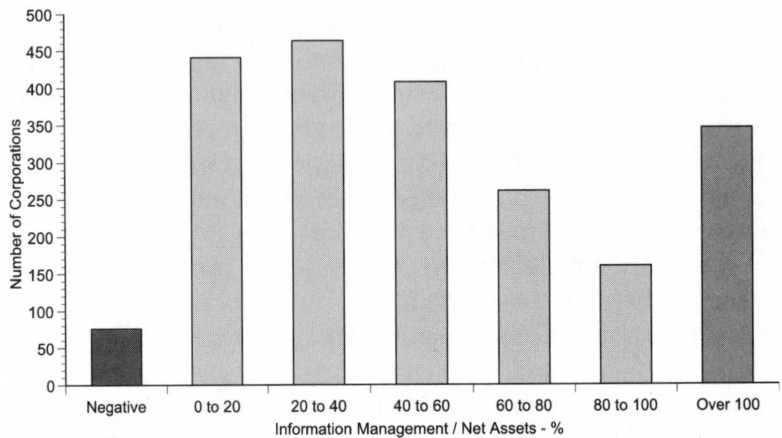

Figure 1-15 – The Information Management/Net Asset Ratio Can Be a High Multiple

Fifteen percent of U.S. industrial corporations incurred annual costs of information management that were greater than total net assets. These were mostly R&D intensive firms and start-up businesses. The 1997 median value of the information management/net asset ratio for all U.S. industrial firms was 44.1%.

It Takes Less Information to Manage Assets

The relationship between information management and net assets over an extended time period is a telling indicator of how the structure of an enterprise changes, as information resources increase in importance. It is now widely claimed that superior information capabilities can be an effective substitute for capital. Whether it is electronic commerce, cooperative outsourcing, just-in-time goods delivery or organizing for rapid customer responses, there are trade-offs that can be made between more money to be spent on infor-

27 Defined as Total Assets minus Total Liabilities.

mation resources so that capital resources can be reduced. Although this tradeoff opportunity has been observed and widely reported in noteworthy case studies, the question remains whether this is true when one examines the historical data for a large collection of U.S. industrial corporations that have been in business for ten years. For these corporations the transitory effects of low-asset and high debt start-up businesses would have been removed by eliminating from the study any short-term data.

One of the most useful ways of checking up on the theory that information can profitably substitute for assets is to examine whether the information management to net assets ratio has decreased. The following shows the ten-year history of median assets employed for every dollar's worth of information management:

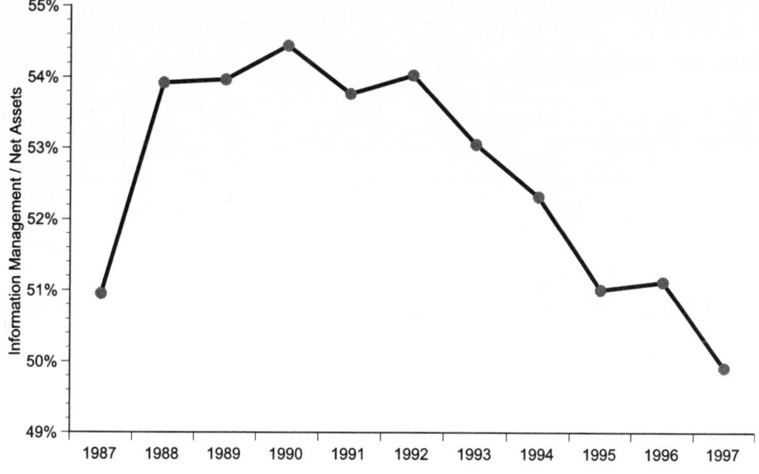

Figure 1-16 – The Information Management/Net Asset Ratio Decreasing Recently

The decline in the ratios can be explained primarily by lower prices for net assets that caused them to grow. The wage costs of information management have not declined during the decade.[28] This suggests that even though anecdotal studies can demonstrate impressive elimination of inventories and increased utilization of processing facilities, data for 1,609 corporations show that the asset structure of U.S. industrial firms does not as yet reflect such benefits:

	1990	1991	1992	1993	1994	1995	1996	1997
Net Assets / Revenue - %	41.10%	41.75%	41.84%	42.03%	41.84%	42.00%	42.41%	43.26%

Figure 1-17–Net Assets Required to Support Revenues have Increased

It Is Less Expensive Now to Own Assets

One plausible explanation for the relative rise in net assets can be found in the steady decline in interest costs, thus diminishing the incentives to substitute costly computerization for the steadily lower

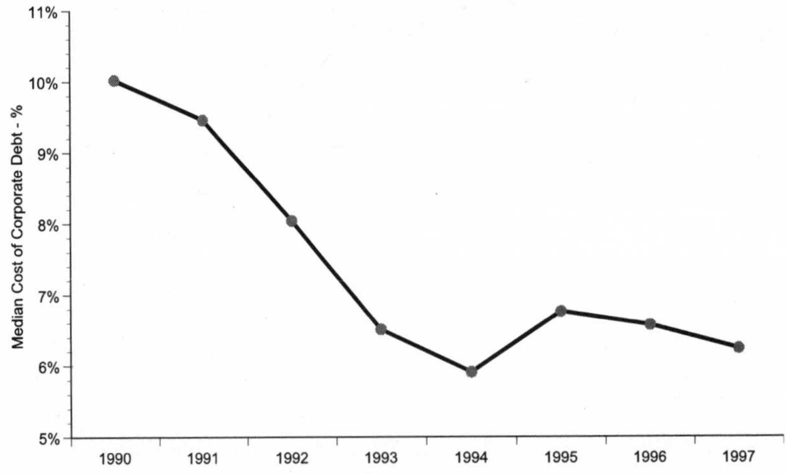

Figure 1-18–Lower Interest Rates Make Asset Increases Attractive [29]

28 Zuckerman, G., "U.S. Corporations Load on Debt at a Rapid Clip," *The Wall Street Journal*, December 31, 1998. The outstanding debt of U.S. non-financial corporations has increased at a faster pace than in the last decade. $292 billion of new corporate bonds were sold in 1998. What is troubling is that 41% of all new bonds sold in 1998 were rated below investment grade and therefore a potentially major drain on profits in the future when business conditions deteriorate. Corporate debt now represents 43% of the GNP and is at the highest levels since 1960.

29 Medians of the effective interest paid by 1,522 industrial corporations for long-term debt.

costs for carrying assets. Since 1989 U.S. firms have found that dropping interest rates made it more attractive to own assets. As interest rates dropped from their peak in 1989 by 22%, assets kept growing at a record rate. Proposals to cut the need for capital by means of investments in improved management methods would be harder to justify under such circumstances.

It remains to be seen what will happen when interest rates rise again—as has always happened before. Computer-derived innovations in information management would again make reductions in capital requirements increasingly enticing.

Although reduced costs of capital may explain most of the rise in net assets employed by U.S. industrial corporations, that still does not demonstrate that information has become an effective substitute for assets. Here we have an example that does not support the frequent assertion that the "information age" may bring about a dematerialization of U.S. corporations as claimed by a number of popular writers. That may happen, but is not as yet apparent.

Coca-Cola Company—An Example of Contributions to Excellence

According to Forbes magazine the Coca-Cola Company ranks as one of the most successful U.S. corporations, as measured in terms of its increase in shareholder value over the last decade.[30]

To illustrate the utility of the information management/net assets ratio as one of the planning, budgeting and effectiveness indicators Figure 1-19 shows those ratios for the Coca-Cola Company.

Unlike the rest of the industrial corporations, where the median information management/net assets declined, the Coca-Cola pattern of a rising ratio suggests a preference by Coca-Cola management to use information resources as a substitute for owning assets.

However, the reversal of this trend since 1992 suggests that Coca-Cola executives ought to explore ways to trade low-cost auto-

30 Gains in shareholder value are measured as annual changes in market capitalization (e.g. share price x number of shares outstanding).

mated systems for potentially more expensive costs of assets in the future.

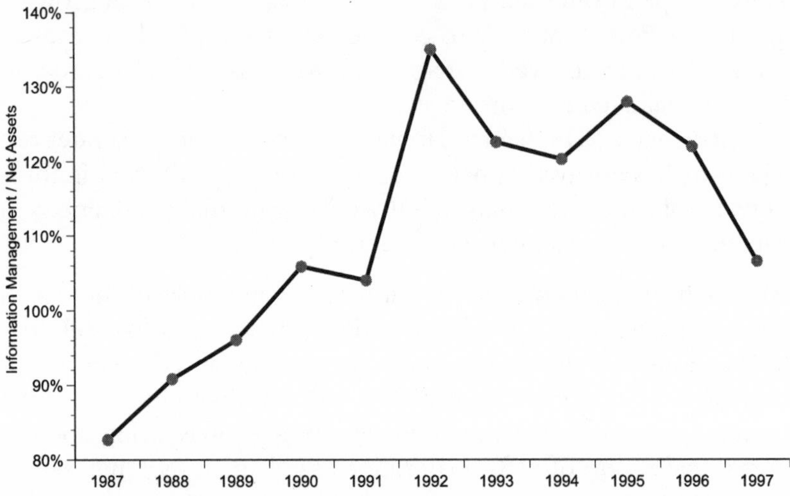

Figure 1-19 – Coca-Cola Ratios Suggest Favorable Tradeoffs

INFORMATION MANAGEMENT AND INFORMATION TECHNOLOGY

The terms "information management" and "information technology" are frequently used interchangeably. In fact, they are different. Information technology amounts to only a fraction of information management spending, though increasingly these terms are indistinguishable as tasks previously performed by information technologists are classified as general administrative expenses.

Perhaps the primary reason for such inconsistent usage is the aspiration of Chief Information Officers to have an all-inclusive title indicating they are in charge of all "information." In reality the CIOs always control only a small share of information management costs as well as a steadily diminishing share of spending for information technologies.

As result of benchmarking engagements, I have collected a large set of data about corporate financial results and spending on information technologies.[31] Statistical analysis of these data reveals that the expected information technology costs for U.S. industrial corporations can be estimated with high levels of confidence based on financial variables and operational data. These costs can be calculated by using the following independent variables: cost of information management; information employment as a ratio of the total workforce; the ratio of professional to clerical workers; the number of personal computers; corporate profits; net assets and salary levels relative to the industry median. Of these variables, the cost of information management is the single largest influence, explaining 42% of the difference between the actual and the estimated expected

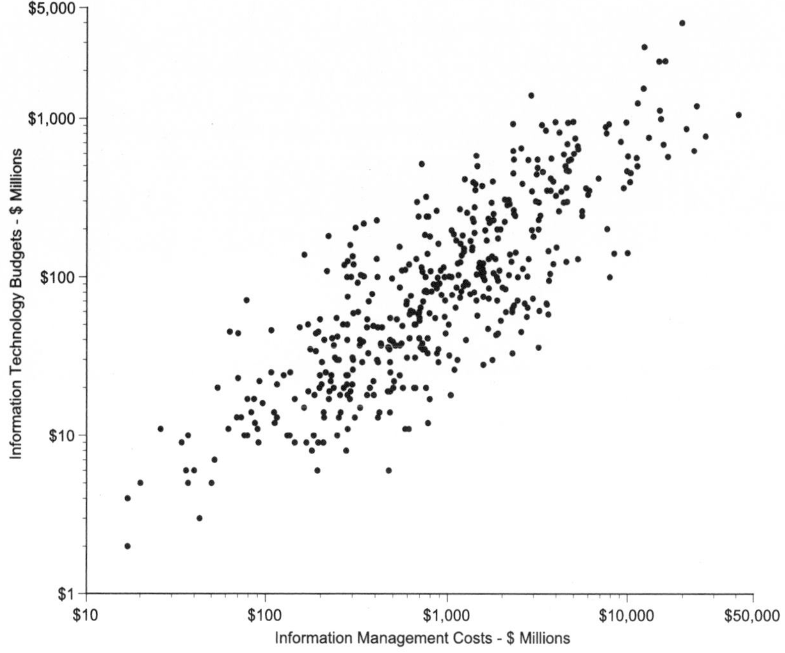

Figure 1-20–Information Technology Averages 11.5% of Information Management Costs

31 A copy of the standard data collection form can be obtained from the worldwide web page of Strassmann, Inc. <http://www.strassmann.com/>

costs. The following diagram shows the relation between Sales, General, Administrative and R&D costs and the corresponding information technology budgets for 459 corporations or operating divisions of corporations:

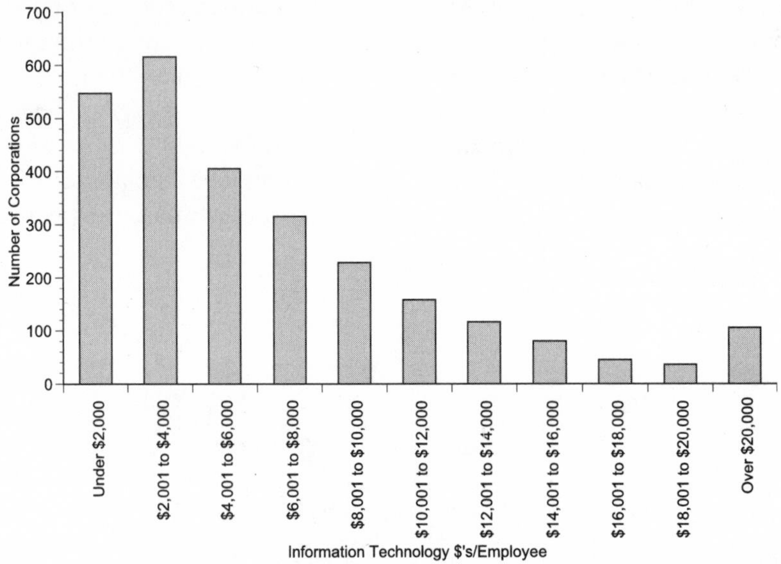

Figure 1-21–Information Technology per Employee Reflect Information Intensity

When all of the variables of the multi-factor estimating equation are applied to the 1997 financial data one obtains a good estimate of the importance of information technology expenses per employee for 2,662 industrial corporations.

The median information technology spending per employee is $4,709. This is 14.3% of average employee compensation in 1997, and is as high as 60% of compensation. This exceeds corporate expenses for corporate employee Social Security contributions. If the employee happens to receive a fully featured networked computer with a total cost of ownership exceeding $8,000, then the information technology expense per employee becomes greater than any other payroll benefit, inclusive of paid leave, insurance, retirement and medical payments.

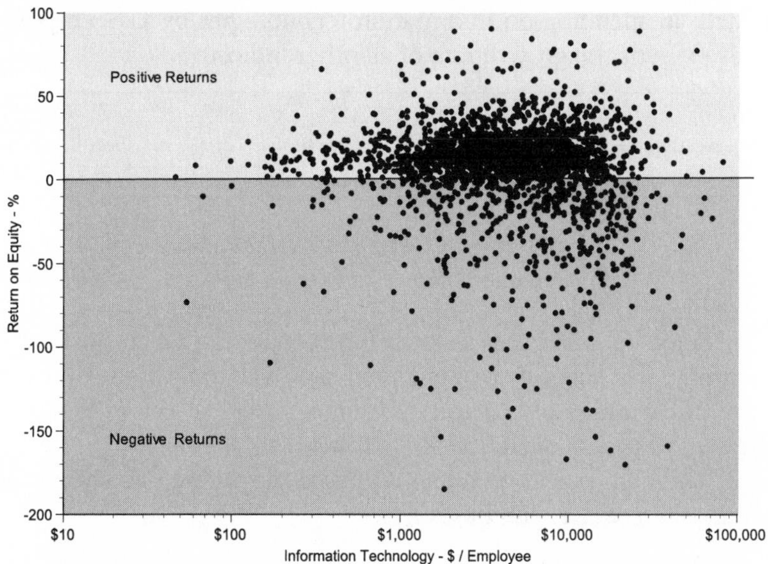

Figure 1-22–Information Technology and Profitability are Unrelated

Information technology spending should be seen only as one of the many essential ingredients of corporate success, but only if managed effectively. As an isolated ratio it has no significance whatsoever, despite numerous attempts to show that greater spending on more advanced technologies somehow enables the generation of superior profits.

As demonstrated in Figure 1-22 the amount of spending on computers has no relationship to profitability: This scatter pattern has remained unchanged ever since I first plotted it in 1984 in my book, Information Payoff. It has kept its form regardless of attempts to apply different measures of profitability and different scales to represent the cost of computers.[32]

Despite the persistence of the "computer paradox"–that computers are everywhere except in the economic indicators–the

32 The chart is a plot of estimated (based on linear regression equation) information technology expenditures for 2,519 firms and the corresponding actual 1997 ROE values.

growth in spending on information technologies by U.S. corporations exceeds the growth rate of all other indicators:[33]

	1990	1991	1992	1993	1994	1995	1996	1997	1998	Total Growth
I.T. Purchases by U.S. Firms - $B	$132	$139	$153	$175	$193	$251	$284	$321	$353	167%
I.T. Purchase Growth Rate	8.27%	4.77%	10.76%	14.02%	10.46%	29.71%	13.29%	13.03%	9.91%	

Figure 1-23–U.S. Corporations' I.T. Purchases Exceed Other Growth Indicators

Since I.T. purchases account for 25-35% of total corporate I.T. spending, this suggests that the total 1988 U.S. corporate I.T. costs were in the range of $1.1 to $1.4 trillion, which is well in excess of the sum of profits of all listed U.S. firms.

The high rise in spending disguises the differences within the composition of I.T. purchases:

I.T. Spending - $ Billions	1990	1991	1992	1993	1994	1995	1996	1997	1998	Total Growth
I.T. Hardware	$67	$66	$71	$82	$90	$109	$131	$144	$153	128%
I.T. Services	$43	$47	$53	$61	$66	$98	$108	$123	$139	224%
I.T. Packaged Software	$22	$25	$30	$32	$37	$43	$46	$54	$61	172%

Figure 1-24–I.T. Purchases Shifting from Hardware to Services and Software

Is the lower rate in the growth in I.T. hardware spending any indication that at least one of the segments of I.T. purchase costs is reaping the benefits of Moore's Law?[34] Whether this is so is an important issue, since much of the publicity that concerns the prospects of rising productivity in the information age is based on frequent references to the enormous gains that can be achieved though inexpensive computing.

Moore's theoretical benefit/cost gains of 33.5% are also reflected in the U.S. government's average information technology

33 McHugh, J., "Big Software takes a detour," *Forbes*, April 5, 1999

34 Moore's Law states that the number of transistors that can be crammed into a single semi-conductor chip doubles every 24 months without increasing its variable manufacturing cost. That means that electronics costs can decline 33.5% annually.

deflation index of 17.5%. The nominal dollars spent are therefore worth more each year, at a 17.5% compound rate of growth, as illustrated in the following:

in $ Billions	1990	1991	1992	1993	1994	1995	1996	1997	1998	Total
I.T. Hardware	$67	$66	$71	$82	$90	$109	$131	$144	$153	$913
Moore's Law Multiplier	100%	118%	138%	162%	191%	224%	263%	309%	363%	
Value of I.T. Spending	$67	$78	$97	$134	$172	$244	$344	$445	$557	$2137
Theoretical Loss	$0	$12	$27	$51	$82	$135	$213	$301	$404	

Figure 1-25–Efficiency of I.T. Hardware Is Low

Whether the $153 billions of I.T. hardware are, in fact, generating the equivalent of $557 billions worth of computing power in 1990 terms is hard to prove. However, it is safe to conclude that since 1990 there has been an enormous expansion of computer capabilities at a declining unit cost of processing power. This growth in capacity was further a steady increase in spending for computing hardware amounting to a 128% increase. If productivity were to show up in the computer hardware it would appear as a steady reduction in purchase costs, not as a large increase. The potential processing capacity of I.T. hardware is then 364% greater than its purchase worth. Such disparity–a theoretical loss–could be justified only if there was a corresponding increase in productivity.[35]

The relatively small increases in Information Productivity found in this book are not attributable to efficiencies that were derived from computer hardware but have origin in economic forces that are largely external to a firm. The enormous increases in the capabilities of computers suggested by Moore's Law were largely squandered by the following practices:

- **Bloated Software:** The widely popular phrase "Moore Delivers and Gates Takes Away" describes one of the major sources of hardware ineffectiveness. Whatever added machine cycles

35 Strassmann's **I.T. Paradox Number** is the difference between a firm's actual computer hardware spending and one that follows Moore's Law. For U.S. corporations this number was $404 billion in 1998, in 1990 terms.

one gets from the producers of electronics are chewed up by software that compensates for its inadequacies by gobbling up all the computing power it can get.

- **Excessive Support Costs:** Hardware maintenance and support costs are included in the reported hardware budgets. The total ownership cost of a desktop computer now includes as little as 10% for hardware depreciation. Almost all of the remaining costs are for expensive support labor to keep the hardware alive and to tranquilize unhappy customers. In fact, the purchases of support services (with an increase of 224% from 1990 to 1998) and of packaged software (with an increase of 172% from 1990 to 1998) attest to the increasing difficulties in installing and maintaining existing computer networks.
- **Negligent Systems Engineering:** Corporate hardware assets are put in place with hardly any configuration management, safeguards against pre-mature obsolescence or provisions how to adapt to different scale of operations. The hardware landscape of most corporations looks to me more like a shanty-town than a metropolis.

The consequences of such inefficiencies then show up in the poor economics and generate the I.T. Paradox Number. Hardware is acquired and junked for no other reason than the inability of I.T. management to cope with what they have in place. What appears as inexpensive hardware is purchased as the preferred solution to the software bloat, uncontrolled support costs and improvised systems engineering.[36]

36 The recent tendency of corporations to engage in comprehensive enterprise-wide software replacement (ERP) projects costing anywhere from $10 to over $100 million magnifies the losses. 28% of ERP projects failed, 46% were over budget or materially late. (see Hunter, R., "GartnerGroup Expects 50% of ERP projects to fail," *Executive Edge*, April, 1999).

LIMITATIONS OF INFORMATION MANAGEMENT INDICATORS

The six information management indicators that are discussed earlier in this chapter could be useful for planning and budget purposes. They can be used for comparing a firm's results against data from look-alike firms. However, if such indicators diverge and if they are considered one at a time, such analysis is likely to be inconclusive.

For U.S. industrial corporations we find that most of the time the information management indicators will point in a different directions:

Indicator	1991	1997	% Change
Information Management/Cost of Goods	32.1%	31.2%	-2.8%
Information Management/Employee	$29,559	$38,304	29.6%
Information Management/Revenue	21.8%	20.6%	-5.3%
Information Mangement/Profit	344.4%	276.7%	-19.7%
Information Management/Net Assets	53.8%	49.9%	-7.2%
Information Technology Purchases - $B	$139	$321	131.7%

Figure 1-26–Contrary Information Management Indicators

For individual corporations information management indicators will diverge without suggesting how such a pattern should be interpreted:

1. **Information Management and Cost of Goods** ratios usually display a large range of values, even for look-alike firms. The significance of a particular value can be judged only as it relates to other trends. A decline in this ratio may signal a reduction in overhead cost (always a good sign). An increase in this ratio may reflect a failure of new businesses to gain acceptance (always a bad sign). If corporate profits keep rising, a lower Information Management/Cost of Goods ratio should be always favored.

2. **Information Management per Employee** ratio reflects the intrinsic complexity of a business. If the

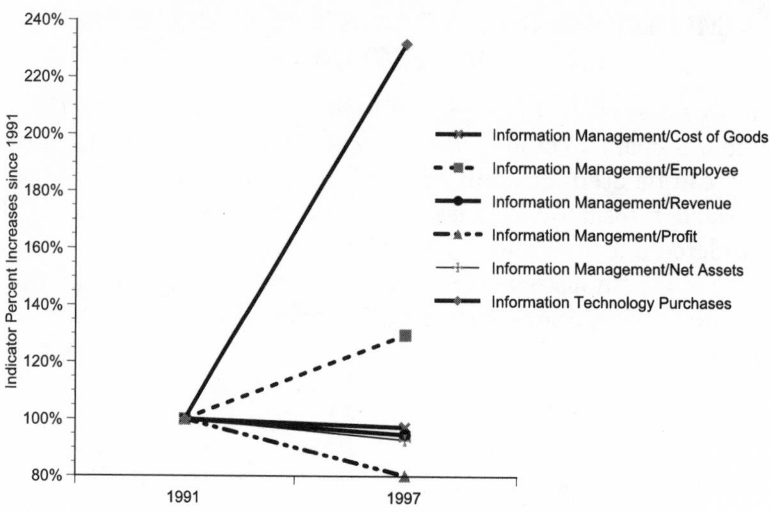

Figure 1-27–Contrary Indicators are Inconclusive

cost of the information overhead keeps rising that is always an unfavorable sign since that adds to the fixed cost and increases the break-even level for business operations. However, there are circumstances–such as in start-up firms or where competitive conditions mandate continued investments in products and in marketing–where high information spending per employee may be desirable to grow profits in the long run.

3. **Information Management and Revenue** ratios are the best available approximations of what constitutes corporate overhead. Chief financial officers and investment analysts have already singled out this indicator for periodic attention and track it and its trends. Accordingly, any increase in this ratio is seen as an adverse development which is generally true, but not always so. This ratio is sensitive to unrelated influences that are outside of management's control, such as changes in interest rates, deflationary effects on cost of materials and the way

the published financial results must account for inventories in order to comply with GAAP (generally accepted accounting principles) rules.

4. **Information Management and Profit** ratios are useful measures for highlighting the relative importance of information management costs during planning and budget exercises. Focusing on this relationship may provide perhaps the incentive for corporate management to adopt "activity based costing" as a standard accounting practice. However, as there is no causal relationship between the amounts of information management spending and corporate profits the best one can say is that a high information management to profit ratio should be always an inducement to examine the direct economic contribution of all information-related activities.

5. **Information Management and Net Assets** ratios reveal what is rarely fully appreciated by economists or accountants. The substitution of an overhead expense item (found on the financial statement) for an asset (found on the balance sheet) calls for innovative methods of investment justification which have not been, as yet, incorporated into the formal budget justification procedures of most corporations. Though most large scale computer investment proposals refer to asset "savings" to be realized from better information flows, it is only this ratio that will ultimately demonstrate whether such benefits have been realized.

6. **Information Management and Information Technology** ratios are perhaps the most frequently abused spending indicators, especially when used during budget reviews to justify additional spending. Basing decisions on information technology spending as a percentage of revenues represents the

> most severe abuse of sound business practices. As a rule, the growth in this ratio should be accepted only if there is a demonstrable correlation with an increase in profitability.

The difficulties with inconclusive and often contradictory indicators are also present in other ranking methods that depend on compilations of check-lists such as we find in the "critical factor method," the "balanced score-sheet" technique and in numerous "best practices" rating schema.

If six (or more) indicators yield contradictory signals, how does one resolve any conflicts about the priorities in resource allocation? Making major improvements in any one of the indicators may be desirable but may not deliver the best overall results. What's needed is a metric that could be used for making tradeoffs on the basis of an indicator that reflects a composite of several conflicting influences. That composite indicator is "productivity" which is the ratio of the output of a corporation divided by what is a critical measure of inputs.

As the first step in determining productivity we must first define what will be the measure of corporate output. It is not revenue, tons of production, miles traveled, profits, customer calls, pages printed or units of production. Each of these, regardless how defined, are only partial measures. To make possible the reconciliation of contrary indicators, this book adopts the dollar value of the Economic Value-Added (EVA)–to be discussed in the chapter that follows–as the measure of corporate output against which all other information management ratios will be evaluated.

2.

Economic Value-Added

Economic Value-Added (EVA) is a more reliable measure of the economic contribution of corporate information management than accounting profits. Information management expenses are a large multiple of the EVA valuation. In judging the performance of corporate information management one must consider that forty percent of U.S. industrial corporations deliver a negative EVA and twenty-one percent of these corporations report accounting profits, while still losing economic value.

Determining Net Output

None of the conventional ratios that measure productivity reveals the company's Economic Value-Added, defined as revenues minus payment for all costs.[37] Economic Value-Added is a more reliable measure of economic output than any other indicator. Without a measure of productivity based on Economic Value-Added, there is no valid way of assessing a firm's overall productivity.

The Economic Value-Added, currently popularized as "EVA," reflects the fundamentals of economic performance because it includes all factors that affect productivity. You calculate EVA by subtracting all economic costs (land, cost of goods, compensation for shareholder capital, taxes and information management) from profits after taxes. What is left is the true economic surplus available for further investment.[38]

37 A number of European firms follow this practice.

38 Taxes are classified here as an involuntary overhead expense, in contrast to information management costs that are a discretionary overhead expense. From a budgetary standpoint taxes and allocations of corporate overhead costs have many similar characteristics–they are often levied by political fiat and without directly demonstrable benefits.

EVA does not equal accounting profits after taxes. The typical financial statements do not reflect the fact that shareholders have investments tied up in the firm. Because they do, shareholders should receive a return on their original capital and interest on all assets in the corporate coffers that has not been paid out as dividends and remains under management control, such as retained earnings, reserves and allowances. In its most sophisticated form the calculation of EVA calls for adjustments to accounting entries such as write-offs, good will, and research expenses. I believe that the most comprehensive description of how to make calculations of EVA is that given in G. B. Stewart's book.[39] The EVA values for the Fortune 1,000 companies are available from Stern Stewart Management Services.[40]

Contrary to claims by a number of consulting firms, the term "Economic Value-Added" is neither original, proprietary or particularly modern. Theoretical economists have used this term for over two hundred years and U.S. corporations have used this concept since the 1950's, such as in the General Electric Corporation where it was called "residual value." GE operating divisions had to reduce their operating profit by an interest charge for their share of invested corporate capital.

The Strategic Planning Institute, an outgrowth of GE, adopted this measure in calculating the profit impact of marketing strategies (PIMS) in the 1970's.[41] I adopted this approach in pursuing a seven-year research program about management productivity as a method for evaluating the business value of computers.[42] The "Management

39 They deserve credit for popularizing EVA concepts, especially by getting their annual rankings published by Fortune magazine and by profuse advertising in leading magazines read by corporate executives. The book by Stewart, G.B., *The Quest for Value*, Harper Business, 1991 is still the best reference source about the intricacies and uses of EVA calculations.

40 The *Stern Stewart Performance 1000 Database*. Published annually.

41 Robert D. Buzzell and Bradley T. Gale, *The PIMS Principles*, The Free Press, 1987

42 I used extensively the term "economic profit" as the proxy for "management value-added" throughout *The Business Value of Computers*, The Information Economics Press, 1990

Value-Added" calculations I used in my 1985 work turned out to be a good approximation of EVA.[43]

Estimating Economic Value-Added

In the absence of detailed financial data or historical information about financial adjustments to shareholder equity, the best one can do is to take accounting profit and subtract from it the accounting value of shareholder equity multiplied by the average cost of shareholder capital.

The EVA defines what remains after all costs–including the costs of ownership of capital assets–have been paid for. Some economists used to call that "residual income." Others have labeled it as the "economic profit" to distinguish this concept from the "accounting profit" by which corporate management prefers to be measured.

In this book EVA is calculated as follows:[44]

EVA = Profit – Cost of Ownership of Capital

Profit = Accounting Profit after Taxes and before Preferred Dividends

Cost of Ownership of Capital = Cost of Capital * Capital

Where:

Cost of Capital = Interest Expense on Debt (Defined as Short Term Debt plus Current Portion of Long Term Debt plus Long Term Debt)[45]

Capital = Total Assets–Total Liabilities

These definitions of Profit, Cost of Capital and Capital comply with generally accepted accounting principles (GAAP) as defined by the Financial Accounting Standards Board (FASB), the accounting profession's self-regulatory body. Conforming to these

43 Paul A. Strassmann, "Information Payoff, The Transformation of Work in the Electronic Age," *The Free Press*, 1985

44 This is "basic EVA" as described in Ehrbar, A., *EVA-The Real Key to Creating Wealth*, Wiley & Sons, 1998.

45 The cost of debt is likely to understate the risk premium for equity financing. Here is another reason why my valuations of EVA will be always overstated.

rules was necessary because the financial data of U.S. industrial corporations are available only in this form. The EVA valuations used in all calculations in this book also could be designated as EVA-GAAP when discussed with financial analysts.

Cost of Capital

When calculating the expected shareholder return from investing in a corporation one of the most difficult choices is the interest rate to be used as the cost of capital. There are many different views how to make such a choice. Each approach reflects a point of view that ultimately becomes reflected in opinions whether a particular corporation's shares are over-valued or under-valued.[46] The following shareholders' cost of capital valuation models are most frequently applied:

- The Treasury Bond Model: The "fair value" of shareholders' cost of capital is the current yield of a 10-year Treasury bond.[47]
- The Capital Asset Pricing Model With Risk Premium: The "fair value" is the current rate of a Treasury Bill plus the "Beta" value of stock market volatility multiplied by the difference between the returns from the stock market minus the "risk free" rate of return on long term Treasury Bonds.[48]
- The Capital Asset Pricing Model Without Risk Premium: This model does not recognize a shareholder's risk premium. The "fair value" is the return

46 Weber, J., and Laderman, J.M., "The Market: Too High? Too Low?," *Business Week*, April 5, 1999

47 At the time (March 1999) the 10-year Treasury bond interest rate was 5.62%.

48 The current rate on Treasury Bills is 4.45%. The difference between the stock market average returns and the Treasury bill interest is also called the market risk premium. At present such risk premium is estimated at about 7%. Since 1926 large company stocks have been producing average returns of 11% whereas the long-term Treasury bonds have returned only 5.2%. (See J.K.Glassman and K.A.Hassett, "Stock Prices Are Still Far Too Low," *The Wall Street Journal*, March 17, 1999). For a detailed discussion on applying this model see Brigham, E.F. and Houston, J.F., *Fundamentals of Financial Management*, The Dryden Press, 8th Edition, 1998, p.176

on long term Treasury Bonds or, and appropriate after tax expected return whichever is higher.[49]

In calculating the value of EVA we have tried to apply each of the above interest valuation models and found it inconsistent with what corporations actually reported at their costs of interest in their annual reports. Individual corporations paid interest charges that could be explained only as a reflection of their particular banking relationships and credit-worthiness than by any of the above three models.

We paid particular attention to the widely used Capital Asset Pricing Model (with risk premium) to verify if the stock market volatility would correlate with the actual interest rates that the firm paid for debt.

There was no correlation at all (R2 = 0.1) based on a sample of 2,873 U.S. industrial corporations, as shown in the following figure that plots the log of 1997 beta values against actual interest rates paid by firms in 1997:[50]

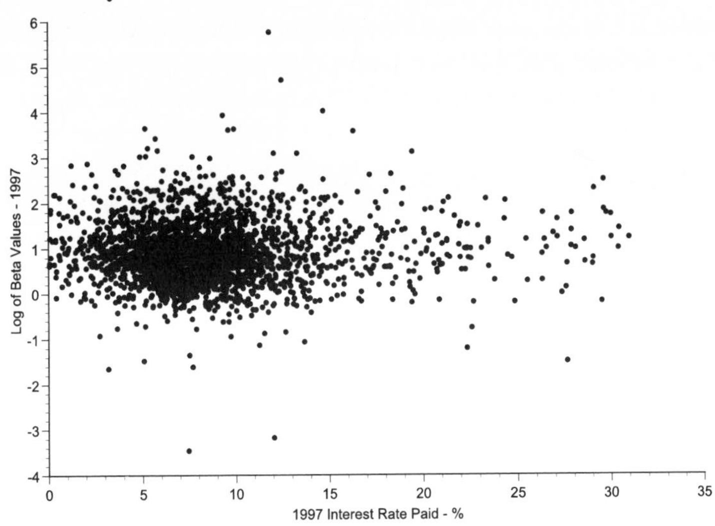

Figure 2-1–Interest Rates Actually Paid Unrelated to Market Volatility

49 B.Lev and S.L.Mintz, "Seeing is Believing," *CFO Journal*, February 1999
50 Beta values from *Worldscope Global Researcher*, Disclosure Corp, February 1999.

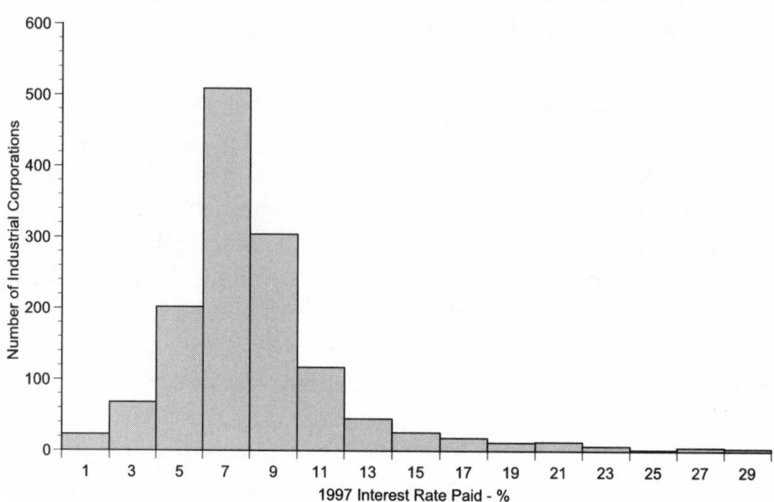

Figure 2-2–Interest Rates Actually Paid by Industrial Corporations

What individual firms incurred as actual interest costs cannot be explained by the capital asset pricing model. After finding similarly unsatisfactory correlation with other models we accepted the principle that financial markets can best dictate what is an appropriate interest rate. What corporations reported as the interest cost they paid for debt is as good a reflection of the costs of capital as any other known theory.

The above diagram displays the wide range in the actual interest rates paid by U.S industrial corporations in 1997. It has a median value of 7.53%, for a total number of 1,376 industrial corporations. It is noteworthy that the median value as well as distribution patterns of interest rates for financial and services corporations differ materially:

The above distribution has a median value of 5.95%, for a total number of 564 financial and services corporations.[51]

51 These rates not used elsewhere in this report except in Appendix E.

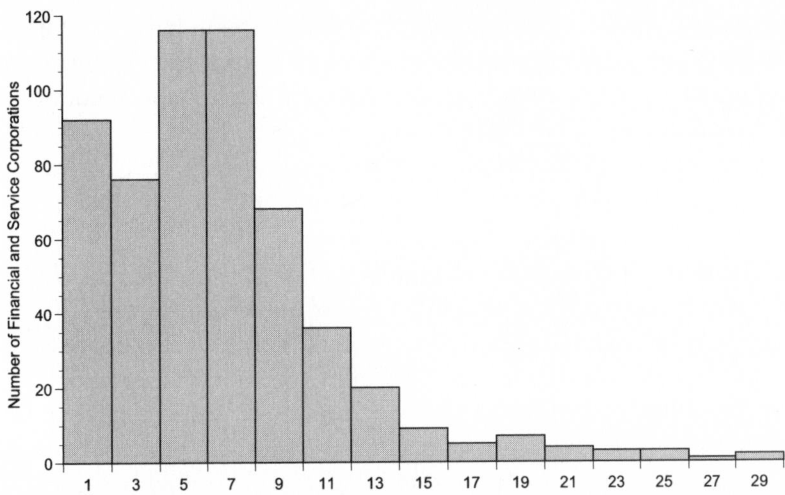

Figure 2-3–Interest Rates Actually Paid by Financial and Services Corporations

The Many Ways of Calculating EVA

The accounting definitions included in GAAP are a mind-boggling collection of rules that favor interpretations that tend to reflect the tangible liquidation value of a firm. GAAP avoids accounting interpretations that may reflect what a firm may be worth as an ongoing concern in the market. GAAP rules are particularly allergic to accounting for anything that may resemble the valuation of Knowledge Capital.[52] Therefore the values of EVA obtained by the calculations in this book are always overstated. Our estimates of Information Productivity are more favorable than a full valuation of all assets would reveal.

According to GAAP rules, the assets as well as liabilities have been reported in a most conservative manner to satisfy the lenders' need to know if they can recover outstanding loan balances in case

52 Strassmann, Inc. has the Registered Trademark for Knowledge Capital® and how to calculate it. It was granted by the Commissioner of Patents and Trademarks, U.S. Department of Commerce in December, 1996.

of bankruptcy.[53] To compensate for the liquidation bias of GAAP a number of consulting firms have developed what they claim to be proprietary adjustments for some or all of the following accounting entries:[54]

- Research and Development expenses that represent future products and processes are capitalized, but not expensed in the current year.
- Software expenses for programs and databases that can be expected to have a long life are capitalized and written off over the useful life and not expensed. As software costs rise to become a major component of information management costs the GAAP practice of writing off software as current cost is the chief culprit in making the prevailing practice of squandering computer resources acceptable simply because it becomes untraceable.[55]
- Good-will write-offs call for depreciation of the difference between the accounting valuation and the acquisition costs of another company. That diminishes both reported earnings as well as assets on the balance sheet. A number of consultants reverse these charges in the belief that shareholders should be measuring the long-term economic value of mergers and acquisitions.
- Changes in Depreciation Charges would account for company-owned assets as leased equipment. This would make replacements with improved models more attractive.
- Restructuring charges have been the source of the worst GAAP-sanctioned distortions in the reported profitability of corporations. Business magazines report weekly about firms that have written off tens of billions of dollars from the

53 GAAP rules have been jokingly referred to as an undertakers' accounting method. The accountant's approach to valuation of net assets has been also called the "carcass" valuation technique–the worth the remaining assets would fetch on the market after a firm's demise.

54 The most noteworthy of these is the article by Dr. Sidney Schoeffler," The Purpose of Full-Value Economic Statements," http://www.mantis-boston.com/FVESintro.htm., March 1998.

55 This matter has been largely neglected because it is in the interest of everyone–but the shareholders–to keep increasing funds flowing into newer and larger computer projects. This practice is treated in considerable detail in Strassmann, P.A., *The Squandered Computer.*

shareholder equity as "restructuring" costs. This practice made it possible to keep up the appearance of high reported operating profits thus justifying bonuses for executives.[56]

- Adjustments for actually paid taxes are necessary because of the large difference between calculated taxes and taxes actually paid out. The presence of this inconsistency usually can be observed by a large entry on the balance sheet that shows up as "deferred taxes." In fact, this is shareholder capital because these taxes will never be paid out, but will be deferred from year to year.

Additional adjustments are often made for transforming EVA-GAAP calculations into any of the proprietary versions of EVA. The differences between the EVA-GAAP and any other version of EVA receives much attention whenever a corporation chooses to adopt an EVA metric to calculate executive compensation incentives.[57]

Unfortunately, the proprietary versions of EVA are always held as private and highly confidential information. The EVA-based evaluations in this book construct the EVA only for comparative benchmarking purposes. For this reason, we have adopted the computation of EVA as a three-year moving average to smooth out the effects of one-time accounting adjustments. The primary benefit of this approach is that it diminishes the impact of immediate write-offs and of restructuring charges which are a frequent phenomenon on the current U.S. industrial scene. It is a compromise among the many possible variations of EVA.

EVA RATIOS

Forty Percent of U.S. Industrial Firms Detract from Shareholder Wealth

Since the Economic Value-Added (EVA) is calculated by subtracting from the reported profits the calculated cost of net invested capital

56 Even the venerable cereal company Kellogg, Inc. has taken "one time" restructuring charges four years in a row to "streamline operations." The total charged to earnings was equivalent to one quarter of Kellogg's net income. See *New York Times*, December 27, 1998, BU8.

57 A common practice for US industrial corporations.

or shareholder equity, the reported EVA number will be always less than the accounting profits that were recorded under GAAP rules.[58] The median value of the information management/economic value ratio for the 736 U.S. industrial corporations (that deliver to shareholders a positive value of EVA) is 602%. This large multiplier of EVA shows that both the expense and the effectiveness of information management costs have potentially greater effect on EVA than any other economic influence.

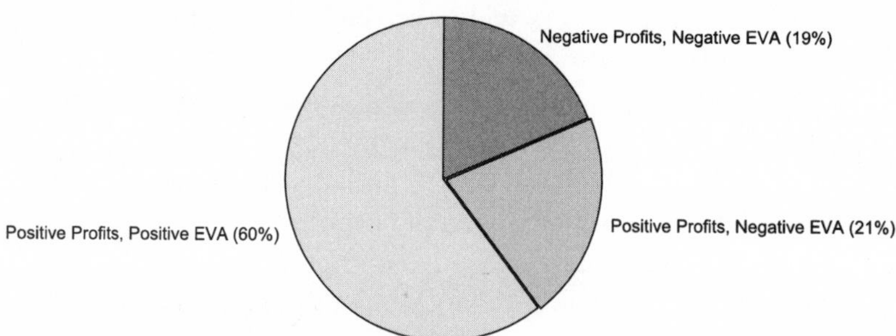

Figure 2-4–40% of Industrial Firms Deliver Negative Economic Value-Added

This large potential impact of information management on EVA causes discomfort for management–especially if a firm that is reporting positive profits to its shareholders is in fact recording a loss in EVA terms. Such a reversal occurred for 21% of U.S. industrial firms, based on the three-year averages for 1995-1997 as shown on Figure 2-4 which represents the shares by the number of firms.

Forty percent of U.S. industrial firms now deliver negative EVA, ironically during a time that represents one of the most prosperous periods in recent U.S. economic history. Such a negative EVA should cause considerable apprehension about the future

58 For the purpose of the analyses in this book the GAAP-reported "shareholder equity" is not used for pricing the cost of capital. A number of corporations set aside reserves that are excluded from the reported "shareholder equity." Regardless of the reason for these exclusions, they are nevertheless capital that has been retained in business and remains under control of management.

prospects of a large number of corporations in the event of an economic decline.[59]

In dollar terms, the U.S. industrial firms with positive profits and positive EVA delivered $137.8 billion of EVA.[60] The firms with negative profits and negative EVA accounted for $23.0 billion in losses, equal to 24.9% of the total EVA generated by all U.S. industrial firms. Firms that claim a profit, but are losing EVA (with positive reported profits and negative EVA) accounted for $11.3 billion of EVA.[61] Whenever the reversal from the prevailing high profit margins takes place more firms will convert from EVA creators to EVA detractors. Should that occur the task of improving the effectiveness of information resources would offer one of the most attractive options for improving financial results. Moreover, corporate executives may then have added incentives to institute long overdue improvements in their firms' information management practices.

Reported Profits Are Not Reliable Performance Indicators

Even firms that can boast about a positive Economic Value-Added will find that their EVA is only fractions of the reported profits after taxes. The median EVA/Profits ratio for 1,118 U.S. industrial corporations (for corporations with a positive EVA) is 47.2%. This relatively low percentage suggests that under GAAP rules, top corporate executives are able to claim at least a 52.8% larger contribution to shareholders than would be allowed if EVA were used as the measure of corporate performance.

59 The reader should remember that my calculations of EVA are based on the most favorable interpretation of the GAAP reported financial results.

60 To place this number in a perspective one should consider that it equals about half of the 1999 budget for the U.S. Department of Defense.

61 There are 680 U.S. industrial corporations that show a negative EVA. These firms spend a median of $4.57 of Information Management expense for every dollar they lose. Turning this enormous drain into positive EVA contributions then offers one of the greatest opportunities for profit improvement.

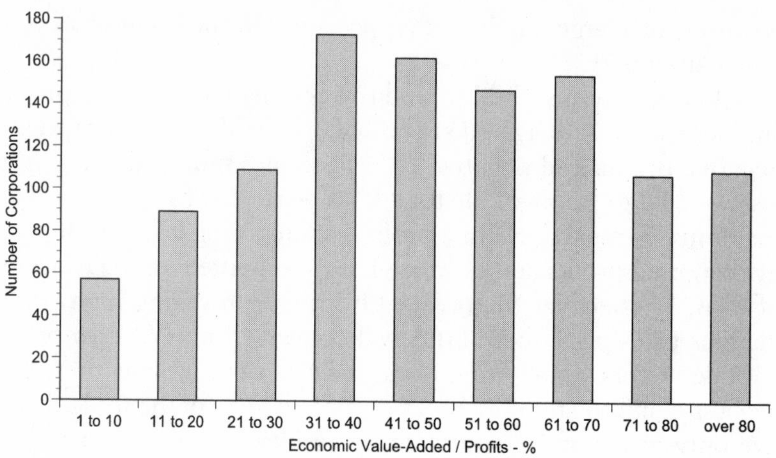

Figure 2-5–Economic Value-Added Is Less than Accounting Profits

If EVA were to be adopted as a standard measure of performance at least 57 CEOs would have to explain why they are delivering less than 90% of the shareholder economic benefits than is accounted for in their annual reports to shareholders. One should recognize that EVA-based reporting is a tough and unpopular taskmaster. It confronts corporate managers with greater economic hurdles for their performance than they faced when they relied on conventional accounting reports.

Information Management Costs Vastly Exceed Economic Value-Added

Information management costs are a very large multiplier of EVA. Therefore, any firm that is attempting to increase its EVA should look to the effective and efficient deployment of these costs as one of greatest sources of leverage for delivering favorable financial results.

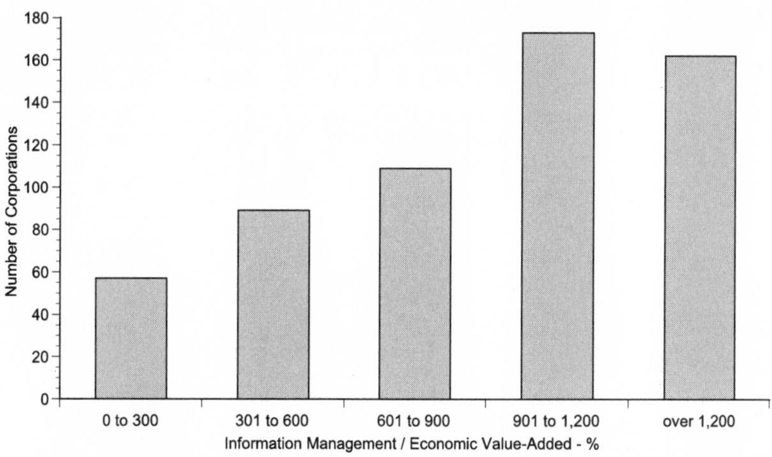

Figure 2-6–Information Management Costs are a Large Multiple of EVA

Summary Observation

A corporation's EVA is the true economic residual cost, after payment for cost-of-goods sold, depreciation, interest cost, taxes and the costs of shareholder equity. It stands for the economic contributions of those factors of production whose value is "intangible", e.g. the value of knowledge, the worth of the accumulated information assets, the intelligence of management, the effects of superior employee morale and competitive superiority gained trough excellent customer care. Therefore, the calculation of a firm's EVA is a prerequisite for assessing the worth of a firms productivity in information management.

3.

Measuring Information Productivity

The most frequently quoted indicators for assessing corporate productivity rely primarily on capital asset ratios, such as Return-on-Assets (ROA), Return-on-Investment (ROI) or Return-on-Equity (ROE). Such metrics are not adequate since capital has ceased to be the most important and scarcest input for a firm. Capital can be now treated just as another commodity that can be obtained at a competitive price. Information management has now overtaken capital both in importance as well as in magnitude. Information, not capital makes the decisive difference in a firm's economic performance.

The Need for Information Productivity Metrics

U.S. companies only rarely report about productivity in their annual reports, even though productivity is frequently touted as one of the firm's objectives. Part of the reason is that conventional accounting is more concerned with the interests of the holders of debt than with the concerns of those who would like to understand how the company could grow and prosper. The holders of debt like to know a great deal about the ratios of current assets to current liabilities, debt coverage and book value. All of these measures represent a banker's view of credit-worthiness in case of failure and subsequent liquidation of assets. In contrast, the purpose of productivity measurement is to judge whether a firm is succeeding in the creation of new wealth.

Rare attempts to report on productivity, such as the Forbes annual ranking of U.S. corporations, measure it in terms of sales per employee.[62] Leading information-age firms, such as IBM, for many

62 "The Forbes 500 Annual Directory," *Forbes*, April 25, 1994

years reported sales per employee as an indicator that its productivity was increasing even though it was accumulating an enormous amount of under-utilized plant capacity while losing market share.

Revenue per employee and profit per employee ratios are not only inconclusive but also usually invalid and misleading for making productivity comparisons. For instance, in one of the mature industries–food processing–the sales per employee for twenty-five firms range from a high of $745,000 to a low of $56,300. Does this range suggest that the highest-ranking firm is more than thirteen times more productive than the lowest ranking firm is? That is not the case, since the company with the high sales per employee deploys ten times more assets per employee, pays its employees higher salaries and purchases most of its packaging and transportation services from others. The company with the low sales per employee is a fully integrated operation, purchasing its ingredients only while employing mostly low-wage personnel. To compare the effectiveness of these two firms requires productivity metrics that take into consideration all of the variables which influence the ability of these firms to create shareholder wealth.

Before one can consider a high sales or high profits per employee ratio as an indication of high productivity, one must also consider the cost of capital, the occupations of employees, purchases and taxes as an input. True increases in productivity are the result of an effective combination of many factors of production, including land, labor, capital and information. Taking any one factor in isolation as an indicator of productivity will be always misleading. Regrettably, such an approach to productivity reporting is still widely used in comparing the performance of most corporations. Government statistical agencies also use such simplified methods for judging productivity gains, such as calculating productivity on the basis of hours worked by the employees. It is my intention to overcome some of the problems caused by an examination of isolated ratios by concentrating on a measure of productivity of what will be shown as the single most important resource of the modern industrial corporation: the costs of information management.

THE IMPORTANCE OF MEASURING PRODUCTIVITY

The chairman of the Federal Reserve, Wall Street bankers and assorted chief business executives have explained the enormous gains in the 1990s stock market as an upward expansion in high-technology industries that are expected to deliver sustainable superior profits from steadily rising productivity gains.

These proponents of the new economy which is based on the productivity of computerization emphasize that the new electronic technologies have been harnessed by the workforce to deliver improved operating results are sustainable for a long time to come.[63] They have concluded that the build-up of information technologies has enabled companies to offset increased payrolls with more efficient processes so that incomes can rise without fueling excessive inflation. To make their case, the optimists rely on a selected assortment of measures as well as anecdotal reports from business magazines.[64] In a poll of two hundred CEOs and chief financial officers, the advances in information technology ranked third in their choice as the enablers behind the economic growth in the 1990s.[65]

A Skeptic's View

The productivity skeptics refer to official government statistics denying that aggregate productivity has been rising. Unfortunately, none of the government reports have been able to sort out which components of the decline have been alleviated by means of

63 Uchitelle, L., "What Goes Up Must Usually, Well, Stop Going Up," *The New York Times*, August 10, 1997 quotes David Wyss "People are looking for an easy explanation of why profits are doing well." One explanation has been summoned:"...the main characteristic of this new era is rising productivity. The new technologies, particularly computers and telecommunications are making workers more productive."

64 Uchitelle, L. "Measuring productivity in the 90s," *The New York Times*, August 2, 1997. *The Economist*, August 9, 1997 echoed this message in an editorial that much of the current market exuberance is due to "...delightful notion that productivity ...is in the throes of a secular rise, thanks to the spread of information technology..." There is one banker, the chief economist of Morgan Stanley Dean Witter, who states that "...there's not a shred of credible evidence in the macro-economic data that supports the notion of a meaningful improvement in America's productivity." See Roach, S.S., "The Worker Backlash," *The New York Times*, August 24, 1997.

65 Hoffman, T., "Feds link IT, productivity but hard evidence is lacking," *Computerworld*, August 25, 1997.

increased efficiencies in information handling.[66] Meanwhile, government economists have been keeping records that show that the annual rate of productivity increases since 1990 has been slowing down as compared with the prior three decades:[67]

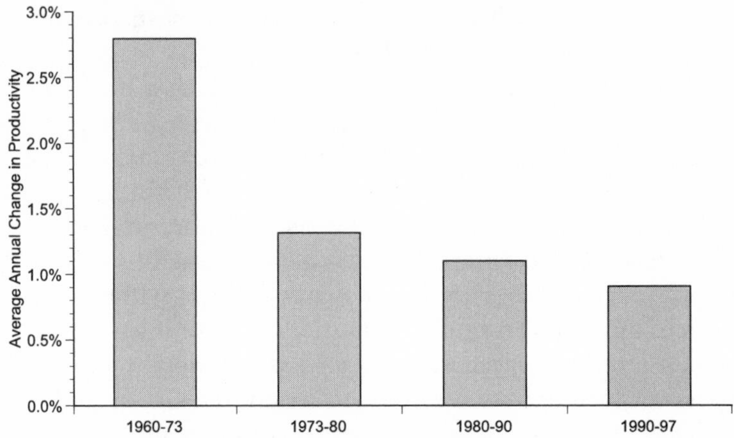

Figure 3-1–Productivity growth reported by U.S. Bureau of Labor Statistics

I do not trust the government's macroeconomic data about productivity because they neglect to account adequately for the output of the service and the public sectors. One should not rely on this data to arrive at verifiable conclusions. Furthermore, corporate management cannot make practical use of these data to make decisions within the context of their own operations.

66 McNamee, M., "The Productivity Boom is Still a Mystery," *Business Week*, August 10, 1997. Melloan, G., "Where Is the Information Technology Payoff," *The Wall Street Journal*, August 11, 1997 echoes the identical view, adding that "...it could be that the gains some businesses are making with computers are being offset by higher costs elsewhere inflicted by government red tape." I have documented the government's waste in Chapter 14 (Workload without Payoff) in *The Squandered Computer*.

67 The Bureau of Labor Statistics, quoted in *The New York Times*, August 2, 1997. This measure of productivity is based on inflation-adjusted value of GNP per million hours worked. It is a metric that does not recognize changes in the composition of the workforce, does not take into consideration stagnation in the wage rates and is particularly deficient in accounting for the work done in the service sector of the economy.

RELEVANCE OF PRODUCTIVITY

The stakes in these debates are enormous. The performance of the stock market, the prospects of achieving a balanced budget and the ability to finance an increasingly expensive government, all depend on the expectation of steadily rising productivity gains. Meanwhile, the presumption that information technologies improve productivity gives legitimacy proposals to invest more money on computers.[68]

The prevailing opinions of the productivity-through-information enthusiasts cannot be supported either by denying the relevance of government statistics or by the selective analysis of the data.[69] Only measures that can be explicitly related to corporate financial performance can settle the arguments about whether the U.S. is either losing or gaining on productivity growth where such measurements are feasible. Reliance on corporate financial data has also the advantage of changing the speculations from unverifiable conjectures to certifiable facts.

IN SEARCH OF EVIDENCE

U.S. industrial corporations include in their financial statements an item known as Sales, General & Administrative Cost (SG&A) which is also inclusive of R&D spending in most public financial statements. It represents the costs of coordinating, controlling, guiding, promoting, motivating, training and managing employees, customers and suppliers, while making and delivering the goods. The S.G.&A with the R&D expense largely accounts for a firm's overhead expenses. It also reflects the costs devoted to the generation and consumption of all data.

68 Encouragement of I.T. spending as a solution to most corporate problems can be found in a large library of books authored by consultants and computer industry executives. Books by Tapscott, D., and Caston, A., *Paradigm Shift–the New Promise of Information Technology*, McGraw-Hill, 1993 and Gates, B., *The Road Ahead*, Viking Penguin, 1995 are characteristic of such advocacy that relies entirely on anecdotes and not on financially sound evidence.

69 Stevenson, R. W., "Greenspan Voices Doubt on Statistics," *The New York Times*, September 6, 1997. Mr. Greenspan, at a speech for the Center for Economic Policy Research cast doubt on the reliability of statistics showing a decline in US productivity while the economy has remained inflation-free.

Evaluating Productivity Gains

Take the case of a paper firm that employs 400 people to produce boxes. It also requires 200 employees in executive, managerial, professional and sales occupations to manage the production, distribution and selling of its products.

An advanced computer system is installed. The company now requires only 300 workers for production and only 180 information-processing employees in information-handling jobs. Profits have increased modestly, but administrative expenses are up to pay for the new computer system. Inventories have been reduced, but assets and debt are higher than before. Meanwhile, the increased responsiveness to customers allows the firm to retain its traditional premium prices for boxes, though a small decline in revenues indicates rising competitive problems.

Do the increased revenues per employee prove that corporate productivity has increased? Does the reduced inventory-to-sales ratio confirm that information has been successfully traded for assets? Does the increased overhead ratio defined in terms of head counts give a contrary sign that information workers are now less productive?

None of these single-ratio indicators can prove much. Together they may offer contradictory findings. To measure corporate productivity requires a composite measure that reflects the interactions of the resources that are put to use in a modern organization. Unfortunately, most of the existing composite measures of corporate productivity are unsatisfactory.

Problems with Existing Measures of Corporate Productivity

The shifting of corporate performance measures from profits, as defined by GAAP, to Economic Value-Added (EVA) has far-reaching implications on the ways in which one should evaluate overall corporate productivity. Before I present my approach it is useful to examine in detail the problems associated with existing measures of corporate productivity.

The most frequently quoted indicators for assessing corporate productivity rely primarily on capital asset ratios, such as Return-on-Assets (ROA), Return-on-Investment (ROI) or Return-on-Equity (ROE). Accordingly, principally the following indicators are now used to evaluate overall corporate productivity:

Return-on-Assets = Accounting Profits/ Total Balance Sheet Assets Employed

Return-on-Investment = Accounting Profits/ Total Investment in Business

Return-on-Equity = Accounting Profits/ GAAP-Defined Shareholder Equity

These ratios are similar in that they reflect a definition of productivity (Output/Input) where only profits matter as output and only capital matters as input. The roles of people and management do not enter into these measures except as an expense and therefore as a subtraction from profits. As with GAAP, these definitions of productivity are biased to reflect the interests of the debt-holding owners who prefer indicators that show how well their assets are protected.

The questionable utility of these measures is dramatized in the stock market valuation of corporations and in the prices organizations can command when acquired. Rarely, if ever, do these transactions reflect the reported accounting profits, the balance sheet assets or the figure recorded as the shareholder equity. The median of the ratio of the market valuation on the stock markets to the "book value" of net assets reveals the extent to which conventional accounts understate corporate marketable worth.

The 1997 median value of the Market Valuation/Book Value of Net Assets for 2,177 U.S. industrial firms was 232%. This ratio demonstrates that what the accountants report is understated by 132% in at least half of the cases. As the ratio of Market Valuation to Assets, Equity and Investment exceeds 500% (which is the case for 470 corporations, or 22% of industrial corporations), the dependence on capital-based ratios becomes less meaningful in assessing corporate productivity.

Most Frequently Used Measures of Productivity Are Faulty and Obsolete

It is the principal thesis of this book that the capital-based approach to evaluating the productivity of firms is fundamentally flawed, obsolete and potentially misleading for the following reasons:

- Capital is no longer the most important economic input for a modern industrial corporation to function.
- The availability of capital from investors has ceased to be the critical resource by virtue of its scarcity. It is now readily available, for a competitive price. The global financial markets make it possible to re-deploy a trillion dollars worth of capital at a moment's notice.
- Capital has become a commodity and is readily available for a price that is commensurate with risk. Capital need not be owned any more–leasing, outsourcing and subcontracting offer a wide range of options to acquire capital through purchases or rentals.
- The most important assets of a corporation are the people who sustain it and the relationships they develop both internally and externally.
- The critical resource of the modern corporation is the management of information, which now exceeds the costs of capital ownership by a large multiplier. Competent information management teams are not easily available and are not easily replaced by other means, such as mergers and acquisitions. Furthermore, the current expenditures for information management are unrelated to results.

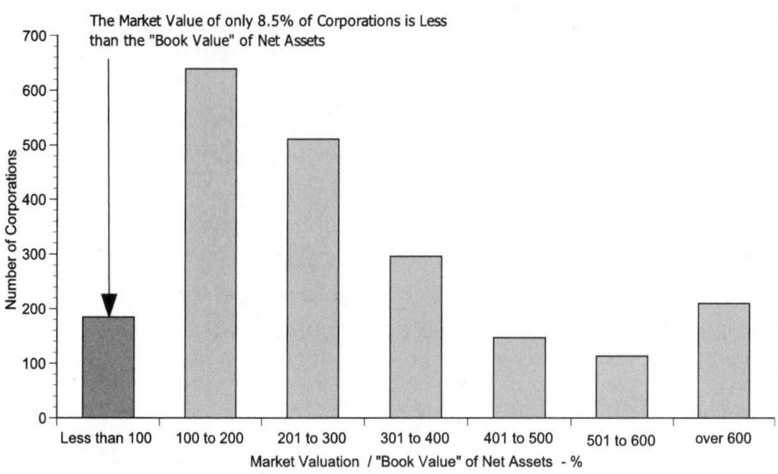

Figure 3-2–Market Valuation Exceeds the Book Value

This book offers an added measure of corporate productivity that will overcome many of the limitations of capital-based measures. It does so by defining Economic Value-Added (EVA) as the measure of economic output and the costs of information management, as the decisive measure of economic input. This measure should be a supplemental indicator for assessing the planning, budgeting proposals as well as for evaluating operating results.

Information Management Costs Exceed Costs of Capital Ownership

The most important argument that favors the designation of information management as the most important discretionary input for productivity analysis is the fact that its leverage is greater than the costs of ownership of capital. That is demonstrated in Figure 3-3. The median value of the Information Management/Cost of Capital Ownership ratio is 595%. Only 130 of the 1,605 U.S. industrial corporations–or 8.1% of the total–had costs of capital ownership greater than their costs of information management. These were mostly firms engaged in a highly capital-intensive production of primary metals

The typical U.S. industrial corporation ceased to be a capital-intensive enterprise over fifty years ago. Its performance cannot (and should not) be judged any more by the returns the corporation realizes on its invested capital (e.g. ROI, ROA or ROE). With capital constituting a significantly smaller input than information, what matters from now on is the productivity of information management.

Ours is not an economy where capital budgeting for investing in tangible assets is the key to success. Rather it is an economy in which information has ceased to be an expense and is increasingly taking on the attributes of long-term capital investments.[70]

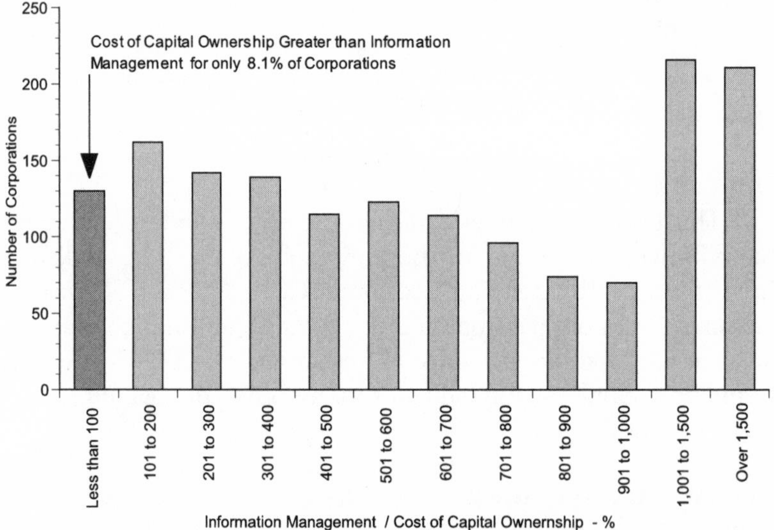

Figure 3-3–Information Management Costs Exceed Cost of Capital Ownership

Today we can observe a change that in every respect is as dramatic as anything is that took place when the industrial era was born. During the transition from an order based on land-ownership to economies based on capital-ownership, many old institutions remained in place that masked the transformation. The asset-based measures of productivity are similar relics. They make it difficult to

70 This topic will be the persistent theme in the follow-on books about information technology and knowledge capital.

observe how the underlying economics of business is changing. Therefore, as the first step towards increased understanding of the productivity of the information resources, we must accept a change in the way productivity is defined and calculated.

MEASURING INFORMATION PRODUCTIVITY

It is only a matter of time before corporate leadership will be forced to shift attention to information management as a resource of greater economic leverage than any other input. In terms of Economic Value-Added the total costs of information will certainly warrant at least the same concentrated attention as is presently bestowed on capital costs. The need to answer the following questions will direct such efforts:

- Is information technology improving the productivity of corporate information resources?
- How does one track gains from investments resulting from changes in management processes and increased employee training?
- What new measures of effectiveness are needed to equip operating management with indicators to guide their decisions investments in training, innovation, market development and business transformation?
- Which indicators support motivation to make the right choices and hence, that could be used for incentive compensation purposes?

Determining Input

Controversies about the valuation of inputs are the principal reason why productivity reporting is not popular. Financial analysts will allege that it is difficult to calculate information productivity because there are no precedents for clearly separating "information" from "production." Accountants prefer to dispense with that question by attaching most of the information management costs as an overhead multiplier to direct expenses. The typical overhead burden rates, sometimes exceeding 400% in factory operations, are very often much larger than the direct costs, thus making accounting for information as an overhead expense inappropriate for making decisions.

The computation of information productivity depends on getting the costs of information approximately right. My definition of information costs is very broad. It includes all costs of managing, coordinating, training, communicating, planning, accounting, marketing and research. Unless an activity is clearly a direct expense associated with delivering to a paying customer a product or service it will be classified as an information expense.[71]

Activity-based costing methods are particularly useful in separating cost elements that are directly related to the production of customer value from those that are engaged in support.[72] This method employs a disciplined and standardized approach to cost analysis. My approach to determining information inputs is to have the client to fill out forms that reveal all the costs according to a prescribed method for separating the direct costs of operations from the supporting costs of information.

Estimating Inputs

In many cases, especially when conducting exploratory studies, top management may not wish to engage in elaborate studies for coming up with preliminary insights as to what is their overall information productivity. In many instances management prefers to use readily available public source data to make the initial productivity estimates.

To come up with approximate valuations of information productivity in this book, we will use the published data on expenses that can be classified largely as costs of information. This approximation is:

71 Exceptions to this rule would be support services such as guards, cafeterias and transportation.

72 James A. Brimson, *Activity Accounting*, John Wiley and National Association of Accountants, New York, 1991

Information Productivity = Output/Input

Where:

Information Output = Economic Value-Added

Information Input = Sales, General, Administrative Costs plus Research & Development

Information Productivity® is a remarkably useful ratio for the purpose of relative ranking and benchmarking comparisons although the above valuations of information inputs will understate the total cost of information, especially if central overhead is improperly allocated to local operations,

PURPOSE OF INFORMATION PRODUCTIVITY ANALYSES

The purpose of information productivity analysis is to shift attention from information technology itself to the effectiveness of the executives who manage it. The key to obtaining business value from computers lies in linking the uses of the technology to business plans. This connection must be explicit by showing how it overcomes existing business problems and how it contributes to future gains. In isolation, computers are just pieces of metal, plastic and glass.

We have to evaluate the contributions of information technologies in terms of their effects on increasing the ratio of management value-added to management costs, which is how we define Information Productivity. If information productivity increases as a result of the deployment of information technologies, what will indicate whether one's computers are producing a business payoff? Focusing on information productivity rather than on information technology will lead to the following improved practices:

• Correctly diagnose conditions that will improve information productivity before making an attempt to re-systemize, reengineer or automate.

• Make management more productive before adding electronic means, by first finding what impairs their business performance.

• Automate only those business processes that are directly linked to measurable improvements in profits

4.

INFORMATION PRODUCTIVITY FINDINGS

The Information Productivity of U.S. Industrial corporations has been improving since 1990. An examination of corporations into groups ranked by Information Productivity offers useful insights about the characteristics of firms with superior and inferior Information Productivity results. The top ranking firms delivered almost seven dollars of EVA for every dollar spent on information management. The bottom ranking firms were losing almost twenty-two dollars for every dollar spent on information management. The Information Productivity metrics is also much more sensitive for the purpose of discrimination of excellence from failure than conventional measures, such as Return-on-Equity and Market-to-Book ratios.

INFORMATION PRODUCTIVITY ANALYSIS

Appendix C contains tabulations of the Information Productivity® (IP) rankings of U.S. industrial corporations. The listings also include key information management ratios, such as information management/cost of goods, information management/net assets and information management/revenue to be used for comparative purposes. All of the data are based on three-year averages (1995-1997) of the reported financial results.

The massive amount of data makes it difficult to discern the key relationships between Information Productivity® and other relevant indictors of financial performance. It is the purpose of this Chapter to highlight some of the more useful insights.

INFORMATION PRODUCTIVITY HAS IMPROVED

Over the last decade the medians of U.S. industrial corporations have displayed the following trends in the relationship between information management costs and other financial indicators:

- Lower information management costs to deliver goods;
- Higher information management costs per employee, rising faster than employee compensation;
- Lower information management costs to support revenue;
- Lower information management costs to deliver profits;
- Lower ratios of information management costs to assets;
- No correlation between the costs of information management and profitability;
- No correlation between the estimated costs of information technology and profitability.

An examination of the most recent Information Productivity trend offers a way of understanding the interactions between the above seven indicators:[73]

Explanation of Information Productivity Gains

Gains in the Economic Value-Added have the greatest influence on any gains in Information Productivity. In calculating the value of EVA the cost of capital is a variable that is largely independent of what corporate information management can influence.

To test the hypothesis that improved management practices as well as efficiencies attributable to computerization explain the productivity gain, we will first remove the effect of lowered interest rates from our calculations.

73 Medians of Information Productivity for 1,522 U.S. industrial corporations for 1990-1997.

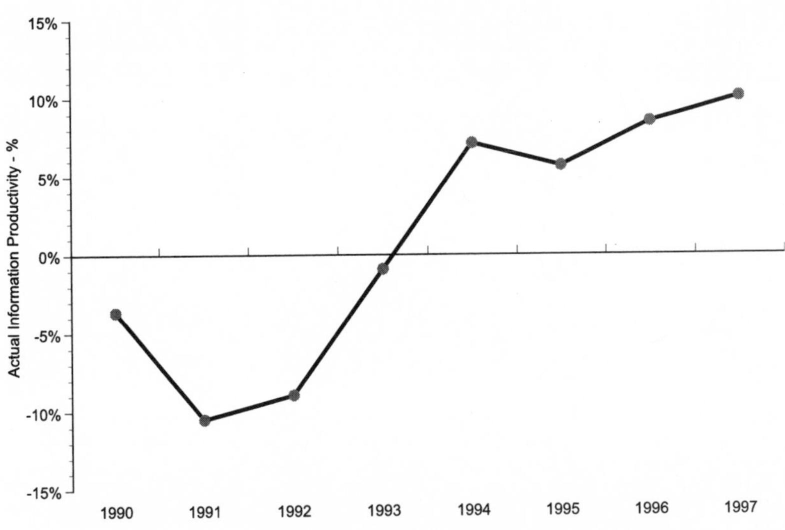

Figure 4-1 - Information Productivity Median Values Show Remarkable Recent Gains

The median interest rates paid by U.S. industrial corporations for debt were as follows:

	1990	1991	1992	1993	1994	1995	1996	1997
Interest Rates Paid for Corporate Debt - %	10.02	9.46	8.04	6.51	5.91	6.76	6.57	6.24

Figure 4-2 - The Decline in the Median Cost of Debt May Explain Productivity Gains

An examination of the trend in the ratio of corporate interest payments to profits before taxes would provide an insight how the reduced cost of debt would account for the rise in corporate profits:

Determining the contribution of lower interest rates to gains in Information Productivity then becomes a simple matter of recalculating the values in constant terms, e.g. as if the interest rates were held constant as of 1990.

However, before one can proceed with calculating the effects of lower costs of debt on corporate profits in 1990 terms, one must take into consideration taxes. Debt is a deductible expense. Lower

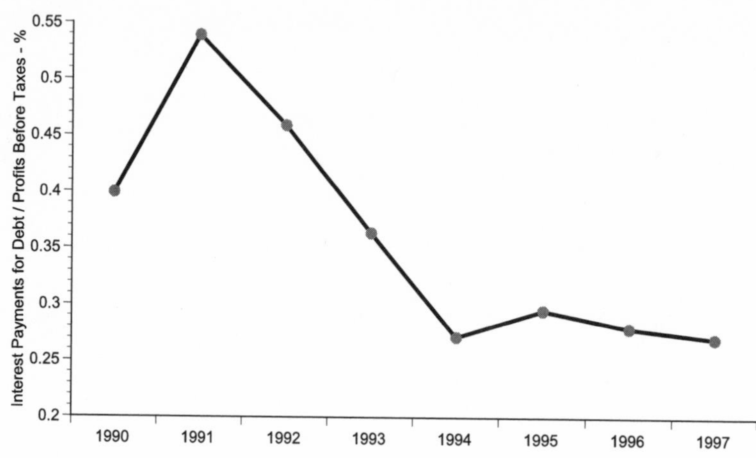

Figure 4-3 - The Reduced Share of Debt Payments Would Explain the Rise in Profits

interest costs would reduce the tax deductions and would have an unfavorable impact on profits after taxes.

The effective corporate tax rate increased from 1990-1997:[74]

	1990	1991	1992	1993	1994	1995	1996	1997
Effective Corporate Tax Rate	35.0%	34.7%	34.5%	34.3%	36.4%	33.9%	36.4%	36.0%

Figure 4-4 - Rising Taxes Offset Some of the Benefits of Lower Interest Rates

In calculating the Information Productivity, in 1990 terms, profits after taxes will be reduced by the differences in the cost of 1990 interest of 10.2% and the actual interest costs incurred. The result would be further adjusted for the loss of tax deductions from lowered interest expense:

	1990	1991	1992	1993	1994	1995	1996	1997
Constant Information Productivity - in 1990 Terms	-3.7%	-12.5%	-16.1%	-14.7%	-10.0%	-7.9%	-6.6%	-7.1%

Figure 4-5 - 1990 Constant Interest Rate Yields Negative Information Productivity

74 This is an example of a national economic policy that can be characterized as "The Fed Gives, the Treasury Takes."

A comparison of the actual and the constant Information Productivity trends suggests that contrary to popular assumptions there is no evidence of U.S. industrial corporations improving their internal information management practices. Whatever gains have occurred recently is the consequence of the monetary and fiscal policies that have resulted in the lowered the cost of interest:

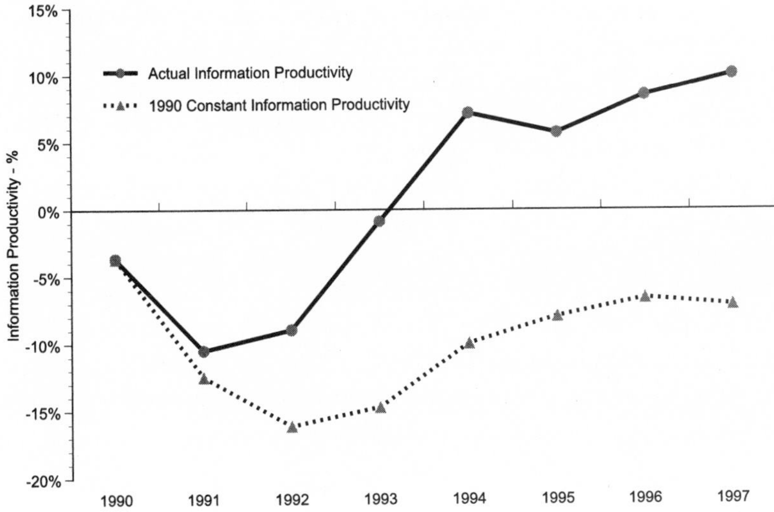

Figure 4-6 - Without Interest Reductions Information Productivity Would be Negative

Conjectures about the influences may that contributed to an increase in actual Information Productivity since 1990 will be arguable, especially by the advocates of computerization who attribute to information technologies most of such gains. Our analysis suggests that it is the reduced cost of capital that offers the simplest, demonstrable and verifiable explanation of any gains in Information Productivity.[75]

It is not corporate management that can claim the actual productivity gains. The reductions in the cost of capital in the period

75 Directly verifiable means that one can test the Information Productivity gains of individual firms to check if changes in the cost of capital explain any of the improvements. Strassmann, Inc. routinely performs such analyses for clients.

from 1990 through 1997 are largely the consequence of to an unusual combination of favorable national and international economic conditions that created the climate in which U.S. corporations found themselves.

The above chart suggests that the claim of a vastly more productive information age (based on Moore's law) has no basis, so far. Our analyses show that the "new economy" has not delivered the improvements in the productivity of the information workforce. The unchanged, and negative levels of information productivity - during a period of unprecedented build-up of computerization - shows that the promise of what the U.S. can expect from information technologies remains unproven.

If the current improvements in Information Productivity do not reflect lasting structural changes within firms, but reflect external influences, that raises the question whether the current levels of Information Productivity are sustainable, or only manifestation of a changeable economic cycle. If the productivity gains realized so far can be fully explained by the effects of fiscal and monetary policies then the sustaining of the current gains is precarious and vulnerable to the vagaries of economic and political forces.

RANKING FIRMS BY INFORMATION PRODUCTIVITY

Our analyses of Information Productivity have so far been based on a study of median values. However, action how to improve productivity is not a matter of averages or medians. It is the result of success or failures at the firm level.

A calculation of the 1990-1997 Information Productivity values based on dollar-weighted financial results showed higher and more volatile results than indicated by the median values. This suggested that the productivity achievements of a few large firms could have an inordinate effect on the economy.[76] Therefore, dividing U.S.

76 Ip, G., "Top-Heavy Stock Market May Become a Drag," *The Wall Street Journal*, January 18, 1999. Fifty largest stocks in the Standard & Poor "500" traded at an average of forty-three times earnings, while the bottom 450 traded at an average of twenty-five times earnings. The differential between the valuations of just a handful of largest corporations and the rest of the firms has never been as large in at least forty years.

industrial firms into ten grouping ranked by Information Productivity offers additional insights as to the characteristics of the top and bottom performers:

Ranking of Firms by Information Productivity	Median Information Productivity	Information Management / Cost of Goods	Information Management / Net Assets	Information Management / Revenue
Top tenth percentile	72.9%	11.2%	13.6%	6.7%
10 to 20th percentile	32.3%	20.6%	32.6%	13.6%
20 to 30th percentile	20.3%	30.6%	44.6%	19.1%
30 to 40th percentile	13.6%	28.9%	52.1%	19.4%
40 to 50th percentile	8.5%	38.7%	66.1%	23.5%
50 to 60th percentile	3.5%	34.5%	76.7%	23.2%
60 to 70th percentile	-2.4%	35.1%	72.6%	23.3%
70 to 80th percentile	-11.7%	34.5%	67.5%	23.0%
90 to 90th percentile	-30.4%	27.5%	48.6%	20.2%
Bottom tenth percentile	-101.5%	21.3%	20.1%	13.4%

Figure 4-7 - Lowest Cost, Asset and Revenue Ratios Yield High Information Productivity

One of the most important characteristics of the Information Productivity index is its unforgiving disclosure of poor performance. The large spread between its top and bottom deciles in productivity reflects the bias of EVA (Economic Value-Added) to penalize unprofitable holders of costly assets.

The above tabulation is a listing of the median values of each of the ten deciles, each consisting of 135 U.S. industrial firms. The top decile contains firms that were ranked #1 through #135 respectively according to their IP values. In the top decile the values of IP ranged from a high of 698% to the low of 73%. The significance of those numbers is that the #1 ranked corporation created $6.98 of EVA for every $1.00 spent on information management. The bottom decile contains firms that were ranked #1,215 through #1,350 respectively according to their IP values. In the bottom decile the value of IP ranged from -47% to the lowest recorded value of IP of -2,164%. The significance of those numbers is that the lowest ranking corporation was losing $21.64 of EVA for every $1.00 spent on information management

The most important finding of this ranking by the criterion of Information Productivity is that the top ranking firms are successful without having high information management costs. The top decile of the firms could show the lowest information management/cost of goods ratio, the lowest information management/net assets ratio and the lowest information management/revenue ratio.

Characteristics of the Information Management Ratios

The median values of the information management ratios reveal a wide range of values. The most sensitive metric is the information management/net asset ratio, which indicates a steep decline after crossing the midpoint of the IP values. Above average performers rapidly cut this ratio from the high of 76.7% to the best value of only 13.6%. The reverse is true for below average performers, who also show reductions as their rankings sink to a low of 20.1%.

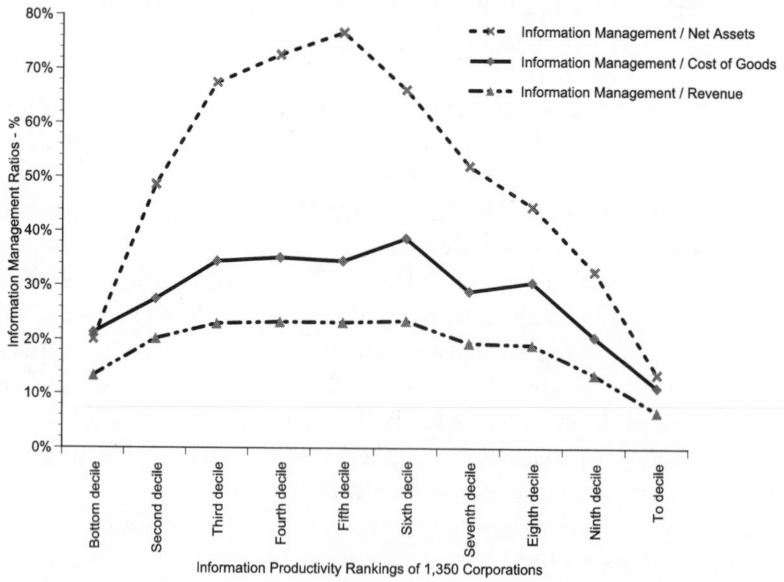

Figure 4-8 - Information Productivity Patterns for 1,350 Corporations

Similar patterns can be also observed for the information management/cost of goods and information management/revenue ratios, though the rise and the decline are not as steep as in the case of the information management/net asset indicator. Three important insights should emerge from a study of the above patterns.

First, just citing that a company has a particular ratio for any one single indicator does not mean much unless one knows its IP value. This observation underscores the fact that quoting the value of any one ratio has little meaning in the absence of some measure that relates to economic value. This is why quoting a ratio such as the information technology budget as a percentage of revenue is misleading because both winners and losers can show identical ratios, but for different reasons.

Second, one should understand why the declining ratios for the losers penalize them while the identical reductions give the winners an added advantage. It all has to do with the observation that while wealth often comes from thrifty habits poor people also spend less because that's all they can afford.

Third, some ratios discriminate between success and failure better than others do. Of all of the indicators for tracking the rise and fall of corporate Sales, General and Administrative costs, the relation to revenue is the least sensitive and should be used only sparingly. Yet, that ratio is the only one the CFO magazine currently tabulates in annual surveys as worthy of attention.[77]

Comparison of IP with ROE

For any new indicator to be accepted by conservative financial professionals, it must show a clear advantage. If IP is to be used in addition to widely adopted ROE (Return-on-Equity) ratio, it must be characterized by a greater sensitivity in assessing the financial health of a corporation than a ROE-based valuation. The following graph shows profiles of ROE and IP calculations medians for individual deciles, for the U.S. industrial corporation in our sample.

77 "SG&A Survey Results," *CFO Magazine*, December 1998.

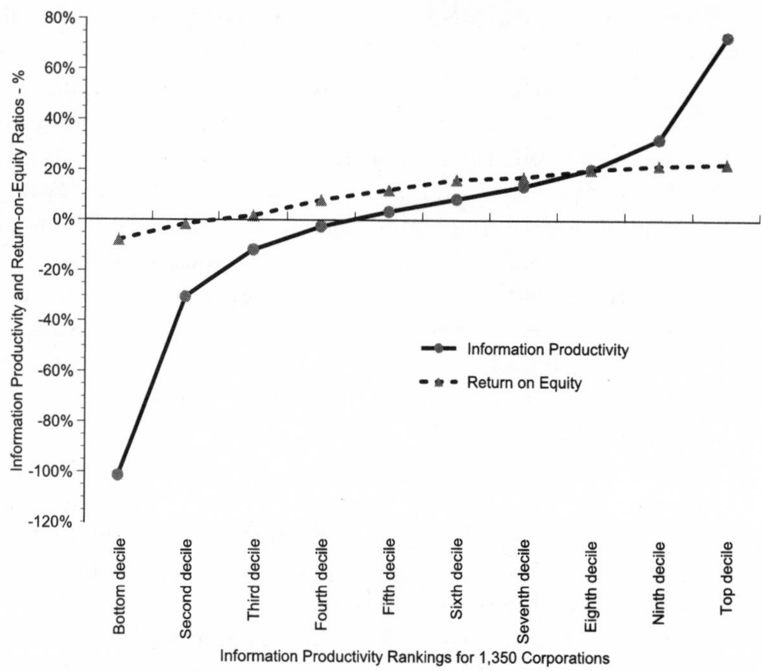

Figure 4-9 - Information Productivity is More Sensitive than ROE

Compared with the calculations of IP the ROE has a much flatter scale of judging the productivity of firms over the entire range of IP values. Because of the effects of EVA, the IP index discriminates more sharply both success and failure, which is desirable in any financial indicator.

A skeptic might argue that this analysis is unfair because the graphic representation has been set into deciles that were defined by IP rankings. How would a similar comparison look to an analyst who does not believe in IP and wishes to slot IP vs. ROE comparisons into decile groups defined by ROE ranking, not by IP ranking?

Even with the bias favoring ROE rankings, the IP indicator is approximately equivalent to ROE valuation for successful firms, but definitely more unforgiving to unsuccessful firms. Since the fastest and least costly path to financial success is to minimize losses, the IP indicator would serve that purpose very well.

The following graph shows such a comparison, but is biased in favor of ROE, with the rankings slotted according to ROE values:

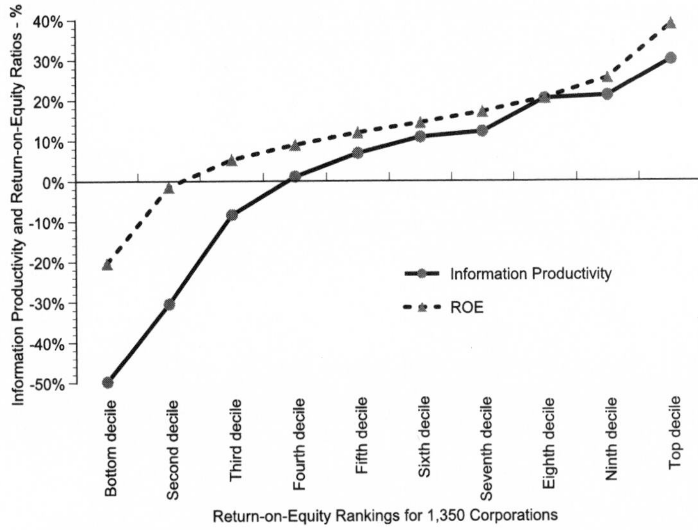

Figure 4-10 - Information Productivity is More Sensitive than the ROE Performance Indicator

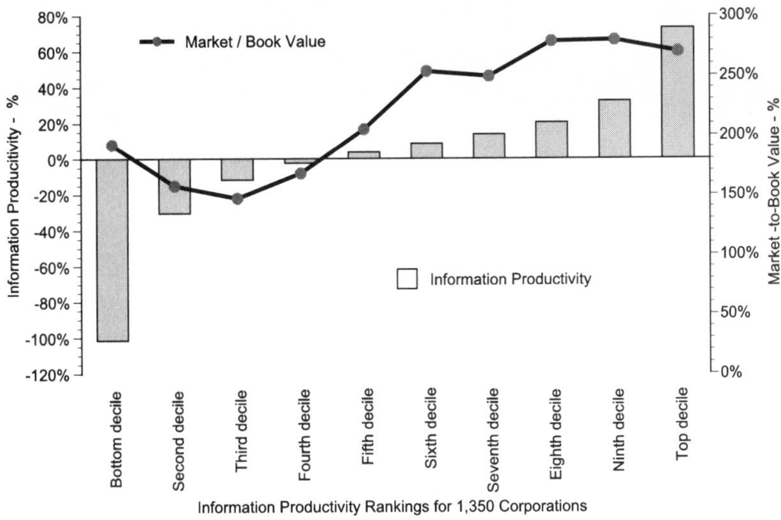

Figure 4-11 - Information Productivity is More Sensitive than the Market/Book Indicator

Comparison of IP with Market-to-Book Valuations

Stock market analysts use market/book ratios as one of several significant indicators of corporate value. How would the IP indicator assist them in making more reliable assessments?

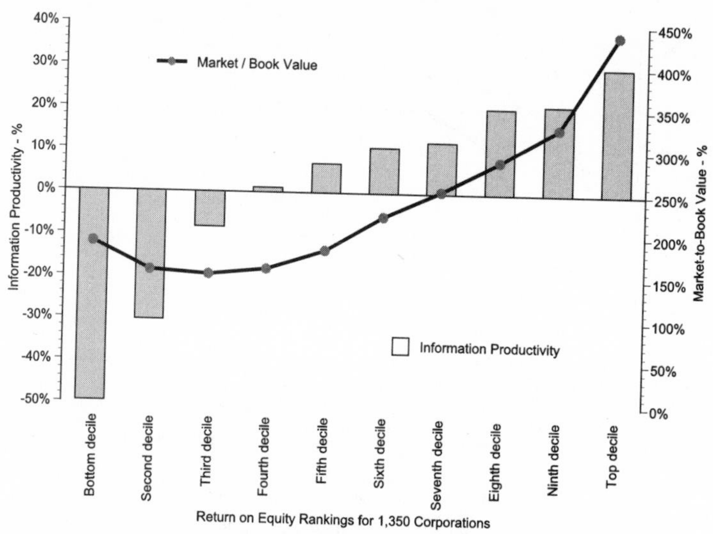

Figure 4-12 - Information Productivity is More Sensitive than the Market/Book Indicator

The preceding graphs show profiles of Market/Book and IP calculations for 1,350 U.S. industrial corporations from our sample. The Market/Book ratio shows a surprisingly insensitive response to fundamentally different characteristics of winners or losers. Slightly above-average performance is well rewarded, truly superior performance is discounted and abysmal results (those of the lowest decile) are given positive market valuations. IP does not do that. Winners are recognized and losers are penalized. Again, we can be criticized that such analyses are unfair because the graphic representations have been set into deciles defined by IP rankings. How would a similar comparison look for an analyst who does not believe in IP and wishes to slot Market/Book ratios as defined by a ROE ranking?

The above graph shows such a comparison, but is biased in favor of ROE measures, with the rankings slotted accordingly. In this case both market/book and IP track financial successes in ways that are equivalent. However, when it comes to failures, the market/book ratio is more lenient than IP. I suppose that reflects the faith of the stock market in the reliability of the accounting system to protect investors against excessive losses, at least in the case of U.S. industrial corporations.

Information Productivity and Company Size

Much has been written about the advantages of small corporations as compared with larger firms. Smaller firms are supposed to be more productive and have lower overhead. Because proprietorships are more profitable and generally smaller than corporations, smaller firms are also supposed to be more profitable than larger firms are. Can these widely held beliefs be substantiated?

The following tabulation suggests that most of the speculations about the benefits of small firms are not always correct:

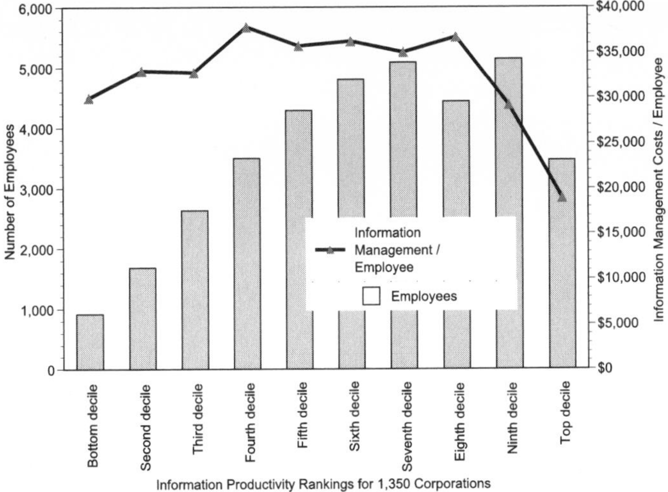

Figure 4-13 - Most Productive Firms are Smaller and Spend Less on Information

The following insights can be gathered from the profile of the U.S. industrial firms in the ten groupings that were arrayed according to their IP rankings:

- When the median size of the firm declines from 5,000 employees to under 1,000 employees, its Information Productivity drops precipitously.
- The Information Management Cost/Employee is almost identical, regardless of size, for 70% of the firms. The exceptions are in the top ranking two deciles, where the ratio declines dramatically and the bottom ranking decile, where the ratio declines moderately.
- The best performing group is of median size and shows the lowest ratio of Information Management Cost/Employee.

The significance of these findings is to confirm that unless one collects sufficient data that constitutes trustworthy evidence, all generalizations without fact remain nothing but appealing, but airy fiction.

5.

Information Productivity Analysis

The Information Productivity metric is useful for planning, budgeting and performance evaluation. An organization should benchmark its performance against "look-alike" firms that would be designated by top management as the models against which the corporation should strive to excel. An analysis of the firm's own historical performance as well as comparison against the Information Productivity record of the industry should provide insights as to the realism of the proposed plans and budgets.

ILLUSTRATIVE CASE STUDY

All the concepts and the findings that we already have presented in this book are of limited value to the reader unless the reader can see how Information Productivity analysis is put into action. It is helpful to study a case about a hypothetical client firm (Pharmaceutical X) that wants to examine its IP performance. This case study will illustrated how to apply IP assessments to an industry-grouping of twenty-three look-alike pharmaceutical preparations manufacturing companies (SIC code 2834).

Step #1: Rank Firms by Information Productivity

All information productivity assessments using my methods start with the selection of look-alike firms that need not be direct competitors. Excellence is not necessarily confined to the existing markets as defined by management. A listing of the key information management indicators, for the last period when public data is available, sets the stage for the analytic sequence that follows.

Since the purpose of Information Productivity assessment is to identify patterns of excellence, comparisons are made against the median indicators of firms that show higher or lower Information Productivity than Pharmaceutical X.

Step #2: Compare with Superior Performers

My comparison of Information Management indicators show that Pharmaceutical X's IP ranking is not a matter of information efficiency (e.g., lower costs of Information Management), but a matter of information effectiveness. The lower values of IP reflect lower business profitability which may reflect pricing, market share or other competitive impediments.

Company	Information Management /Cost of Goods	Information Management /Net Assets	Information Managemen t/Revenue	Information Managemen t/Employee	Information Productivity
WATSON PHARMACEUTICALS	59%	12%	20%	$67.639	130.7%
AMGEN	607%	52%	46%	$209.985	47.3%
ABBOTT LABORATORIES	92%	80%	34%	$73.180	46.3%
BRISTOL-MYERS SQUIBB	201%	108%	47%	$145.504	35.1%
REXALL SUNDOWN	122%	60%	43%	$139.412	24.4%
ALLERGAN	173%	70%	51%	$96.770	16.0%
ICN PHARMACEUTICALS	81%	28%	35%	$16.700	14.3%
BARR LABORATORIES	17%	36%	14%	$79.073	12.9%
SYNCOR INTERNATIONAL	23%	77%	18%	$29.467	9.1%
NATURE'S SUNSHINE	419%	297%	71%	$199.486	7.9%
CHATTEM	239%	1796%	55%	$259.007	6.9%
Pharmaceutical X	**64%**	**69%**	**33%**	**$63.137**	**0.5%**
CENTOCOR	173%	42%	55%	$171.156	-5.1%
LILLY (ELI) AND	199%	77%	43%	$118.855	-23.4%
SEQUUS PHARMACEUTICALS	1122%	224%	144%	$221.750	-43.0%
SCIOS	434%	104%	132%	$178.934	-68.4%
IVAX	60%	60%	45%	$59.959	-109.5%
GENSIA SICOR	85%	38%	49%	$225.651	-112.1%
ALZA	326%	69%	45%	$134.987	-134.9%
PERRIGO	25%	34%	17%	$35.135	-177.7%
AXYS PHARMACEUTICALS	27%	16%	29%	$18.109	-188.0%
VERTEX PHARMACEUTICALS	24%	4%	38%	$51.955	-338.7%

Figure 5-1–Eleven Look-alike Firms Show Superior Information Productivity

The firms that are materially superior in IP values show median values that are twice the Information Management/Cost of Goods ratios, 32% higher Information Management/Revenue ratios and 53% higher Information Management/Employee ratios. Only the Information Management/Net Assets ratios are at approximate parity.

Size of employment or scale of operations does not differentiate Pharmaceutical X from its higher performing look-alikes. Clearly, what needs attention is the intrinsic profitability of products, not primarily information-related issues. From a planning and budgeting standpoint, such insights would be of great value, for instance, in assessing how to invest in information technologies. Based on these indicators, value-creation, rather than information cost reduction, ought to receive the highest priority.

Eleven firms show superior and ten firms show inferior Information Productivity as compared with Pharmaceutical X median values.

Company	Information Management/ Cost of Goods	Information Management/ Net Assets	Information Management/ Revenue	Information Management/ Employee	Information Productivity
11 Firms with Superior	107.2%	64.9%	39.2%	$87,922	20%
Pharmaceutical X	**63.5%**	**68.8%**	**32.8%**	**$63,137**	**1%**
10 Firms with Inferior IP	172.9%	60.0%	44.8%	$134,987	-110%

Figure 5-2–Pharmaceutical X Indicators Suggest Low Information Effectiveness

Three indicators–related to cost of goods, revenue and employees–confirm that Pharmaceutical X does not spend an excessive amount of money on information management. That suggests that cutbacks on sales, general, administrative, research and development costs are not likely to result in improved information productivity. While Pharmaceutical X spends less on information management that does not translate into higher productivity. Pharmaceutical X may be efficient but its management is not effective.

The relatively higher information management/net assets ratio can be interpreted only as an indication that Pharmaceutical X employs lower asset level than its competitors. This then leads to an examination whether the problem with Pharmaceutical X is one of insufficient scale to make it competitive.

Company	Employment	Market Value - $000	Net Assets - $000	Market /Book Value	ROE - %	Revenue Growth/Year
11 Firms with Superior IP	3,795	$2,262,000	$703,797	6.8	32.8	67%
Pharmaceutical X	**2,600**	**$551,000**	**$238,473**	**2.3**	**9.4**	**48%**
10 Firms with Inferior IP	640	$820,000	$257,835	6.3	-27.1	83%

Figure 5-3–Low Assets and Substandard Growth Rate Explain Operating Results

Step #3: Review Critical Indicator Trends

Benchmarking based only on one year's worth of data can be problematic inasmuch as it may highlight conditions that are only temporary. To assess the consistency of the analysis shown in Figure 5-3 the following shows critical indicator trends for several years:

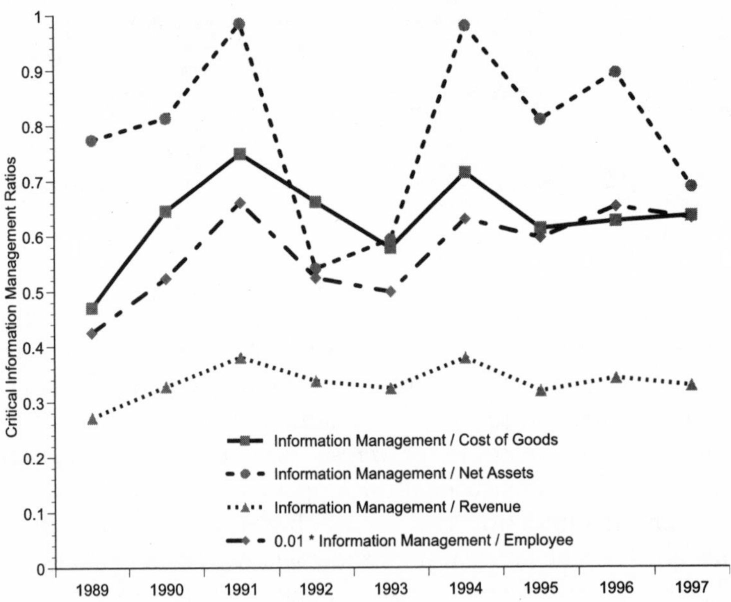

Figure 5-4–Trends in Critical Information Management Indicators

Nine years of information management ratios show a remarkable consistency and do not reveal formation of a major trend. Subject to further analysis of non-financial data one can therefore concluded that the assessments of the internal productivity indicators are reasonable.

As a further verification of the consistency of judgements we also examine trends in financial indicators which largely reflect external influences:

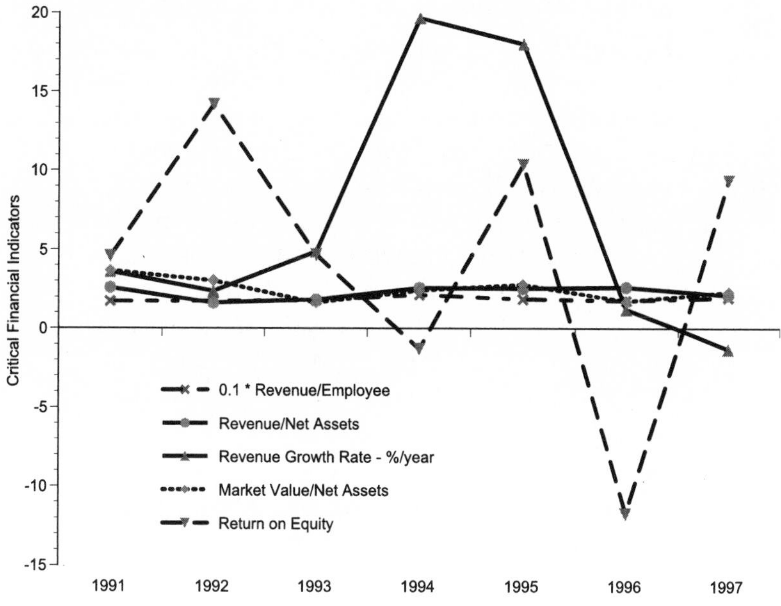

Figure 5-5 – Trends in Critical Financial Indicators

It is remarkable that the stock market valuation of Pharmaceutical X remains consistent regardless of the large swings in Return-on-Equity and revenue growth rates. Again, the ratios show no trend and therefore one may conclude that the productivity diagnosis is reasonably reliable.

An examination of Pharmaceutical X look-alike firms and trends of critical indicators leads to the following insights:

- **Scale of operations.** As suggested by the higher employment numbers for the high-performance firms, this firm needs greater scale of operations to achieve superior levels of Information Productivity.

- **Growth rate**. The stock market often rewards revenue growth rather than of productivity, operational effectiveness and profitability. The only redeeming characteristics of the low-performance start-up firms are their extraordinary growth rates. This firm requires a faster growth rate to compensate for its unfavorable market valuation.
- **Efficiency vs. Effectiveness**. Pharmaceutical X has neither the characteristics of a venture nor the attributes of a mature firm. Its employment levels approach those of a superior firm, whereas its profitability and asset levels are neither that of a high growth start-up nor one that would make it look like a major competitor in this industry segment. All of the diagnostics therefore point towards difficulties that are external to the firm (e.g. marketing and product problems) rather than internal to the firm that can be remedied by making investments in improving the efficiency of information resources.

A financial analysis of Pharmaceutical X using more conventional metrics could conceivably arrive at similar conclusions, but not necessarily. Given the unsatisfactory Information Productivity performance management may be tempted to look to computerization as a remedy. The above diagnostics would suggest that such an approach would warrant only a lower priority.

As noted in the prior Chapter, the application of Information Productivity methods offers a sharper focus on the differences between a corporation that is subject to productivity benchmarking and its superior or inferior competitors. Most importantly, Information Productivity is more likely to shed light on whether overhead cost reductions and cut-backs in information-related expenditures would remedy an unsatisfactory condition.

However, the greatest benefit from applying Information Productivity reviews come from their use when plans and budgets are prepared. Calculating how Information Productivity would change as consequence of a proposed plan offers a way how judge the credibility of budgetary commitments.

Step #4: Examine Proposed Plans for Consistency with Benchmark Trends

The analysis of Information Productivity trends can be of great value when planning and budgeting for the re-allocation of resources and priorities.

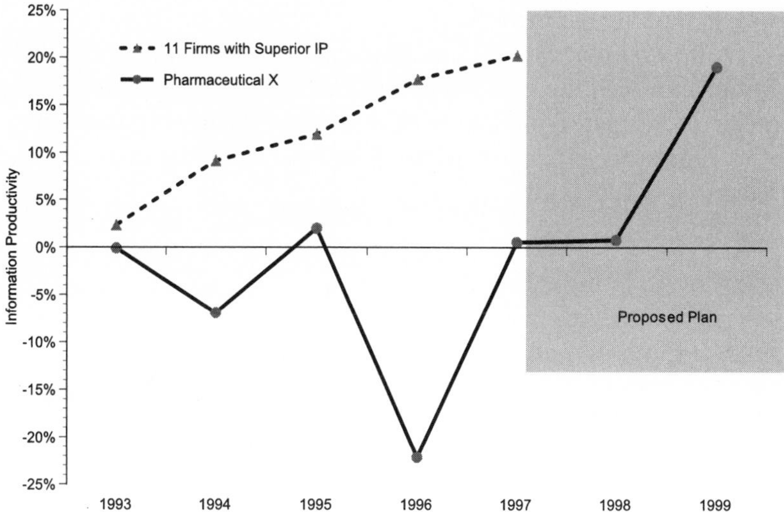

Figure 5-6–Gap in Past Performance Makes Forecast Questionable [78]

The most useful such analysis is an examination of past Information Productivity trends, coupled with a verification of whether the proposed plans will result in a credible improvement.

A display of trends as illustrated in Figure 5-6 would lead to an examination of what dramatic moves have been proposed in the

78 The 1998 and 1998 projections of IP values are hypothetical and for illustrative purposes only.

two-year plan for FY 1998 and 1999 to put Pharmaceutical X in a situation of matching or bettering the median productivity levels of superior look-alike firms.

Similar analyses can be also performed to examine the effects of management decisions on particularly sensitive ratios, such as in the case of the proposed new levels for the information management/cost of goods ratio.

Which of the many possible Information Productivity indicators will be of value in decision-making cannot be determined in advance for any particular case. The introduction of Information Productivity metrics into the planning, budgeting and performance metrics can give rise to many indicators that are unique to conditions in a particular firm.

The Pharmaceutical X example provides a glimpse how one should approach the construction of such indicators.[79] Customizing information-related indicators to address specific corporate situations is best accomplished when drafting the annual planning and budgeting instructions.

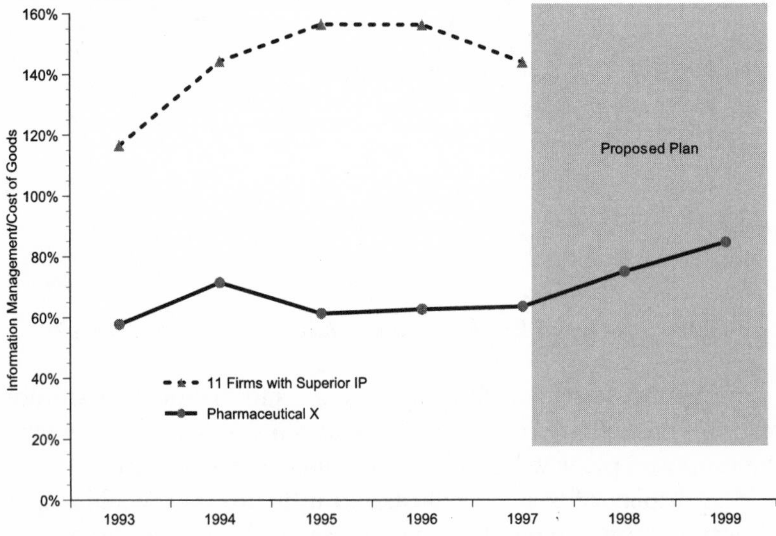

Figure 5-7–The Proposed Plan Narrows the Difference in one of the Ratios

Information Productivity measurements and indicators should be seen as a refinement and enhancement of the conventional metrics that are already in use. They are a potent and useful addition to an improved understanding of the rising importance of information management resources in affecting financial results.

Concluding Observations

It is only fitting to end this book, which concentrates almost entirely on the financial and economic aspects of information work, with the recognition that we do not live by economics alone. Increasing productivity is not the principal reason why people will commit their most productive years working for corporations. Nevertheless, as we build an economy based primarily on information work, it is imperative that we grasp the critical prerequisite for creating wealth and for propelling the U.S. society towards greater prosperity: the need to increase the productivity of our information workforce.

As the prosperity of the U.S. is at historically unprecedented levels of achievement many have doubts as to how much longer can our society sustain its current rate of economic growth. When one examines the enormous disparity between the top ranking U.S. industrial firms and the bottom laggards one cannot fail to realize that a very large share of U.S. industrial firms are not productive in terms that apply to the information age. The bottom ranking firms spend huge sums on information management that does not deliver results and that acts as drag on further progress. It is this realization that leads me to conclude that we are not even close to reaching the limits of what is achievable if we managed our information resources with greater effectiveness.

Without sustained increases in productivity, the real incomes of the population cannot grow. Thus, the challenge for corporate management is to find ways of harnessing and enhancing steadily increasing Information Productivity in the service of fulfilling all of the related hopes and ambitions that depend on it.

To continue this society's journey on the path that builds and exploits an information-based economy, we need mileposts to help us know how much progress has been made and how much farther we are able to proceed. As the rate of social and economic change accelerates, such mileposts become a necessity. It is my hope that this exploration of the productivity of U.S. industrial information management resources may truly become one such milepost in providing a valid understanding of the present and an achievable vision for the future.

Appendix A

The Productivity Context

THE GLOBAL CONTEXT

U.S. Corporations are the Primary Contributors to the U.S. Global Position

It is essential that we first view the role of U.S. industrial corporations in a global context:[79]

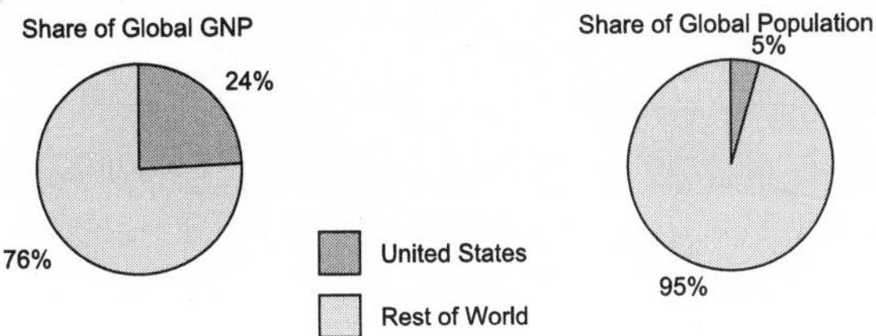

Figure A1 – The U.S. Economy Remains Dominant in the World [80]

The percent share of global GNP of the U.S. relative to the rest of the world was 24.2% in 1995. That marks a moderate decline from the global share of 26.7% in 1985.[81] Meanwhile the global population has grown faster than the U.S. population. The U.S. share of the global population declined from 5.1% to 4.57%. Nevertheless, the slower population growth in the U.S. more than offset the declining share of the global GNP. In terms of GNP per capita the prosperity of the U.S. population has therefore gained relative to the

79 I have already started work on a volume that will address global corporate economics.

80 U.S. Bureau of the Census, *Statistical Abstract of the United States*: 1997, Washington, DC, 1998, Table 1347–Gross National Product, by Country, for 1995 current dollars and Table 1334–Population by Country for 1997

81 That decline is a statistical aberration, not a reflection of economic strength because former Soviet controlled states did not report any GNP until 1985, but show a small but significant GNP contribution by 1995.

rest of the world. It is the favorable performance of U.S. corporations over the present decade that was the primary source of these economic gains. In this book we will examine the economic indicators that reflect these accomplishments.

U.S. Corporations Have an Extraordinary Share of Global Corporate Wealth

As can be readily recognized, the wealth-producing engines of the developed global economies are the major corporations. The U.S. can boast having 153 firms among the world's 500 largest corporations (31% of largest corporations). As Figure A2 illustrates, these U.S. firms have revenues that are 28% of the total global revenues and account for a whopping 49% of all global profits:

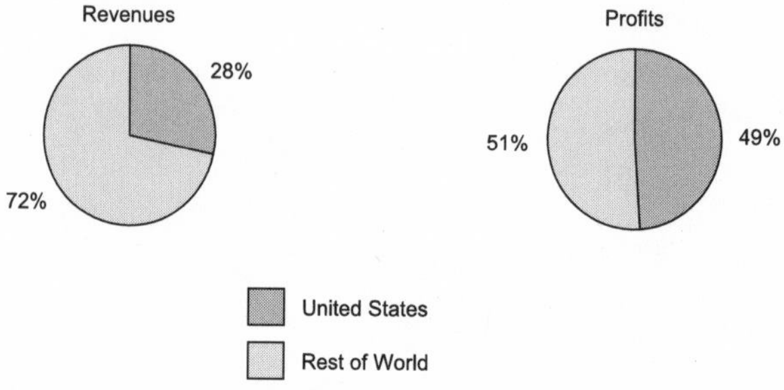

Figure A2 – U.S. Corporations Account for Significant Profits of Largest Global Firms [82]

The high share of profits is a testimonial to the superior economic performance of U.S. firms. By the same token, the economic role of the world's 500 largest corporations is also remarkable. Their total revenues are $11,378 billion, which equal 38% of the global GNP of $29,950 billion. To check the estimates based on a sample of five hundred largest corporations, we have also examined the financial reports for 13,241 public firms. The 1997 financial data from fifty-

82 *Statistical Abstract*, Table 1367 – World's Largest Corporations by Country, 1995. The 153 US corporations had revenues of $3,221 billion and profits of $158 billion in 1995. Stock market valuations confirm the importance of U.S. corporations. At the end of 1997 there were 3,678 major listed U.S. firms that accounted for 50.4% of the total global stock market valuation of $22.5 trillion for a total of 14,001 corporations.

four developed countries confirm that the U.S. corporations possess the largest share of corporate wealth as defined in terms of revenues, profits, assets and employees.[83] Figure A3 shows the key economic indicators of U.S. firms relative to the rest of the world:

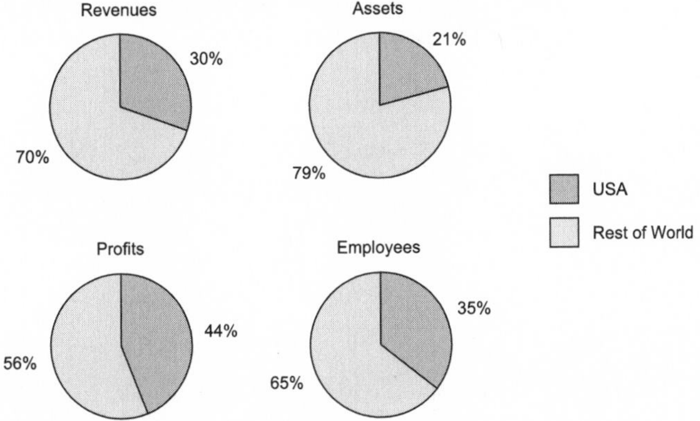

Figure A3–U.S. Corporations Account for Most of the Profits of the 13,241 Global Firms [84]

THERE WILL BE ANOTHER BOOK ON THE NON-INDUSTRIAL FIRMS

The share of corporations in various sectors of the economy, as a percent of total firms, reflects the structure of a national economy. It defines how people will be primarily employed in various occupations.

The U.S. share of global revenues, profits and assets is not the consequence of being weighted in favor of non-industrial corporations. The origins of the U.S. advantage, as compared with the rest

83 The global totals for 13,241 public corporations (in 1997 US$): Revenues $19,744 billion; Profits $832 billion; Assets $53,856 billion; Employees 70 million. Global Researcher Worldscope Database, November 1998, Disclosure Corporation, Bethesda, Md. The prosperity of these organizations is, however, increasingly vulnereable to global financial instability such as from rapid shifts in the values of currencies. The average daily global currency trading is now $1,500 billion (See "Choppy Current of a World Cash Ocean," *The New York Times*, February 15, 1999.

84 *Statistical Abstract*, Table 1367–World's Largest Corporations by Country, 1995. The 153 US corporations had revenues of $3,221 billion and profits of $158 billion in 1995.

of the world, comes from its size, marketing power, management practices and utilization of human resources. Despite opinions that the U.S. is now a "third wave" information age economy with diminishing dependency on industrial firms, that is not the case.

Figure A4 illustrates national differences in revenue-weighted shares for non-industrial firms:

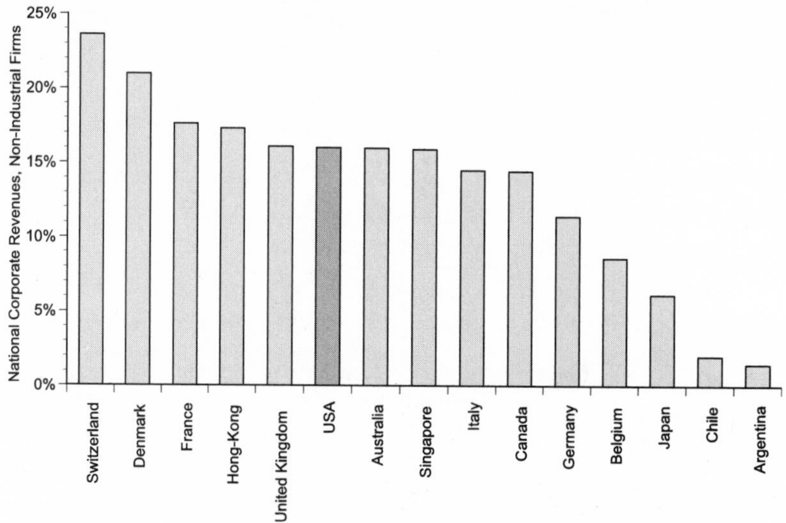

Figure A4–National Revenue Shares of Non-industrial Firms

Switzerland, Denmark, France and Hong-Kong for example have a higher ratio of non-industrial firms than the U.S. In composition of firms, the U.S. is not much different than the U.K., Australia, Singapore, Italy and Canada.

What is the "Information Economy"?

There were 10,593 corporations classified as "industrial" in the global database of 14,494 corporations, which includes both developed as well as also under-developed countries.[85] The remaining firms were "services" firms. Such classification confirms that the corporate economy of the world remains concentrated in the industrial sectors.

With 73% of firms making up the global industrial economy and the remaining 27% belonging to the service economy what is then the meaning of the phrase "the information economy"? One of the primary objectives of this book is to place the role of "information" into the appropriate defining framework.

The classification of the economy into industrial versus service sectors has always been the way in which corporations used to identify what they were delivering to customers. Corporations are typically known as oil, steel, food, chemical or retail organizations. That classification scheme serves a useful purpose.

Employees, however, no longer identify themselves with oil, steel, food, chemicals or retail trade as an adequate description of what they do. Instead, when asked about their jobs they are now more likely to label themselves as accountants, engineers, administrators, craftsmen or laborers. The classification of the economy in terms of its "industrial" and "service" sectors has now become inadequate in describing how the economy has become transformed.

Presently, the creation, distribution and management of information work now influences the activities of every employee. This situation holds true for corporations, private proprietorships, the self-employed or the government.

I base my categorization of an "information economy" on an examination of the resources that are consumed to create goods and services. In this book we will concentrate on the use of information resources as the most critical input needed for the delivery of goods and services.

85 *Global Researcher Worldscope Database*, November 1998, Disclosure Corporation, Bethesda, Md. The Global Research is one of the most comprehensive sources of public information about ownership, financial performance and earning information. It provides data that has been released to comply with regulatory or stock exchange listing requirements.

THE U.S. CONTEXT

Employment Characteristics

Information-Related Occupations Dominate the U.S. Workforce

Studying the occupations of the U.S. workforce offers an insight into the relative importance of information-producing resources. Fifty-five percent of the workforce is in occupations that are almost exclusively engaged in information processing, information coordination, information creation and information distribution:[86]

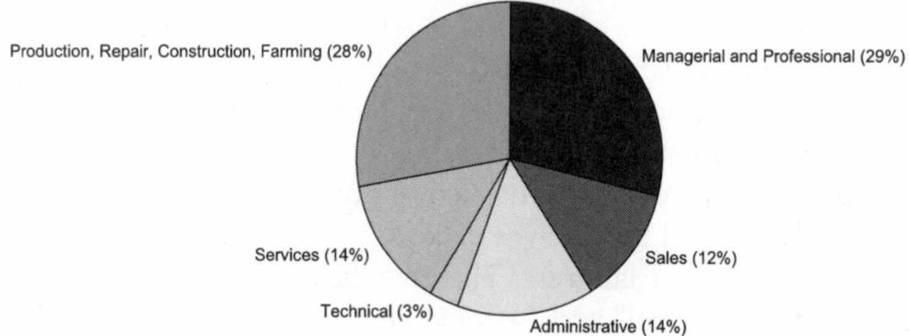

Figure A5–55% of U.S. Workforce Employed in Information Occupations [87]

The above figure understates the amount of information processing that actually takes place in the U.S. economy. Studies of production, services and technical operatives show that they also devote a significant amount of their working hours to information tasks, such as filling forms, reporting about their activities, participating in meetings and engaging in a wide range of administrative tasks.[88]

86 U.S.workers receive on average 190 e-mail, fax, phone and mail messages a day ("Execs Worldwide Complain of Information Overload," *InforWorld*, September 15,1998 citing Institute for the Future study.)

87 U.S. Bureau of the Census, *Statistical Abstract of the United States*: 1997, Washington, DC, 1998, Table 645–Employed Civilians, by Occupation.

88 In a 1975 study of Xerox service technicians it was found that over 35% of their time was devoted to meetings, training, filling out reports and keeping track of spare parts. During a 1994 visit to a 200 acre corn growing farm in Illinois, my host showed me elaborate computer equipment for keeping track of irrigation schedules, inventories, commodity trading and government accounts. The farmer was spending at least 10% of his time on information processing tasks.

GROWTH CONCENTRATED IN THE INFORMATION OCCUPATIONS

The distribution of occupation in the U.S. economy is a dynamic phenomenon. Highly compensated information occupations (e.g. managerial, professional and sales positions) are growing faster than the average for all occupations in the workforce:

Civilian Occupations (1,000)	1983	1996	Growth Rate
Managerial and Professional	23,592	36,497	55%
Sales	11,818	15,404	30%
Administrative	16,395	18,353	12%
Technical	3,053	3,926	29%
Services	13,857	17,177	24%
Production, Repair, Construction, Farming	32,119	35,350	10%
Total	100,834	126,707	26%

Figure A6–Information Occupations Show High Growth Rates [89]

Most significantly, the occupations that used to dominate the economy (e.g. in production, construction, repair, etc.) are gaining at a slower rate than the entire working population. This difference accelerates the shift to a largely information-based workforce, as summarized in the following tabulation:

Civilian Occupations (1,000)	1983	1996	Growth Rate
Information Occupations	51,805	70,254	36%
All Others	49,029	56,453	15%
Total Employment	100,834	126,707	26%

Figure A7–Information Occupations Show High Growth Rates [90]

89 U.S. Bureau of the Census, *Statistical Abstract of the United States*: 1997, Washington, DC, 1998, Table 636–Self Employed Workers, by Occupation

90 U.S. Bureau of the Census, *Statistical Abstract of the United States*: 1997, Washington, DC, 1998, Table 636–Self Employed Workers, by Occupation

Dollar-Weighted Share Shows Importance of Information Occupations

Employment counts are insufficient to display the relative importance of information occupations. The average wages, salaries and benefits of the information workforce are higher than the average compensation levels of those received by all other workers.

A compensation-weighted share of total employment offers a better understanding of the impact of information workers on the economy because it shows what is the relative importance of the information workforce in monetary terms. As shown in Figure A7, on a dollar weighted basis, the information occupations account for 64% of the compensation of the U.S. workforce, thus making them the dominant influence in the economy.

How Productive is an Economy Where Most Workers are Managers?

The fact that in sheer numbers the managers and professionals now constitute the single largest occupational category–which is also the fastest growing occupational group–should raise concerns about the limits of such occupational expansion.

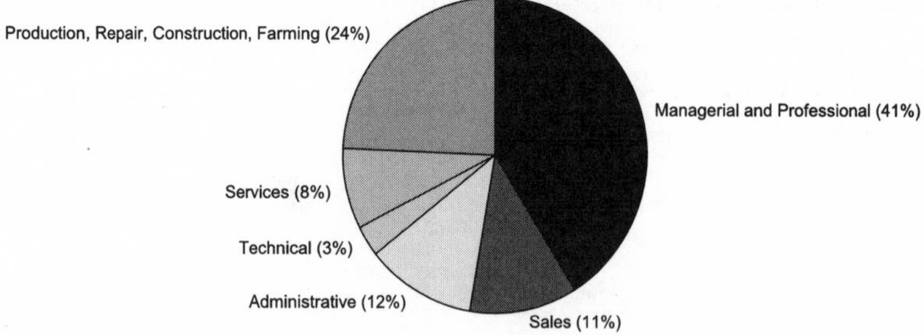

Figure A8–Information Occupations Earn 64% of All Salaries & Wages

Culturally and economically a nation whose workforce is made up of mostly managers and professionals is likely to end up with a different set of values and priorities than a society that depends on agriculture and manufacturing occupations to create wealth.[91] However, the most important problem of a largely managerial and professional workforce relates to concerns whether it can create a steady growth in wealth instead of just consuming wealth as unproductive overhead expense. Thus, the key issue of the "information economy" deals with the question how to measure and evaluate the contributions of managers and professionals. Unless information age metrics assess the productivity of information work it will not be feasible to discern which information activities produce wealth and which become a wealth-diminishing burden.

Sector Characteristics

The source of employment by economic sector also offers an improved understanding about the changing structure of the U.S. economy.

As Figure A8 underscores, the sectors of the economy that concentrate on information services and information management tasks (e.g. business, public administration and professional services) account for the highest growth and the single largest component of the U.S. economy.

For the period from 1970 through 1996 the information-intensive finance, insurance and real estate sectors grew by 104.7% and personal or business services grew by 121%. It is remarkable that manufacturing employment declined by 1.1% while the entire workforce grew by 61% in the period from 1970 through 1996.[92]

As shown in the above Figure, the sectors whose primary occupation is to produce tangible output (agriculture, mining, construction with 9% and manufacturing with 16% of the workforce) now employ only 25% of the U.S. workforce:

91 A nation of information-handlers, whose success depends on the acceptance of what they say and not necessarily on what they can measurably produce, is likely to be beset with conflicts.

92 The public administration number reporting 5.8 million employees disguises the fact that much of the work done for the government is passed on to contractors. For instance, the U.S. Federal government, which claims to have only 1.8 millions civil servants actually pays for the workforce of 17 million through contracts and transfer payments. See Paul C. Light, "The True Size of Government," *The Government Executive*, January 1999. State and local government follow a similar practice.

Sector employment (000's)	1970	1996	Growth
Agriculture, mining, construction	8,797	11,955	35.9%
Manufacturing	20,746	20,518	-1.1%
Transportation, communication, utilities	5,320	8,817	65.7%
Wholesale and retail trade	15,008	26,497	76.6%
Finance, insurance, real estate	3,945	8,076	104.7%
Personal and business services	20,385	45,043	121.0%
Public administration	4,476	5,802	29.6%
Total employed	78,677	126,708	61.0%

Figure A9 – Goods Producing Sectors Stagnated While Total Employment Grew 61% [93]

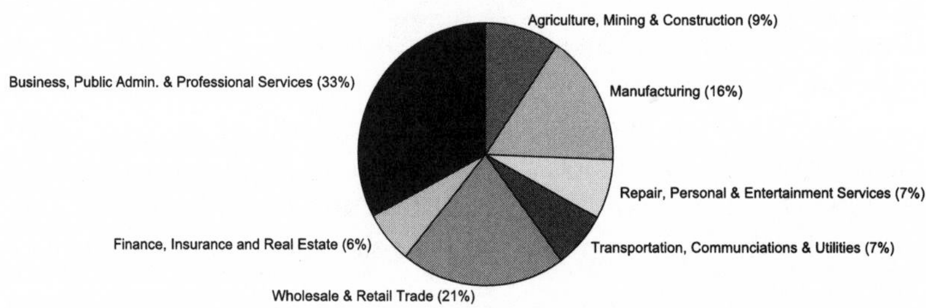

Figure A10 – Goods Producing Sectors Account for Only 25% of Employment

It is difficult to conceive how the business, public administration and professional services sectors will increase their share of the economy beyond the present levels. This single largest sector (with 33% of the workforce) doubled its employment in the period from 1970 through 1996.

It is the information sectors that account for most of the social or corporate overhead of the U.S. economy. It is the information sectors that derive their economic sustenance by means of taxation (for the public sector) or payroll and purchases that end up in a firm's overhead accounts (for corporations). What is perhaps less understood is the link between the paperwork burdens imposed by the public sector and the growth in administrative staffs that has

93 U.S. Bureau of the Census, *Statistical Abstract of the United States*: 1997, Washington, DC, 1998, Table 649–Employment, by Industry.

stimulated the growth in corporate overhead costs. Despite enormous investments in computerization the government has shifted sufficient paperwork to corporations to diminish their potential productivity gains from business process automation.[94]

The decisive time for the business, public administration and professional services sector is when budgets are prepared. This is when the purchasers must decide how, where and when to spend the funds that are essential as inputs for the cost of goods and services.[95]

Unfortunately, better methods for judging the productivity of information resources are not in general use.[96] The existing budgetary tools have focused primarily on dealing with the effectiveness of capital or labor resources. That limitation is increasingly unsatisfactory as the importance of information costs gains relative to all other resources.

THE CORPORATE CONTEXT

CORPORATIONS PROVIDE MOST OF U.S. EMPLOYMENT OPPORTUNITIES

While the analysis in this book will concentrate only on the characteristics of information management in U.S. industrial corporations, it is important to have an understanding of the relative importance of U.S. corporations in the U.S. economy. The first view is to examine the employment shares for corporations, partnerships, proprietorships, self-employed persons and the civilian employment in the public sector.

94 In *The Squandered Computer* I showed that government paperwork compliance costs were equal to 124% of corporate profits and 322% of corporate tax payments in 1994. See Chapter 14 "Workload without Payoff." Fifty-five percent of 3,477 major US firms spent more on paperwork to comply with federal regulations than they paid in taxes.

95 "Company politics" offers perhaps the best description of the prevailing budgetary approaches for allocating overhead funds. This disconnection between making resource investments and planning for realization of their economic value is perhaps the single most damaging characteristic of current corporate planning and budgeting practices.

96 Perhaps the best tool for applying methods of capital budgeting to the unique characteristics of investments in business process improvement is the *BizCase* software published by SRA International in 1996. For more information see http://www.strassmann.com/consulting/bizcase.html.

The employment shares in Figure A10 represent the shares of civilian employment totaling an U.S. workforce of 126.7 million in 1996. Therefore, the generalizations that will be developed in this book will apply only to 78% of the economy.

Keep in mind that a scarcity of data exists about the characteristics of segments of the economy that lie outside of the corporate economy. Where such data are available, it suggests that the observations that are made in this book will not always apply to those segments that are not bound by the same reporting requirements as public corporations. A few examples that illustrate the differences between the corporate and other sectors of the economy will follow in this chapter.

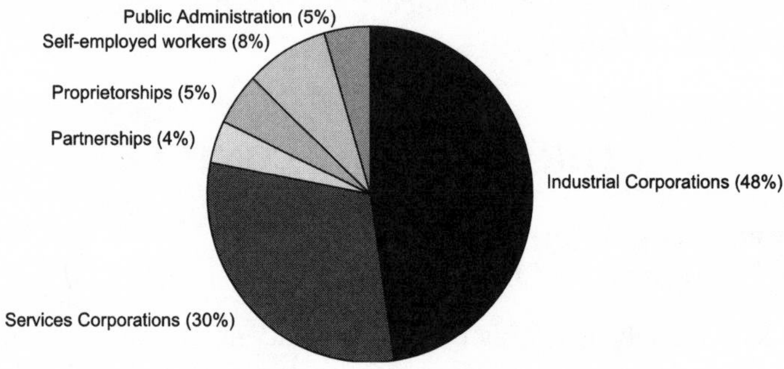

Figure A11–Industrial Corporations Offer Most Jobs[97]

Self Employed Workers are in Production and Services

Self-employed workers make up 8.3% of the civilian workforce but hold less than 7% of the information occupations. For this reason that information occupations will tend to concentrate in corporations, in not-for-profit institutions and in the public sector where organizational complexity requires that additional resources be expended in the coordination of work.

97 U.S. Bureau of the Census, *Statistical Abstract of the United States*: 1997, Washington, DC, 1998. Table 645–Employed Civilians, by Occupation.

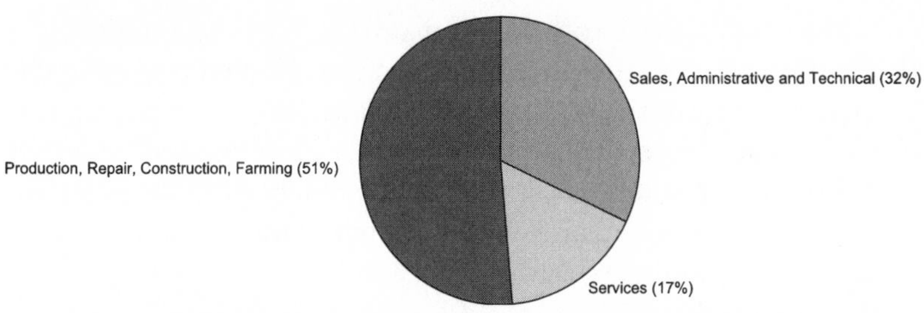

Figure A12–Self-Employed Workers Are Mostly in Production and Services

The employment patterns for self-employed workers are not comparable to the distribution of jobs in the rest of the economy, per Figure A11.

Partnerships and Proprietorships are More Profitable

Information about the employment patterns and economic performance outside of the corporate segment is scarce.

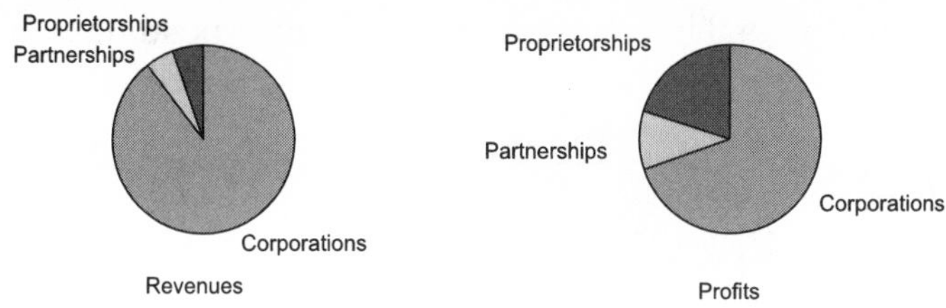

Figure A13–Proprietorships Earn an Exceptional Share of Total Business Profits [98]

Nevertheless, the roles of the corporate segment of the U.S. economy can be placed into a better perspective when one compares the relative shares of revenues and profits for various types of businesses.

98 U.S. Bureau of the Census, *Statistical Abstract of the United States*: 1997, Washington, DC, 1998, Table 834.

The exceptional profitability of private proprietorships raises the question whether their structure of information employment differs materially from the occupational profiles one finds in corporations. One can only speculate that it is their close concentration on the delivery of products and services and inability to afford excessive overhead costs that explains why business owners are more profitable as shown in Figure A12.

A Few Corporations have Most of the Costs

The high correlation between annual expenditures for information technology spending and the costs of information management should make the statistical distribution of these costs a matter of considerable interest to business executives.

Figure A13 shows that the large number of small firms (defined as firms with total employment of less than 5,000, amounting to a total of 72% of all corporations) account for only 15% of the total information management expenditures. By contrast, the medium to large firms (defined as firms with total employment of over than 10,000, account for a total of 16% of all corporations) will incur 76% of the total information management expenditures.

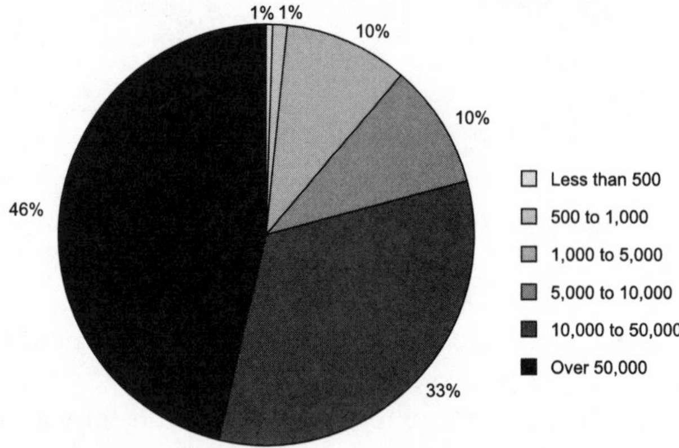

Figure A14 – Large Corporations Incur Most Information Management Costs [99]

99 Worldscope/Disclosure, *Global Researcher Database*, August 1998, U.S. Corporation Search, by Employment Size.

The implications of this highly skewed distribution of costs are far-reaching for the overall information productivity of the USA. Any gains will be largely a reflection of how well large firms manage the productivity of their information resources. That also suggests that the economic effects of computerization will be largely the reflection of what productivity gains will be delivered by a relatively small number of very large enterprises.

Spending on Information Management is Concentrated

The dollar costs associated with each class of firms (by employment size) illustrated in Figure A14 can be also seen in Figure A15:

Employment Size Class	Number of Corporations	% of Corporations	Information Management Costs ($000)	% of Total Information Management Costs
Less than 500	792	25.1%	23,226,003	2.2%
500 to 1,000	446	14.1%	20,446,916	1.9%
1,000 to 5,000	1,040	33.0%	114,236,567	10.9%
5,000 to 10,000	356	11.3%	96,493,483	9.2%
10,000 to 50,000	414	13.1%	348,602,565	33.2%
Over 50,000	108	3.4%	448,105,223	42.6%
Total	3,156	100.0%	1,051,110,757	100.0%

Figure A15–43% of Information Management Costs in 108 Corporations

Because information management costs are so highly concentrated, one will also find that the largest share of all U.S. computer spending is to be found in only a few firms. How these few firms manage their computers is then a matter that warrants most of the attention from shareholders, the stock market, vendors, the computer press and the government.

Employment Opportunities are in Large Corporations

The concentration of employees within a few large firms reveals a pattern that has remained unchanged over the last decade despite rapid changes in the economy, the creation of new ventures and the tendency of large firms to consolidate through mergers and acquisitions:

Employment Size Class	Number of Corporations	% of Corporations	Number of Employees	% of Employees
Less than 500	848	23.9%	157,401	0.5%
500 to 1,000	486	13.7%	346,669	1.1%
1,000 to 5,000	1,202	33.9%	2,962,940	9.6%
5,000 to 10,000	419	11.8%	2,951,827	9.6%
10,000 to 50,000	470	13.2%	10,073,048	32.8%
Over 50,000	125	3.5%	14,235,098	46.3%
Total	3,550	100.0%	30,726,983	100.0%

Figure A16–46.3% of Employment in 125 Corporations

When computer vendors and technical magazines feature articles about remarkable contributions of information technologies to the prosperity of a particular firm, the size of the firm should be noted. Even recent high-technology start-up ventures that have shown astronomical gains in the stock market cannot have much of an effect on the overall productivity of the U.S. economy as long as their revenues, profits and employment remain very small.

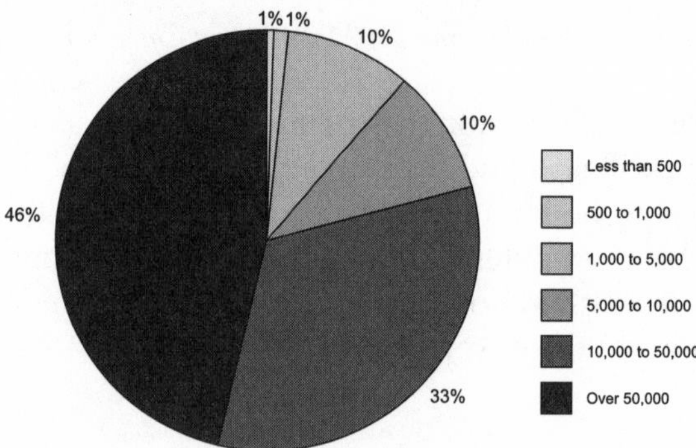

Figure A17–Large and Medium Corporations Employ the Most Workers

The relative share of the various employment size classes tabulated above are perhaps best understood by an examination of the table above which shows that 46% of the U.S. corporate industrial workforce is in organizations with total employment greater than 50,000.

Employment and Payroll Trends

Increasing revenues without a corresponding increase in employment is the most distinctive characteristic of recent U.S. corporate history. Figure A18 is based on seven years of revenue and employment data for 1,773 U.S. industrial corporations with total revenues of $4.7 trillion and 19.1 million employees in 1997:

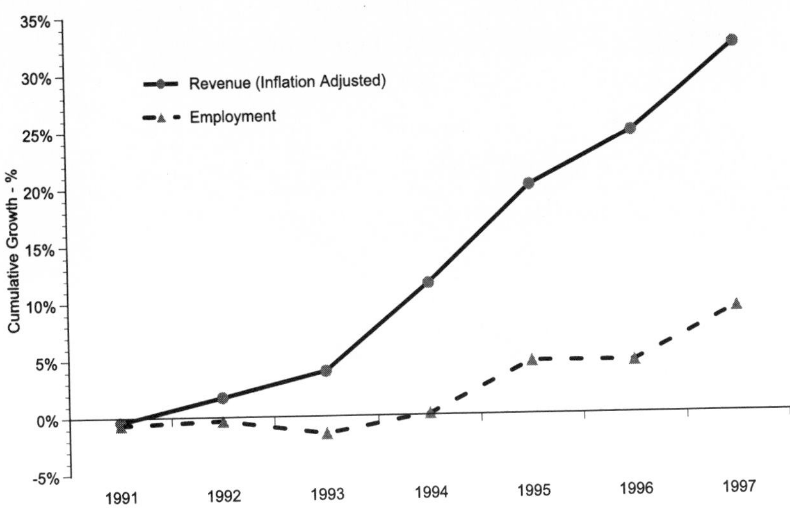

Figure A18–Revenue Growth Unrelated to Employment Growth

Even after making an allowance for an inflation-adjustment of revenues, there remains a significant difference between total employment growth of 9.4% from 1990 through 1997 and the corresponding revenue growth of 52.9% (in actual dollar terms) and a growth of 36.6% (in deflated terms) for this period.

	1990	1991	1992	1993	1994	1995	1996	1997	Growth
Revenues - $ Billions	3,105	3,155	3,263	3,377	3,655	4,042	4,341	4,748	52.9%
Revenues (Inflation-adjusted)	3,105	3,091	3,158	3,228	3,472	3,767	3,943	4,240	36.6%
Employment - Millions	17.46	17.34	17.39	17.19	17.47	18.26	18.25	19.09	9.4%

Figure A19 – Comparison of Revenues and Inflation-Adjusted Revenues

In view of the disparity between revenue and employment growth one can wonder whether the limited additions to payrolls have delivered corresponding gains in profits. In fact, that was not the case. Whatever savings were realized from lower levels of employment were spent on increasing the average compensation levels of employees at a rate that was faster than consumer prices as well as prices realized by industrial corporations.[100]

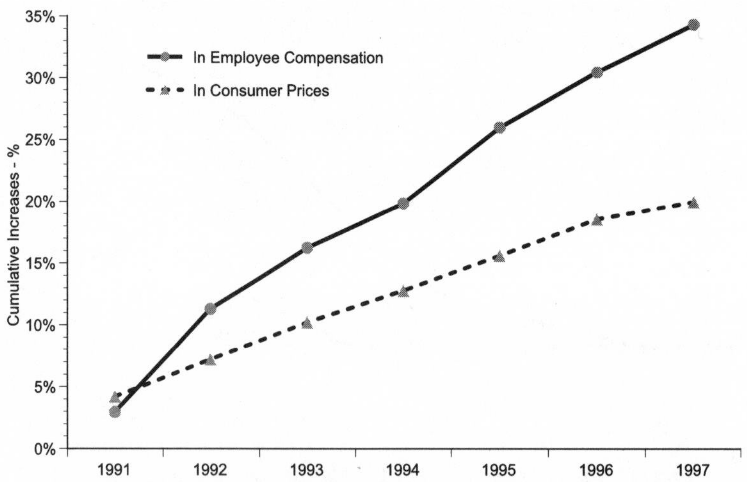

Figure A20 – Employee Compensation Grew Faster than Inflation

The share of revenue spent on payrolls increased from 1990 to 1993, but that trend reversed in the period from 1993 through 1997. At the end of this cycle the share of revenue devoted to pay-

100Median salaries and wages were as follows: 1990=$29,935; 1991=$30,817; 1992=33,389; 1993=$35,041; 1994=$36, 296; 1995=$38,534; 1996=$40,254; 1997=$41,816.

rolls is the same as it was at the start of the decade, despite the large increases in revenues per employee.

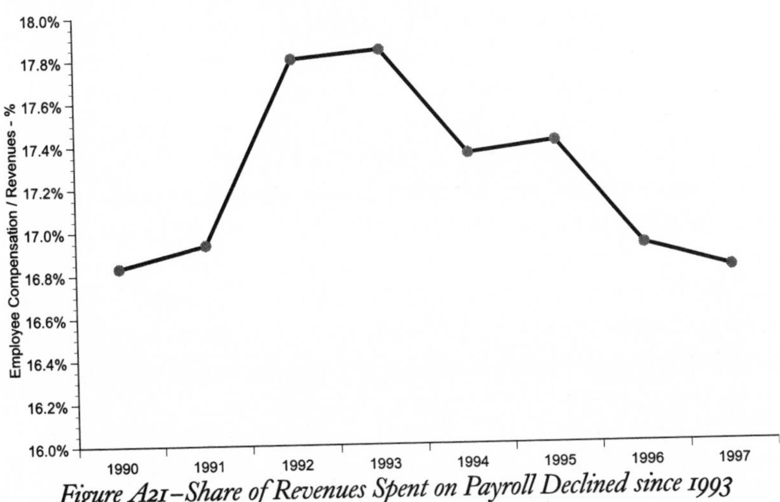

Figure A21–Share of Revenues Spent on Payroll Declined since 1993

The only plausible explanation for this phenomenon is the change in the composition of the workforce as employees shift from lower paid occupations to jobs with higher compensation such as in managerial and professional positions. Any claims that labor productivity increased because revenue per employee has risen has no merit if the compensation of a smaller workforce rises faster than revenues.

Following the period of intensive computerization since 1990 there is no evidence that automation has displaced labor costs. Although the "headcount" of U.S. industrial corporations grew at a slower rate than revenues, the net effect has been to end up with a workforce that is better compensated. An unchanged ratio of employee compensation to revenues would be then an indicator that the results of any automation investments would have to show improvements in value-added rather than in labor savings.

STUDY OF U.S. INDUSTRIAL FIRMS

Defining the Scope of Industrial Firms

This book deals only with U.S. industrial firms that are listed on stock exchanges. These firms disclose standard financial data to conform to regulations of the Security Exchange Commission. Therefore, the statistics in this book exclude the economic role of privately owned firms, partnerships, corporations registered for the purpose of self-employment, not-for-profit organizations and public services. The industrial economy includes SIC (Standard Industrial Classification) codes that are predominantly engaged in the manufacture and distribution of tangible goods.[101] Figure A22 summarizes the classification of the sectors of the economy, grouped by SIC codes.

Excluded from this book are firms classified as banking, insurance, real estate and medical service enterprises.[102] These sectors of the U.S. economy, identified as SIC codes from 60 through 89, are predominantly engaged in the performance of intangible tasks. The financial structure of these firms is materially different–in terms of the cost of goods, capital and information–from that of industrial firms. Therefore, these sectors will be grouped into a separate book that will deal entirely with the productivity of the service economy. This new volume, to follow shortly after this book, will be dedicated entirely to an examination of the characteristics of such firms.

The segmentation of the economy into its principal resource inputs–natural resources (land and raw materials), labor, capital and now "information"–is a way to label the inputs that are necessary both for the industrial as well as the service economy. Our purpose in this book is to demonstrate how the quality of the "information" resources determines whether an organization will be economically successful.

The Industrial Economy includes SIC codes that are engaged in the manufacture and distribution of tangible goods. The following figure summarizes the classification of the major sectors of the economy, grouped by SIC codes.

101For total 1997 employment in listed industrial corporations of 20.8 million.
102For total 1997 employment in listed non-industrial corporations of 7.4 million.

Major Industry Sectors	Primary SIC Code
Agriculture. Timber. Fishing. Mining. Petroleum. Gas. Minerals	010 - 1499
Construction. Furniture	150 - 1799
Food Products. Tobacco	201 - 2141
Textiles. Apparel.	220 - 2399
Wood Products. Furniture. Paper Products. Printing.	240 - 2796
Chemicals. Synthetics. Drugs	281 - 2899
Oil. Gas. Coal. Plastics. Glass. Cement. Brick. Ceramics	291 - 3299
Steel. Iron. Metal Products	331 - 3499
Machinery. Equipment. Automotive. Engines. Electrical Motors	351 - 3629
Appliances. Electrical and Electronic Equipment	363 - 3699
Automotive. Airplanes. Aerospace. Instrumentation	371 - 3799
Health Care Equipment and Instrumentation	384 - 3999
Transportation. Utilities. Telecommunication	401 - 4961
Wholesale and Retail Trade. Food Services	500 - 5999

Figure A22–Description of Industrial Sectors

VERTICAL INTEGRATION OF U.S. INDUSTRIAL FIRMS

The share of revenues allocated to employee compensation, depreciation, interest and profits is one of the most important metrics for defining the scope of a firm's information management tasks. Whatever is not fully accountable as a directly supervised resource of the organization is, by definition, a purchased activity. This includes procurement of raw materials, energy, parts, components, transportation, supplies, consultants and services. Therefore, the scope of a firm's information management effort is not determined by its revenue–a frequently mistaken assumption–but by the extent of its "vertical integration" that is defined as what is directly paid for, supervised, managed, motivated, developed and guided.

Figure A23 shows that the median "vertical integration" of U.S. industrial firms is about 30%, although that number varies over a wide range.[103] Because firms, even in the same industry, pursue different strategies of what they decide to make or own and what to buy, their expenditures for information management and for information technologies are never comparable except when one also has the data about vertical integration.

When a corporation makes purchases the purchase cost already includes compensation for the supplier's information management. Information management is already included in the purchase price. Any claims to include purchased amounts as a justification for added computer spending, such as using revenues instead of costs as a way of defining the scope of what needs to be managed, results in double counting. Although an allowance should be always made for the costs of procurement and for vendor coordination, that should not equal the level of effort that must be devoted to managing a firm's own resources.

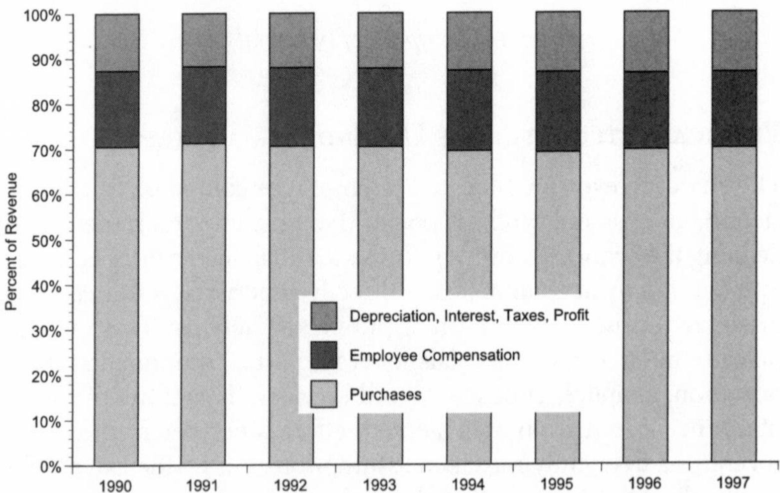

Figure A23 – Corporate Revenues Are Mostly Allocated for Purchases

103 Based on seven years of financial data for 1,502 U.S. industrial corporations with a total 1997 revenue of $4.3 trillion.

Cost elements that make up vertical integration are affected by a number of influences that may materially influence what will remain at the firm's profit after all payments are made.

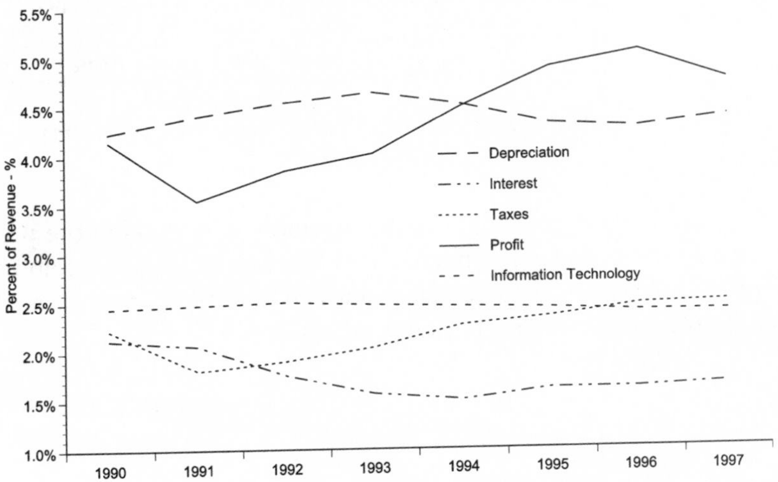

Figure A24–Rise in Taxation Offsets Reduced Costs of Debt

Depreciation expenses can be lower by acquiring assets that have a longer life expectancy. Whatever will reduce the depreciation through extending the useful service life will increased profits while minimizing write-offs. Depreciation charges are comparable to the amount of profits. This makes prudent management of assets for long economic life a key management objective. Interest payments are affected by prevailing economic conditions and can improve profitability if the rates fall, as has been the case in recent history and as is illustrated in the above Figure.

Taxes can be also seen as an "involuntary purchase" rather than as an element of vertical integration as suggested by a number of economists.[104] As can be seen in the following Figure the rise in taxes more than offset favorable trends in the cost of debt. An estimate of

104 The origin of all taxation is payment of protection money, which can be also seen as a form of state-sanctioned extortion. The current high levels of taxation, exceeding more than one third of all wealth in advanced industrial countries is unprecedented in over two thousand years of history.

information technology costs is also included as a comparison with the expenditures for taxes, which are of the similar magnitude.

	1990	1991	1992	1993	1994	1995	1996	1997
Value-Added/Revenue	29.6%	28.8%	29.9%	30.1%	30.1%	30.6%	30.3%	30.1%
Purchases/Revenue	70.4%	71.2%	70.1%	69.9%	69.9%	69.4%	69.7%	69.9%

Figure A25 – Corporations Increased Vertical Integration by Reducing Purchasing Costs

The biggest challenge for management is in making the purchasing processes more effective and value enhancing. The above Figure shows that it is here where one can find the sources of much of the recent gains in corporate profitability.

Appendix B

Women in Information Management

Women are now the dominant influence in the information economy. They constitute the majority of the users of information technologies. That's not the case with the promoters of computers. They are overwhelmingly male.

While collecting demographic data for this book, we uncovered data that either challenges a number of commonly accepted beliefs. Because the costs of information management have been significantly affected by the addition of lower-cost female workers, an analysis of this phenomenon is an appropriate addition to any discussion of productivity trends.

Lead in Information Management

One of the most interesting aspects of the transformation of the U.S. economy to an information-based society is the remarkable increase in the female participation in information occupations:

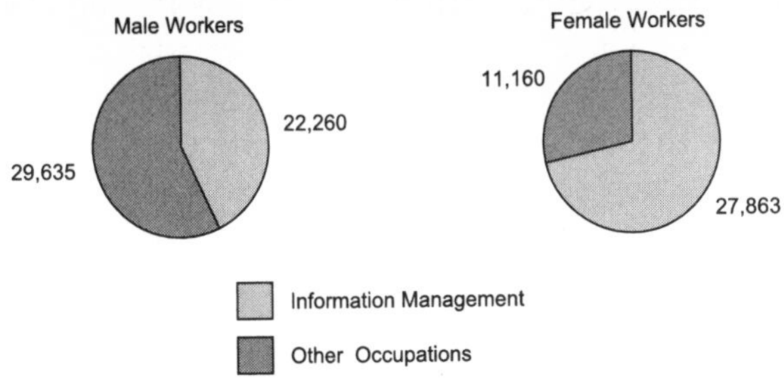

Figure B1–Number of Male and Female Workers [105]

105 U.S. Bureau of the Census, *Statistical Abstract of the United States*: 1997, Washington, DC, 1998, Table 671–Full-Time Wage and Salary Workers–Composition by Demographic Characteristics

As shown earlier in this book, the information management workforce now makes up 55% of total US employment and earns 64% of all wages and salaries. The information workforce also has been growing twice as fast as all other occupations and getting better raises than workers do in other occupations. Information management is where a large number of women have made their careers and the statistics show they have already achieved remarkable success.

Let us first look at the employment ratios of participation in information occupations by male and female workers.

Civilian Occupations	Male Workers - 1985 (000)	Female Workers - 1985 (000)	Male Workers - 1996 (000)	Female Workers - 1996 (000)	85-96 Gains-Male	85-96 Gains-Female
Managerial and Professional	11.078	8.302	13.934	13.288	26%	60%
Sales	4.227	2.929	5.114	3.927	21%	34%
Administrative	3.013	10.494	3.212	10.648	7%	1%
Technical	1.563	1.200	1.662	1.553	6%	29%
Services	3.947	3.963	4.958	5.000	26%	26%
Production & Other	21.761	4.526	23.015	4.607	6%	2%
Total	45.589	31.414	51.895	39.023	14%	24%

Figure B2 – Occupational Growth for Male and Female Workers

There are 5.6 million more women than men in information occupations. Are these women mostly in low-paying clerical jobs? The facts, as the Figure below illustrates, suggests an entirely different scenario:

By 1996 (the last time for which such numbers are available) women had attained parity in numbers in the premium-priced managerial and professional jobs. Their numbers, as well as growth rates in the lowest-paying occupations have been average or substantially below average:

By a wide margin women employed in corporations make their livelihood in information management occupations. On average, men's earnings still remain significantly higher in non-information occupations. On account of the differences in occupational participation rates and compensation levels, the relative importance of information work is, therefore, expressed best on a dollar wages weighted basis.

Civilian Occupations	Male Workers (000)	Female Workers (000)	Median Weekly Earnings - Male	Median Weekly Earnings - Female	Male/Female Compensation Ratio
Managerial and Professional	13,934	13,288	852	616	138%
Sales	5,114	3,927	589	353	167%
Administrative	3,212	10,648	489	391	125%
Technical	1,662	1,553	650	394	165%
Services	4,958	5,000	357	273	131%
Production & All Other	23,015	4,607	475	319	149%
Total	51,895	39,023			

Figure B3–Comparison of Median Earnings for Male and Female Workers [106]

On a wage-weighted basis, the relative position of women in information management positions is 80% vs. men's ratio of only 54%.

As women's compensation picks up with seniority and if the current growth rates continue, one can expect that a compensation-attractive career for a woman will be almost totally in information occupations. The prevailing high female/male ratios of attendance at colleges and universities indicate that women are responding to these prospects.

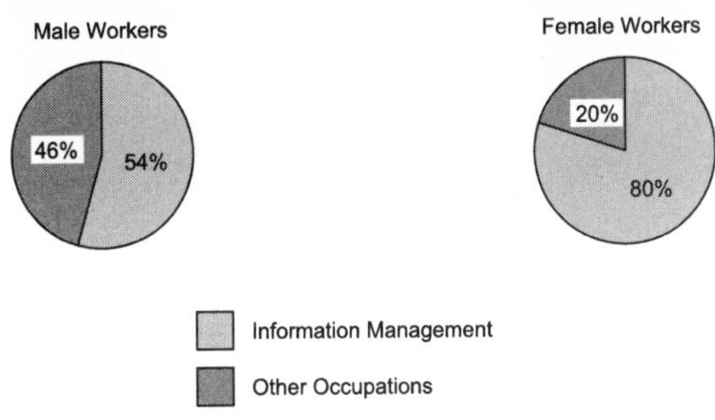

Figure B4–Dollar Weighted Share in Occupations for Male and Female Workers [107]

106 U.S. Bureau of the Census, *Statistical Abstract of the United States*: 1997, Washington, DC, 1998, Table 671–Full-Time Wage and Salary Workers–Number and Earnings

107 U.S. Bureau of the Census, *Statistical Abstract of the United States*: 1997, Washington, DC, 1998, Table 671–Full-Time Wage and Salary Workers–Composition by Demographic Characteristics

Males Continue to Dominate Information Technologies

The corporate careers of women will increasingly depend on their ability to manage the adoption and uses of information technologies as computer-enhanced work takes over an increasing share of information management tasks. This is where the patterns of an overwhelmingly female influence–as the most numerous users of information technologies–do not match the overwhelmingly male influence wherein men are the "pushers" of information technologies. The computer industry, especially in marketing and sales, has been always male-dominated, as illustrated in the Figure below.

The female participation rate in I.T. occupations has actually declined from 31% in 1983 to 29% in 1996. Perhaps that is because there are more influential positions available to women in the huge information management sector than in the small (1.3% of total employment) I.T. occupations.

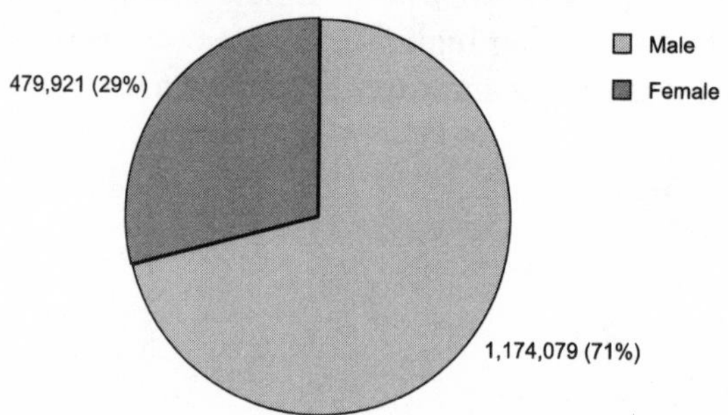

Figure B5–Males Dominate Information Technology Occupations [108]

As the power shifts from the I.T. producers to the I.T. consumers, it seems that women are making the right bet by moving to positions of increasing influence in the corporate arena.

Since the advent of the computer, the dominant theme of that industry has been to promote bigger and better technologies under

108 U.S. Bureau of the Census, *Statistical Abstract of the United States*: 1997, Washington, DC, 1998, Table 671–Full-Time Wage and Salary Workers–Composition by Demographic Characteristics

conditions of aggressive competition that were perhaps matched in U.S. industrial history only during the era when railroads were the primary drivers of economic expansion. Some of the aggressive competitive confrontations between computer executives perhaps are better explained by their compulsions to dominate the marketplace than by the economic benefits that their customers have been able to reap. Often, the urgency to replace technologies can be explained better by the dynamics of an arms race than by demonstrable profitability.

	1983 Employed 000	Female %	Male %	1996 Employed 000	Female %	Male %
Computer systems analysts, scientists	276	28%	72%	1,093	28%	72%
Computer programmers	443	33%	67%	561	31%	69%
Total I.T. Employment	719	31%	69%	1,654	29%	71%
I.T. Occupations as % of total workforce	0.713%			1.305%		

Figure B6–The Female Share of I.T. Occupations Has Decreased since 1983

The marketing methods that have prevailed in the I.T. industry over the last fifty years have often reflected tactics one could observe during a military campaign. Such methods may not be acceptable to an increasingly female population of information workers who may not have the same inclination as their male colleagues to put up with computer systems that are unfriendly, failure-proof and rapidly obsolescent.

The current build-and-junk attitudes that characterize the economics of I.T. are unlikely to continue because the human costs and disruptive influences on organizational performance now far exceed the costs of the technology itself. That shift will occur for no other reason than that concentration on purely technological superiority will cease to be affordable.

Appendix C

Information Productivity Listing

INFORMATION PRODUCTIVITY

IP Rank	Company	SIC	EMPLOYEES	Information Management/ Cost of Goods	Information Management/ Net Assets	Information Management/ Revenue	Information Management/ Employee	Information Productivity
913	360 COMMUNICATIONS	4812	4,400	216%	94%	42%	$120,397	2.8%
519	3COM	357	7,109	82%	80%	35%	$153,841	15.8%
1,131	AAR	5088	2,100	14%	26%	11%	$28,707	-6.1%
178	ABBOTT LABORATORIES	2834	54,487	90%	77%	33%	$69,537	45.8%
528	ABC RAIL PRODUCTS	3312	1,600	6%	20%	5%	$8,509	15.6%
347	ABT BUILDING PRODUCTS	2493	1,700	22%	41%	15%	$25,651	25.6%
1,337	ACC	4813	1,268	49%	88%	29%	$91,182	-21.9%
191	ACE HARDWARE	5072	4,685	5%	53%	5%	$28,761	42.9%
444	ACETO	5169	75	9%	21%	8%	$159,084	19.4%
1,114	ACME ELECTRIC	3621	660	28%	123%	21%	$26,084	-4.9%
1,581	ACME METALS	331	2,471	8%	16%	7%	$13,705	-104.0%
1,429	ACME UNITED	3421	433	38%	176%	27%	$30,117	-35.6%
1,051	ACT MANUFACTURING	3672	985	6%	24%	5%	$13,023	-2.1%
1,541	ACX TECHNOLOGIES	2671	5,600	17%	22%	13%	$20,126	-72.4%
1,015	ADAC LABORATORIES	3845	880	48%	63%	27%	$84,640	-0.8%
231	ADAPTEC INC	3577	3,276	92%	42%	34%	$107,213	36.3%
1,361	ADC TELECOMMUNICATIONS	5065	5,924	64%	42%	31%	$58,817	-24.7%
1,487	ADELPHIA COMMUNICATIONS	4841	3,895	56%	-8%	18%	$24,768	-47.1%
166	ADTRAN	3661	1,008	53%	35%	26%	$68,066	48.1%
782	ADVANCED ENERGY INDUSTRIES	3629	1,059	44%	47%	25%	$35,583	6.9%
1,221	ADVANCED MICRO DEVICES	3674	12,800	73%	39%	36%	$64,051	-11.4%
1,504	ADVANCED POLYMER SYSTEMS	2834	94	158%	194%	75%	$148,601	-56.6%
1,580	ADVANCED TISSUE SCIENCES	2835	238	2737%	97%	284%	$149,722	-101.5%
765	AEP INDUSTRIES	3081	4,200	21%	100%	16%	$20,127	7.4%
1,374	AERO SYSTEMS ENGINEERING	3724	147	30%	100%	22%	$31,703	-26.9%
1,403	AEROFLEX	367	790	35%	47%	22%	$24,233	-30.8%
418	AEROQUIP-VICKERS INC	3089	14,780	23%	73%	16%	$21,855	20.6%
50	AES	4911	10,000	7%	3%	4%	$6,788	114.0%
460	AFC CABLE SYSTEMS	364	1,196	22%	33%	16%	$32,340	18.4%
959	AFP IMAGING	3861	190	44%	109%	28%	$49,855	1.2%
678	AG-CHEM EQUIPMENT	3523	1,741	31%	107%	21%	$36,254	10.2%
253	AGCO	3523	11,000	14%	34%	10%	$32,889	33.2%
136	AGL RESOURCES	4924	3,035	4%	5%	3%	$9,820	55.8%
1,102	AGWAY	202	7,100	10%	90%	9%	$19,967	-4.2%
1,505	AIR & WATER TECHNOLOGIES	4959	2,900	22%	3809%	17%	$31,834	-56.8%
544	AIR EXPRESS INTERNATIONAL	4731	7,419	12%	59%	10%	$20,820	14.9%
382	AIR PRODUCTS AND CHEMICALS	2813	16,400	51%	42%	25%	$68,341	22.9%
865	AIRBORNE FREIGHT	4522	22,500	13%	50%	10%	$17,327	4.6%
889	AIRGAS	4924	8,100	62%	111%	33%	$56,842	3.6%
1,012	AIRTOUCH COMMUNICATIONS	4812	8,800	204%	23%	47%	$144,680	-0.8%
1,544	AIRTRAN HOLDINGS	4512	3,500	25%	37%	18%	$18,987	-73.1%
64	AK STEEL HOLDING	3312	5,800	6%	15%	5%	$19,929	103.8%
534	ALAMO GROUP	3523	1,414	20%	28%	15%	$19,940	15.4%
1,376	ALARIS MEDICAL	384	2,588	73%	158%	33%	$45,189	-27.3%
604	ALBANY INTERNATIONAL	2297	5,881	56%	60%	29%	$33,707	12.3%
1,363	ALBA-WALDENSIAN	3842	692	27%	46%	20%	$17,056	-25.1%
182	ALBEMARLE	2824	2,700	24%	27%	15%	$52,997	44.9%
850	ALBERTO-CULVER	2844	11,000	89%	157%	43%	$64,058	5.0%
610	ALBERTSON'S	5411	94,000	28%	123%	20%	$30,998	12.3%
594	ALEXANDER & BALDWIN	4449	2,930	14%	17%	10%	$38,629	12.9%
262	ALICO	0174	124	14%	3%	7%	$20,995	32.4%
173	ALLEGHENY TELEDYNE	3312	22,000	16%	47%	12%	$20,463	47.0%
659	ALLEN TELECOM	3663	3,300	39%	35%	23%	$27,944	10.6%
680	ALLERGAN	2834	6,100	189%	77%	52%	$95,099	10.1%
291	ALLIANT TECHSYSTEMS	3764	6,550	12%	47%	9%	$14,441	30.2%
155	ALLIED PRODUCTS	352	1,500	17%	36%	13%	$22,169	51.1%
1,167	ALLIED RESEARCH	3483	448	22%	53%	17%	$35,059	-7.7%
1,553	ALLIED WASTE INDUSTRIES	4953	5,400	24%	17%	13%	$14,130	-81.1%
202	ALLIEDSIGNAL	3728	70,500	14%	38%	11%	$19,503	41.4%
548	ALLTEL	481	16,393	376%	76%	49%	$97,774	14.7%
533	ALLTRISTA	3353	1,100	22%	46%	15%	$34,031	15.5%
1,435	ALOETTE COSMETICS	2844	31	82%	57%	41%	$163,011	-37.1%
1,311	ALPHA INDUSTRIES	3674	800	45%	64%	29%	$33,224	-19.4%
1,222	ALPHA TECHNOLOGIES GROUP	3679	814	27%	68%	20%	$17,976	-11.4%
1,141	ALPHARMA	2834	2,600	62%	79%	33%	$62,593	-6.6%
545	ALPINE GROUP	3661	3,809	9%	58%	7%	$11,431	14.9%

Appendix C–Information Productivity Listing

IP Rank	Company	SIC	EMPLOYEES	Information Management/ Cost of Goods	Information Management/ Net Assets	Information Management/ Revenue	Information Management/ Employee	Information Productivity
1,280	ALT ULTRASOUNDS	3845	2,669	89%	82%	43%	$67,920	-16.6%
104	ALTERA	3674	1,086	78%	36%	27%	$143,141	68.0%
98	ALTRON	3679	1,210	11%	13%	8%	$11,226	69.8%
536	ALUMAX	3353	14,400	10%	16%	8%	$17,335	15.4%
245	ALUMINUM OF AMERICA	3334	81,600	9%	14%	7%	$11,011	34.2%
1,413	ALZA	2834	1,532	305%	40%	45%	$116,682	-32.6%
1,622	AMATI COMMUNICATIONS	357	48	129%	158%	71%	$156,918	-169.5%
1,665	AMAX GOLD	1041	1,353	7%	3%	5%	$7,451	-619.0%
426	AMCAST INDUSTRIAL	3321	4,040	16%	30%	12%	$13,972	20.3%
587	AMCOL INTERNATIONAL	3295	1,546	18%	31%	13%	$35,547	13.2%
1,359	AMERADA HESS	2911	9,216	10%	21%	8%	$68,252	-24.3%
1,250	AMERICA WEST HOLDINGS	4512	8,921	27%	38%	14%	$27,369	-13.7%
1,399	AMERICAN BANKNOTE	2759	3,390	23%	69%	16%	$14,813	-30.5%
1,008	AMERICAN BILTRITE	1752	3,030	37%	129%	24%	$34,739	-0.6%
933	AMERICAN BUSINESS PRODUCTS	275	3,202	33%	77%	22%	$35,564	1.9%
1,602	AMERICAN ECOLOGY	4953	305	40%	102%	31%	$48,687	-131.1%
1,000	AMERICAN FREIGHTWAYS	4212	12,201	413%	211%	61%	$42,866	-0.1%
833	AMERICAN GREETINGS	2771	20,400	149%	81%	50%	$50,853	5.6%
457	AMERICAN HOME PRODUCTS	283	60,523	180%	93%	48%	$107,263	18.6%
683	AMERICAN HOMESTAR	1521	2,661	34%	106%	23%	$33,787	10.0%
1,627	AMERICAN MOBILE SATELLITE	481	477	232%	38%	239%	$172,727	-193.0%
1,660	AMERICAN RADIO SYSTEMS	4832	2,655	4%	1%	3%	$3,369	-502.6%
542	AMERICAN SAFETY RAZOR	3421	2,257	33%	121%	21%	$26,565	15.0%
654	AMERICAN STANDARD	3585	51,000	22%	-198%	16%	$19,842	10.7%
725	AMERICAN STATES WATER	4941	467	47%	19%	19%	$58,430	8.8%
907	AMERICAN STORES	5411	121,000	32%	177%	23%	$34,506	2.9%
899	AMERICAN TECHNICAL CERAMICS	3675	322	44%	36%	25%	$24,952	3.2%
1,644	AMERICAN TELECASTING	4841	410	82%	1031%	47%	$41,166	-275.0%
1,618	AMERICAN WASTE SERVICES	4953	529	17%	16%	14%	$22,382	-162.3%
685	AMERICAN WOODMARK	2434	2,154	26%	100%	19%	$17,175	9.9%
1,556	AMERIQUEST TECHNOLOGIES	5045	80	14%	-223%	13%	$130,962	-84.5%
474	AMERISOURCE HEALTH	5122	3,700	4%	-387%	3%	$65,770	17.9%
1,225	AMERIWOOD INDUSTRIES INTERNATIONAL	2511	700	24%	51%	19%	$26,899	-11.6%
908	AMERON INTERNATIONAL	327	2,761	28%	70%	20%	$36,905	2.9%
1,094	AMES DEPARTMENT STORES	5311	20,500	36%	465%	26%	$27,152	-3.8%
148	AMETEK	3621	6,700	11%	58%	9%	$11,175	52.5%
157	AMGEN	2834	5,308	537%	52%	45%	$213,114	50.2%
508	AMISTAR	3599	193	44%	46%	27%	$40,006	16.4%
103	AMOCO	2911	43,451	13%	14%	7%	$51,164	68.4%
372	AMP	3678	46,526	29%	35%	18%	$22,346	23.7%
78	AMPEX	3572	509	89%	-146%	44%	$77,331	85.1%
317	AMPHENOL	3357	6,900	23%	98%	14%	$19,066	27.5%
809	ANADARKO PETROLEUM	1311	1,386	53%	7%	12%	$54,381	6.4%
1,344	ANADIGICS	3674	580	67%	25%	30%	$50,766	-22.8%
243	ANALOG DEVICES	3674	7,500	76%	41%	32%	$52,970	34.4%
1,096	ANALOGIC	3825	1,500	63%	34%	34%	$51,719	-3.9%
1,466	ANAREN MICROWAVE	3679	217	51%	32%	31%	$30,260	-42.0%
1,116	ANDERSEN GROUP	3679	192	63%	47%	37%	$48,444	-5.0%
1,248	ANDREA ELECTRONICS	3842	93	64%	59%	38%	$60,088	-13.5%
420	ANDREW	366	4,227	43%	40%	23%	$43,597	20.5%
1,260	ANGELICA	2326	9,400	29%	56%	21%	$10,576	-14.5%
217	ANHEUSER-BUSCH	2082	24,326	29%	44%	17%	$75,608	38.9%
1,329	ANNTAYLOR STORES	5699	6,300	72%	68%	38%	$46,640	-21.0%
1,348	ANTEC	3663	2,500	26%	43%	20%	$52,282	-23.4%
1,436	APACHE	1311	1,287	10%	3%	4%	$30,506	-37.2%
1,214	APOGEE ENTERPRISES	1793	6,672	15%	78%	12%	$17,016	-11.0%
1,392	APPLE COMPUTER	3571	8,437	27%	100%	22%	$188,784	-29.6%
338	APPLE SOUTH	5812	28,500	9%	12%	5%	$1,307	26.0%
293	APPLEBEE'S INTERNATIONAL	5812	18,150	15%	18%	11%	$2,768	30.0%
901	APPLIED INDUSTRIAL TECHNOLOGIES	5085	4,101	30%	131%	22%	$59,802	3.1%
116	APPLIED MAGNETICS	3572	8,500	22%	33%	14%	$7,811	61.1%
195	APPLIED MATERIALS	3674	13,924	52%	41%	26%	$80,513	42.5%
706	APPLIED POWER	3492	4,235	46%	95%	27%	$47,566	9.4%
1,283	APS HOLDING	5013	5,400	47%	270%	31%	$36,999	-16.8%
491	APTARGROUP	3089	4,100	26%	31%	17%	$26,401	16.9%
349	AQUARION	4941	393	57%	14%	16%	$35,816	25.5%

INFORMATION PRODUCTIVITY

IP Rank	Company	SIC	EMPLOYEES	Information Management/ Cost of Goods	Information Management/ Net Assets	Information Management/ Revenue	Information Management/ Employee	Information Productivity
133	AQUILA GAS PIPELINE	4923	310	3%	9%	2%	$55,037	56.4%
849	ARBOR DRUGS	5912	7,000	29%	94%	21%	$26,433	5.1%
1,443	ARCH COAL	122	3,366	5%	6%	4%	$12,906	-38.1%
1,576	ARCH COMMUNICATIONS GROUP	4812	2,800	141%	96%	40%	$48,062	-99.8%
560	ARCHER DANIELS MIDLAND	204	17,160	4%	8%	3%	$29,559	14.2%
221	ARCO CHEMICAL	280	4,200	12%	16%	8%	$78,951	38.6%
964	ARDEN GROUP	5411	1,670	61%	175%	36%	$56,493	1.1%
1,406	ARMATRON INTERNATIONAL	3524	130	24%	862%	20%	$19,808	-31.6%
100	ARMCO	3316	6,000	7%	-49%	6%	$16,145	68.7%
321	ARMSTRONG WORLD INDUSTRIES	3253	10,600	30%	50%	19%	$36,746	27.3%
1,401	ARROW AUTOMOTIVE INDUSTRIES	3714	1,259	28%	78%	22%	$14,900	-30.6%
608	ARROW ELECTRONICS	5065	9,800	11%	45%	9%	$75,935	12.3%
433	ARTESYN TECHNOLOGIES	362	4,200	30%	60%	20%	$25,165	19.9%
288	ARTRA GROUP	2671	1,000	18%	-139%	15%	$18,730	30.6%
1,371	ARTS-WAY MANUFACTURING	3523	190	36%	71%	26%	$22,597	-26.5%
1,196	ARVIN INDUSTRIES	3714	14,324	10%	35%	8%	$13,150	-9.6%
84	ASA HOLDINGS	4512	2,504	25%	19%	14%	$21,241	79.4%
1,393	ASARCO	3331	6,900	8%	8%	6%	$16,547	-30.1%
1,014	ASHLAND	2911	37,200	13%	63%	10%	$36,456	-0.8%
1,262	ASPECT TELECOMMUNICATIONS	3661	1,600	98%	57%	38%	$87,988	-14.8%
1,586	ASSOCIATED GROUP	4812	761	447%	9%	247%	$107,374	-110.3%
1,041	ASTREX	5065	52	28%	99%	21%	$54,838	-1.8%
435	ASTRONICS	3647	443	31%	46%	19%	$16,159	19.6%
599	AT&T	481	128,000	62%	97%	32%	$105,392	12.6%
1,489	ATHEY PRODUCTS	3711	263	25%	25%	20%	$16,617	-48.6%
105	ATLANTIC RICHFIELD	2911	24,000	17%	15%	7%	$56,613	67.6%
257	ATMEL	3672	4,589	58%	30%	25%	$57,213	32.6%
1,048	ATMI	3674	376	81%	50%	37%	$89,056	-2.1%
845	ATMOS ENERGY	4924	2,679	31%	55%	20%	$60,295	5.1%
72	ATWOOD OCEANICS	1381	700	11%	5%	7%	$7,849	91.5%
1,386	AUSPEX SYSTEMS	3577	619	101%	60%	40%	$124,899	-28.7%
1,294	AUTHENTIC FITNESS	2329	1,211	37%	56%	25%	$42,999	-17.9%
422	AUTOZONE	5531	28,700	54%	76%	30%	$26,424	20.4%
567	AVERY DENNISON	2891	16,200	34%	86%	22%	$45,095	14.0%
1,578	AVIALL	5088	700	29%	76%	21%	$53,754	-100.6%
1,274	AVID TECHNOLOGY	3861	1,599	107%	89%	48%	$131,973	-16.2%
503	AVNET	5065	9,400	14%	41%	12%	$62,525	16.5%
620	AVON PRODUCTS	2844	34,995	127%	835%	49%	$70,134	11.9%
278	AVONDALE INDUSTRIES	3731	5,500	7%	20%	6%	$6,815	31.3%
113	AVX	3675	13,500	13%	15%	9%	$8,563	63.1%
1,437	AXIOHM TRANSACTION SOLUTIONS	3577	1,513	32%	54%	19%	$20,337	-37.2%
1,646	AXYS PHARMACEUTICALS	2834	395	28%	16%	27%	$24,575	-279.1%
808	BADGER METER	3823	972	49%	94%	29%	$36,813	6.4%
1,480	BADGER PAPER MILLS	2621	363	6%	21%	5%	$10,444	-45.6%
595	BAIRNCO	367	505	41%	76%	25%	$52,408	12.8%
1,286	BAKER (J.)	5661	6,630	67%	292%	39%	$33,860	-17.1%
1,016	BAKER HUGHES	3532	21,250	56%	49%	30%	$53,025	-1.0%
331	BALDOR ELECTRIC	3621	3,843	25%	39%	17%	$23,480	26.5%
1,145	BALDWIN PIANO & ORGAN	3931	1,520	28%	48%	21%	$18,212	-6.6%
1,347	BALDWIN TECHNOLOGY	3555	1,047	44%	82%	29%	$60,459	-23.0%
1,351	BALL	3411	10,300	6%	18%	5%	$13,261	-23.5%
1,278	BALTEK	2436	1,138	28%	34%	20%	$8,864	-16.3%
313	BALTIMORE GAS AND ELECTRIC	4911	9,000	22%	10%	10%	$41,891	27.7%
1,444	BANDAG	3011	4,507	46%	45%	25%	$60,185	-38.1%
577	BANTA	275	7,000	16%	32%	12%	$20,992	13.6%
708	BARD, (C.R.)	384	9,550	88%	78%	38%	$46,943	9.3%
1,139	BARNES & NOBLE	5942	31,500	37%	128%	25%	$23,164	-6.5%
546	BARNES GROUP	3495	3,900	42%	100%	26%	$40,381	14.8%
999	BARR LABORATORIES	2834	467	18%	39%	14%	$82,588	-0.1%
635	BARRETT RESOURCES	1311	207	15%	6%	8%	$106,480	11.2%
1,055	BARRY (R.G.)	3142	3,300	66%	88%	35%	$16,381	-2.3%
1,654	BATTLE MOUNTAIN GOLD	1041	1,810	6%	3%	4%	$7,974	-400.3%
1,036	BAUSCH & LOMB	3851	13,000	109%	64%	43%	$62,386	-1.6%
396	BAXTER INTERNATIONAL	5047	41,000	57%	53%	28%	$41,048	21.8%
692	BAY STATE GAS	4924	1,005	42%	44%	23%	$97,604	9.7%
897	BCT INTERNATIONAL	279	90	52%	58%	32%	$54,915	3.3%

Appendix C–Information Productivity Listing

IP Rank	Company	SIC	EMPLOYEES	Information Management/ Cost of Goods	Information Management/ Net Assets	Information Management/ Revenue	Information Management/ Employee	Information Productivity
1,383	BE AEROSPACE	3728	3,600	42%	72%	26%	$31,040	-28.1%
1,176	BEAZER HOMES USA	1521	1,143	12%	47%	10%	$78,071	-8.2%
1,270	BECKMAN COULTER	3845	11,100	105%	157%	41%	$56,982	-15.8%
421	BECTON, DICKINSON AND	384	18,900	74%	66%	33%	$49,559	20.4%
1,317	BEI MEDICAL SYSTEMS CO	3841	94	46%	69%	30%	$39,509	-19.8%
129	BELDEN	367	4,500	16%	43%	12%	$17,879	57.3%
956	BELL INDUSTRIES	5065	1,900	22%	85%	17%	$64,352	1.4%
535	BELLSOUTH	4813	81,000	72%	32%	23%	$53,283	15.4%
285	BEMIS	267	9,300	16%	33%	12%	$22,466	30.9%
1,025	BEN & JERRY'S HOMEMADE	2024	736	43%	55%	27%	$63,071	-1.4%
80	BENIHANA	5812	2,274	6%	18%	5%	$2,075	83.5%
448	BENTON OIL AND GAS	1311	71	67%	10%	14%	$196,776	19.2%
1,029	BERG ELECTRONICS	5065	7,000	38%	115%	22%	$26,216	-1.5%
752	BERGEN BRUNSWIG	5122	5,100	4%	72%	4%	$85,372	7.8%
1,053	BERKSHIRE GAS	4924	153	19%	12%	9%	$27,313	-2.2%
1,107	BEST BUY	5731	39,000	15%	140%	13%	$27,251	-4.6%
562	BESTFOODS	2034	44,200	52%	138%	29%	$50,500	14.1%
70	BET HOLDINGS	4841	460	26%	19%	12%	$36,151	92.8%
1,520	BETHLEHEM STEEL	3312	15,600	3%	10%	2%	$6,327	-66.2%
611	BETZDEARBORN	2899	6,405	140%	118%	45%	$81,523	12.2%
175	BHC COMMUNICATIONS	4833	1,181	122%	7%	28%	$40,053	46.2%
1,419	BIG FLOWER HOLDINGS	2752	8,500	11%	78%	9%	$13,733	-33.6%
1,078	BINDLEY WESTERN INDUSTRIES	512	1,283	1%	27%	1%	$68,811	-3.1%
1,373	BINKS SAMES	3563	1,260	43%	112%	29%	$48,922	-26.8%
379	BIOGEN	2836	797	1302%	41%	71%	$288,282	23.1%
215	BIOMATRIX	2834	223	552%	48%	58%	$81,456	39.0%
1,258	BIOMET	384	2,550	145%	42%	41%	$93,138	-14.3%
1,003	BIO-RAD LABORATORIES	3841	2,650	121%	110%	48%	$77,307	-0.4%
1,454	BIO-TECHNOLOGY GENERAL	2833	247	368%	43%	54%	$109,257	-40.2%
1,325	BIRMINGHAM STEEL	3312	1,520	5%	8%	4%	$24,546	-20.7%
810	BJ SERVICES	1389	8,453	12%	13%	9%	$13,773	6.3%
755	BLACK & DECKER	3634	28,600	45%	81%	27%	$44,947	7.7%
541	BLACK BOX	367	892	67%	76%	31%	$102,713	15.1%
37	BLACK HILLS	4911	446	9%	5%	5%	$22,919	132.9%
948	BLAIR	5961	2,200	91%	113%	44%	$107,195	1.5%
929	BLOCK DRUG	2844	3,380	206%	78%	61%	$139,586	2.2%
571	BLYTH INDUSTRIES	3999	2,400	96%	107%	41%	$96,640	13.9%
631	BOB EVANS FARMS	5812	29,375	43%	51%	26%	$7,295	11.5%
1,122	BOISE CASCADE	5112	22,514	14%	33%	11%	$28,290	-5.5%
673	BOOKS-A-MILLION	5942	2,600	25%	53%	18%	$18,249	10.3%
34	BORDEN CHEMICALS & PLASTICS	2821	800	4%	12%	3%	$29,269	137.0%
1,302	BORDERS GROUP	5942	24,300	30%	79%	21%	$19,736	-19.0%
484	BORG-WARNER AUTOMOTIVE	3714	10,400	10%	18%	8%	$12,240	17.2%
977	BOSTON BEER	5181	335	92%	121%	44%	$261,494	0.5%
731	BOSTON SCIENTIFIC	3841	11,000	163%	70%	42%	$67,280	8.6%
234	BOWATER	262	5,000	11%	10%	7%	$24,056	35.7%
1,035	BOWNE &	275	4,975	49%	50%	27%	$39,284	-1.6%
1,356	BRADLEES	5137	10,000	43%	-245%	31%	$39,949	-24.1%
928	BRADY (W.H.)	2672	2,500	99%	82%	42%	$67,161	2.2%
138	BREED TECHNOLOGIES	3714	11,100	20%	28%	13%	$9,246	54.8%
180	BRIGGS & STRATTON	3519	7,661	11%	25%	8%	$15,019	45.4%
878	BRINKER INTERNATIONAL	5812	800	208%	126%	58%	$21,985	4.0%
294	BRISTOL-MYERS SQUIBB	2834	53,600	204%	109%	47%	$139,538	30.0%
1,582	BROADBAND TECHNOLOGIES	3661	300	251%	139%	176%	$114,007	-104.1%
710	BROOKE GROUP LTD.	2111	1,556	149%	-48%	57%	$128,273	9.2%
1,234	BROWN & SHARPE MANUFACTURING	3545	2,409	46%	83%	29%	$47,476	-12.3%
1,079	BROWN GROUP	5661	11,600	56%	235%	34%	$45,979	-3.1%
452	BROWN-FORMAN	208	7,500	99%	93%	39%	$80,140	18.8%
1,069	BROWNING-FERRIS INDUSTRIES	4952	40,000	23%	32%	15%	$20,073	-2.8%
650	BRUNSWICK	3732	25,300	27%	51%	18%	$26,233	10.9%
829	BRUSH WELLMAN	3339	2,160	28%	34%	19%	$37,142	5.7%
1,057	BT OFFICE PRODUCTS INTERNATIONAL	5021	6,650	33%	124%	24%	$54,395	-2.4%
114	BUCKEYE PARTNERS,	4613	543	14%	4%	7%	$21,894	62.9%
61	BUCKEYE TECHNOLOGIES INC	2611	1,725	10%	25%	7%	$21,613	105.4%
763	BUFFETS	5812	24,830	7%	18%	6%	$1,909	7.5%
1,060	BUILDING MATERIALS HOLDING	521	3,500	25%	97%	19%	$41,204	-2.5%

INFORMATION PRODUCTIVITY

IP Rank	Company	SIC	EMPLOYEES	Information Management/ Cost of Goods	Information Management/ Net Assets	Information Management/ Revenue	Information Management/ Employee	Information Productivity
1,070	BURLINGTON COAT FACTORY	5331	17,600	45%	117%	30%	$29,572	-2.8%
789	BURLINGTON INDUSTRIES	2231	20,100	10%	27%	8%	$7,921	6.9%
652	BURLINGTON NORTHERN SANTA FE	4011	44,500	90%	41%	32%	$55,102	10.8%
346	BURR-BROWN	3674	1,308	76%	41%	34%	$55,992	25.6%
747	BUSH BOAKE ALLEN	2087	1,964	42%	44%	25%	$56,670	8.0%
386	BUSH INDUSTRIES	2511	3,250	28%	59%	19%	$20,748	22.7%
522	BUTLER MANUFACTURING	1521	5,177	16%	87%	13%	$24,595	15.7%
384	C&D TECHNOLOGIES	3691	2,596	21%	51%	15%	$20,722	22.8%
1,543	C.P. CLARE	3625	1,719	38%	39%	24%	$21,194	-72.8%
374	CABLE DESIGN TECHNOLOGIES	3669	2,900	27%	47%	18%	$31,867	23.5%
1,297	CABLEVISION SYSTEMS	4841	9,818	61%	-32%	25%	$52,914	-18.7%
265	CABOT	2895	4,800	26%	40%	17%	$64,677	32.2%
1,598	CABOT OIL & GAS	4923	342	30%	13%	11%	$60,279	-125.3%
1,140	CADMUS COMMUNICATIONS	275	3,000	24%	66%	18%	$20,490	-6.6%
573	CAGLE'S	2015	3,500	5%	33%	5%	$4,938	13.8%
1,655	CAI WIRELESS SYSTEMS	4841	128	220%	22%	101%	$141,689	-405.1%
375	CALGON CARBON	2819	1,341	31%	27%	19%	$47,423	23.5%
1,213	CALIFORNIA AMPLIFIER	3663	226	40%	61%	26%	$41,134	-10.9%
1,396	CALIFORNIA MICROWAVE	3661	1,412	33%	62%	23%	$44,712	-30.4%
412	CALIFORNIA WATER SERVICE GROUP	4941	649	48%	19%	17%	$47,349	20.9%
1,445	CALMAT	5032	1,880	12%	12%	10%	$22,245	-38.3%
1,621	CALPROP	152	18	12%	27%	12%	$97,344	-167.5%
1,415	CALTON	1521	85	14%	55%	12%	$136,106	-33.0%
651	CAMBREX	2833	1,790	25%	27%	16%	$39,300	10.9%
704	CAMCO INTERNATIONAL	3533	5,500	49%	38%	26%	$40,242	9.4%
301	CAMPBELL SOUP	2032	37,000	48%	83%	25%	$47,492	29.3%
895	CANANDAIGUA BRANDS	2084	2,500	26%	53%	18%	$83,897	3.4%
601	CANNONDALE	3751	762	39%	56%	24%	$46,441	12.4%
161	CARAUSTAR INDUSTRIES	2655	4,701	19%	43%	13%	$18,825	49.2%
74	CARBIDE/GRAPHITE GROUP	3624	1,193	7%	19%	5%	$11,524	90.4%
624	CARDINAL HEALTH	5122	11,000	5%	44%	5%	$63,015	11.8%
344	CARLISLE	3357	8,500	18%	45%	14%	$19,916	25.8%
38	CARNIVAL	4481	18,100	22%	9%	12%	$15,925	132.4%
343	CARPENTER TECHNOLOGY	3312	5,081	19%	33%	13%	$24,843	25.8%
1,105	CARR-GOTTSTEIN FOODS	5411	3,000	24%	349%	17%	$30,414	-4.3%
1,540	CARVER	3651	60	50%	93%	39%	$76,132	-72.3%
376	CASCADE	3537	2,322	26%	44%	18%	$30,587	23.3%
309	CASE	3523	18,300	19%	38%	14%	$42,951	28.2%
814	CASEY'S GENERAL STORES	5411	3,728	23%	67%	17%	$20,559	6.1%
1,327	CASH AMERICA INTERNATIONAL	5932	2,787	17%	12%	7%	$7,618	-20.9%
1,275	CATALINA LIGHTING	3645	225	17%	59%	13%	$89,039	-16.2%
179	CATERPILLAR	3531	59,863	21%	60%	14%	$42,402	45.6%
722	CAVALIER HOMES	1521	5,051	15%	58%	12%	$13,462	8.8%
1,276	CBS	4841	51,444	39%	33%	25%	$27,157	-16.3%
1,001	C-COR ELECTRONICS	3663	1,200	25%	54%	18%	$19,434	-0.2%
1,206	C-CUBE MICROSYSTEMS	3674	750	71%	61%	30%	$139,680	-10.1%
1,043	CEC ENTERTAINMENT	5812	13,600	32%	33%	16%	$3,939	-2.0%
1,604	CELLPRO	3841	137	592%	46%	239%	$173,654	-132.6%
561	CELLSTAR	5065	1,100	10%	78%	9%	$70,239	14.1%
1,609	CENTENNIAL CELLULAR	4812	1,100	133%	11%	34%	$51,507	-137.8%
1,587	CENTENNIAL TECHNOLOGIES	3572	119	45%	34%	29%	$69,688	-112.2%
1,635	CENTEX CONSTRUCTION PRODUCTS	3241	1,076	11%	7%	7%	$16,193	-216.3%
1,432	CENTOCOR	2834	640	239%	63%	71%	$174,880	-36.0%
1,087	CENTRAL GARDEN & PET	5083	2,700	15%	53%	12%	$40,475	-3.4%
983	CENTRAL SPRINKLER	3569	1,575	35%	85%	23%	$35,262	0.4%
1,427	CHAMPION INTERNATIONAL	2611	23,969	8%	11%	6%	$15,752	-35.4%
1,570	CHAMPION PARTS	3714	430	20%	-165%	19%	$7,917	-94.5%
1,661	CHANCELLOR MEDIA	4832	4,300	6%	1%	3%	$4,780	-555.6%
1,370	CHARMING SHOPPES	5621	12,600	33%	62%	25%	$18,872	-26.3%
1,624	CHART HOUSE ENTERPRISES	5812	275	28%	20%	9%	$40,653	-182.4%
159	CHART INDUSTRIES	3443	1,290	22%	54%	15%	$21,399	50.1%
42	CHASE INDUSTRIES	3351	700	4%	16%	3%	$21,375	124.4%
623	CHATTEM	2834	303	227%	-997%	56%	$222,567	11.8%
1,458	CHAUS (BERNARD)	2339	482	30%	-97%	25%	$78,577	-40.8%
1,597	CHECKERS DRIVE-IN RESTAURANTS	5812	5,000	26%	55%	19%	$5,317	-124.5%
984	CHECKPOINT SYSTEMS	3669	3,605	65%	39%	34%	$31,906	0.4%

IP Rank	Company	SIC	EMPLOYEES	Information Management/ Cost of Goods	Information Management/ Net Assets	Information Management/ Revenue	Information Management/ Employee	Information Productivity
818	CHEMED	284	6,849	44%	69%	28%	$22,145	5.9%
268	CHEMFIRST	281	1,175	15%	22%	10%	$47,407	31.8%
854	CHERRY	3643	4,453	32%	55%	21%	$21,257	5.0%
516	CHESAPEAKE	083	5,184	18%	33%	13%	$25,605	16.0%
1,672	CHESAPEAKE ENERGY	1381	362	12%	3%	4%	$18,993	-1054.3%
81	CHEVRON	1311	39,362	5%	9%	4%	$34,854	83.2%
1,310	CHIC BY H.I.S	2339	3,850	27%	68%	20%	$16,239	-19.4%
1,384	CHIQUITA BRANDS INTERNATIONAL	0179	40,000	16%	44%	13%	$8,559	-28.4%
1,343	CHIRON	3851	6,482	243%	93%	66%	$103,905	-22.8%
1,054	CHOCK FULL O'NUTS	2095	1,400	35%	120%	24%	$63,096	-2.3%
627	CHRISTIANA	4222	746	13%	14%	10%	$13,111	11.7%
389	CHROMCRAFT REVINGTON	2511	2,300	19%	32%	14%	$11,891	22.5%
212	CHRYSLER	3711	121,000	10%	41%	8%	$36,866	40.3%
859	CHURCH & DWIGHT	281	1,137	67%	119%	37%	$196,285	4.8%
797	CHYRON	3663	459	88%	64%	39%	$83,810	6.7%
518	CINCINNATI MILACRON	3229	12,957	25%	77%	18%	$25,430	15.8%
914	CIRCLE INTERNATIONAL GROUP	4731	3,910	62%	117%	36%	$60,389	2.7%
1,197	CIRCON	3845	1,204	122%	79%	48%	$63,425	-9.6%
955	CIRCUIT CITY STORES - MAIN	5731	29,622	26%	106%	20%	$43,437	1.4%
906	CIRCUIT CITY STORES - CIRCUIT CITY	5731	26,840	27%	106%	20%	$43,558	2.9%
436	CITATION	3321	5,778	12%	30%	9%	$9,223	19.6%
967	CKE RESTAURANTS	5812	46,500	34%	61%	22%	$6,413	0.9%
365	CLARCOR	3569	2,872	25%	38%	17%	$22,116	24.4%
149	CLEAR CHANNEL COMMUNICATIONS	4832	5,400	5%	1%	3%	$3,541	52.2%
19	CLEVELAND-CLIFFS INC	1011	5,776	5%	4%	3%	$2,707	212.2%
439	CLOROX	2842	5,500	92%	85%	37%	$159,442	19.5%
694	CMI	3531	1,590	29%	44%	21%	$21,599	9.7%
1,282	CML GROUP	5941	3,100	163%	320%	64%	$71,155	-16.8%
106	CMS ENERGY	4911	9,659	6%	8%	4%	$18,303	67.0%
846	CNF TRANSPORTATION	421	26,300	15%	86%	12%	$17,497	5.1%
918	COACHMEN INDUSTRIES	3711	4,274	10%	34%	8%	$13,088	2.6%
224	COASTAL	4922	13,200	1%	2%	1%	$4,502	37.8%
1,135	COBRA ELECTRONICS	3663	125	21%	74%	17%	$112,473	-6.3%
200	COCA-COLA	208	29,500	123%	118%	40%	$254,703	42.0%
842	COCA-COLA BOTTLING CONSOLIDATED	2086	5,500	51%	972%	29%	$45,403	5.3%
976	COCA-COLA ENTERPRISES	2086	56,000	56%	167%	31%	$60,363	0.6%
1,653	COEUR D'ALENE MINES	1044	949	16%	4%	12%	$11,203	-362.1%
1,353	COGNITRONICS	357	94	78%	64%	35%	$85,849	-23.8%
581	COHERENT	3845	2,131	87%	68%	39%	$74,998	13.4%
1,169	COHO ENERGY	1382	166	61%	7%	13%	$45,896	-7.7%
909	COLD METAL PRODUCTS	3316	834	6%	44%	6%	$18,524	2.9%
1,076	COLE NATIONAL	5995	14,000	172%	759%	57%	$33,373	-3.0%
1,188	COLEMAN	3648	5,125	29%	85%	20%	$48,954	-8.7%
642	COLGATE-PALMOLIVE	284	37,800	74%	144%	35%	$81,139	11.1%
41	COLLINS & AIKMAN	2396	15,100	11%	-70%	9%	$8,655	125.9%
630	COLLINS INDUSTRIES	3711	900	12%	105%	10%	$16,808	11.5%
355	COLONIAL GAS	4924	490	39%	31%	20%	$73,538	25.1%
92	COLTEC INDUSTRIES INC	3728	9,100	19%	-39%	12%	$17,845	74.8%
1,417	COLUMBIA ENERGY GROUP	1311	8,529	4%	6%	3%	$10,729	-33.1%
1,319	COLUMBUS MCKINNON	3536	4,100	21%	35%	15%	$16,650	-20.0%
1,314	COMCAST	4841	17,600	37%	171%	19%	$50,828	-19.6%
874	COMDIAL	3661	865	50%	77%	29%	$34,813	4.2%
558	COMMERCIAL INTERTECH	3492	3,805	29%	86%	20%	$26,817	14.3%
1,272	COMMNET CELLULAR	4812	596	163%	81%	45%	$103,372	-15.9%
1,493	COMMONWEALTH INDUSTRIES	3334	2,015	4%	12%	4%	$18,299	-50.4%
819	COMPUCOM SYSTEMS	5045	4,300	10%	93%	9%	$45,769	5.9%
233	COMPUSA	5734	14,251	2%	24%	2%	$7,015	35.9%
1,628	COMSAT	4899	2,732	8%	4%	5%	$12,609	-195.6%
131	COMSTOCK RESOURCES	1382	47	8%	3%	3%	$46,527	56.6%
892	CONAGRA	201	80,000	11%	74%	9%	$27,000	3.5%
1,227	CONCORD FABRICS	2231	365	30%	78%	22%	$83,217	-11.7%
1,381	CONE MILLS	2211	6,100	13%	40%	11%	$12,872	-27.9%
622	CONGOLEUM	3996	1,234	34%	202%	23%	$45,740	11.8%
32	CONNECTICUT ENERGY	4924	501	3%	3%	1%	$7,202	141.1%
332	CONSOLIDATED GRAPHICS	2752	2,400	27%	37%	18%	$16,812	26.4%
27	CONSOLIDATED PAPERS	2671	7,244	7%	6%	5%	$12,041	165.7%

IP Rank	Company	SIC	EMPLOYEES	Information Management/ Cost of Goods	Information Management/ Net Assets	Information Management/ Revenue	Information Management/ Employee	Information Productivity
393	CONSOLIDATED PRODUCTS	5812	12,000	20%	50%	14%	$3,046	22.3%
1,061	CONSOLIDATED STORES	5331	50,324	60%	134%	34%	$25,704	-2.5%
612	CONTINENTAL HOMES HOLDING	1521	646	14%	50%	11%	$122,559	12.2%
1,155	CONTINENTAL MATERIALS	3585	685	21%	47%	16%	$20,035	-7.1%
1,335	CONVERSE	3021	2,956	44%	-355%	32%	$50,689	-21.6%
510	COOKER RESTAURANT	5812	5,527	7%	9%	6%	$1,385	16.3%
1,062	COOPER	3851	1,400	54%	80%	29%	$28,488	-2.6%
1,530	COOPER CAMERON	3559	9,600	19%	37%	14%	$23,012	-69.1%
564	COOPER INDUSTRIES	3646	41,200	27%	44%	17%	$21,769	14.0%
143	COOPER TIRE & RUBBER	3061	10,456	7%	11%	5%	$9,367	53.6%
1,017	COORS (ADOLPH)	2082	5,800	55%	76%	31%	$91,651	-1.0%
1,472	COPLEY PHARMACEUTICAL	2834	404	31%	26%	21%	$59,773	-43.7%
727	CORCOM	3677	672	46%	48%	27%	$13,342	8.7%
362	CORDANT TECHNOLOGIES	3764	5,300	12%	19%	10%	$14,293	24.6%
1,340	CORECOMM	4812	750	322%	40%	47%	$91,449	-22.3%
898	CORNING	3669	20,500	43%	47%	23%	$37,134	3.3%
836	COSTCO	5331	57,000	10%	86%	9%	$31,627	5.5%
871	COURIER	2732	1,202	21%	49%	15%	$17,271	4.4%
415	COVENANT TRANSPORT	4213	3,965	15%	29%	10%	$7,097	20.7%
1,465	COX COMMUNICATIONS	4841	7,700	88%	18%	29%	$58,398	-42.0%
877	CPAC	2842	662	64%	66%	33%	$53,701	4.0%
634	CRACKER BARREL OLD COUNTRY STORE	5812	35,805	198%	88%	53%	$16,182	11.3%
449	CRANE	349	11,000	21%	63%	15%	$28,048	19.1%
582	CROMPTON & KNOWLES	2865	5,519	26%	615%	18%	$54,480	13.4%
358	CROSS TIMBERS OIL	1311	349	34%	11%	10%	$51,323	24.9%
1,590	CROWN BOOKS	5942	1,600	24%	84%	20%	$29,451	-116.0%
1,485	CROWN CENTRAL PETROLEUM	2911	2,819	6%	46%	6%	$30,657	-46.9%
832	CROWN CORK & SEAL	3411	40,985	5%	10%	4%	$8,868	5.6%
953	CROWN CRAFTS	2391	2,559	20%	44%	15%	$17,379	1.4%
1,637	CRYSTAL OIL	4922	24	273%	3%	29%	$134,907	-219.6%
588	CSS INDUSTRIES	2761	2,054	37%	45%	24%	$34,321	13.1%
261	CSX	4011	46,911	18%	25%	12%	$26,620	32.4%
876	CTG RESOURCES	4924	612	34%	34%	19%	$90,416	4.1%
530	CTS	3678	5,044	23%	36%	16%	$12,876	15.5%
1,198	CUBIC	3829	3,500	26%	44%	19%	$21,863	-9.7%
1,309	CULLIGAN WATER TECHNOLOGIES	3589	4,758	57%	60%	30%	$36,270	-19.3%
540	CULP	2221	3,146	14%	45%	11%	$13,421	15.3%
568	CUMMINS ENGINE	351	26,300	25%	74%	18%	$39,622	14.0%
241	CURTISS-WRIGHT	3724	1,884	33%	20%	21%	$21,803	34.5%
1,266	CVS	5912	90,000	33%	123%	23%	$28,038	-15.3%
1,410	CYBEX INTERNATIONAL	3842	532	78%	92%	43%	$58,331	-32.1%
1,564	CYGNUS	2835	157	385%	163%	107%	$183,230	-89.3%
429	CYPRESS SEMICONDUCTOR	3674	2,770	69%	28%	28%	$67,750	20.2%
1,542	CYPRUS AMAX MINERALS	1021	10,500	6%	5%	4%	$12,788	-72.7%
211	CYTEC INDUSTRIES	2819	5,200	28%	65%	18%	$45,852	40.4%
339	D.R. HORTON	1522	1,160	13%	34%	10%	$81,574	26.0%
1,075	DAIRY MART CONVENIENCE STORES	5411	3,500	38%	1726%	26%	$34,767	-2.9%
916	DAISYTEK INTERNATIONAL	5044	971	7%	44%	6%	$57,068	2.7%
300	DANA	3714	49,100	11%	45%	9%	$15,573	29.3%
250	DANAHER	3423	13,200	29%	44%	19%	$28,736	33.5%
1,231	DANIEL INDUSTRIES	382	1,800	48%	49%	29%	$41,232	-12.0%
1,292	DARDEN RESTAURANTS	5812	114,600	14%	31%	11%	$3,016	-17.8%
733	DATAPOINT	357	641	50%	-82%	32%	$67,719	8.5%
1,330	DATRON SYSTEMS	3663	319	41%	50%	28%	$48,046	-21.0%
1,160	DATUM	3812	656	59%	74%	33%	$49,137	-7.5%
883	DAYTON HUDSON	5311	230,000	23%	109%	17%	$19,500	3.8%
1,083	DDL ELECTRONICS	3672	500	17%	202%	14%	$11,917	-3.3%
1,066	DEAN FOODS	202	11,800	24%	90%	18%	$42,565	-2.6%
1,021	DEB SHOPS	5621	2,600	27%	51%	21%	$15,055	-1.2%
225	DEERE &	3523	34,420	21%	42%	13%	$45,015	37.7%
618	DEFIANCE	3714	729	17%	32%	12%	$14,152	12.0%
875	DEKALB GENETICS	011	2,000	82%	93%	40%	$80,298	4.1%
866	DEL LABORATORIES	2844	1,480	134%	263%	51%	$89,165	4.6%
1,187	DELCHAMPS	5311	7,934	31%	212%	23%	$29,533	-8.7%
151	DELL COMPUTER	3571	16,000	15%	95%	11%	$83,655	51.6%
1,478	DELTA WOODSIDE INDUSTRIES	2211	7,400	15%	32%	12%	$10,316	-45.1%

IP Rank	Company	SIC	EMPLOYEES	Information Management/ Cost of Goods	Information Management/ Net Assets	Information Management/ Revenue	Information Management/ Employee	Information Productivity
949	DELUXE	2782	18,900	91%	106%	39%	$38,408	1.5%
616	DENTSPLY INTERNATIONAL	3843	5,300	70%	56%	32%	$40,181	12.1%
1,321	DEP	2844	300	174%	1147%	59%	$207,256	-20.2%
142	DEPARTMENT 56	5199	220	50%	27%	21%	$233,021	53.8%
1,418	DESIGNS	5651	3,200	31%	63%	23%	$23,473	-33.1%
1,229	DETREX	281	353	26%	97%	20%	$54,351	-11.7%
1,056	DETROIT DIESEL	3519	6,500	26%	126%	20%	$65,409	-2.3%
1,562	DEVCON INTERNATIONAL	5032	459	29%	24%	21%	$24,727	-88.3%
912	DEXTER	2833	4,800	40%	59%	25%	$58,018	2.8%
1,136	DIGITAL EQUIPMENT	3571	54,900	49%	120%	31%	$73,207	-6.4%
311	DII GROUP	367	6,350	12%	31%	9%	$10,554	27.7%
927	DILLARDS	531	44,616	37%	58%	25%	$35,862	2.3%
886	DIMON	5194	6,700	7%	42%	6%	$30,273	3.7%
798	DISCOUNT AUTO PARTS	5531	3,677	43%	44%	25%	$25,436	6.6%
1,426	DIXIE GROUP	2273	4,600	15%	67%	12%	$15,399	-34.9%
993	DIXON TICONDEROGA	3952	1,170	42%	140%	26%	$23,245	0.1%
657	DOLE FOOD	203	44,000	12%	64%	10%	$8,738	10.7%
591	DOLLAR GENERAL	5331	27,400	28%	86%	20%	$17,877	13.0%
1,246	DOLLAR TREE STORES	5331	13,000	36%	110%	23%	$10,667	-13.3%
529	DONALDSON	3569	6,230	29%	64%	19%	$27,132	15.6%
1,170	DONNELLEY (R.R.) & SONS	275	25,800	14%	34%	10%	$17,608	-7.8%
1,299	DONNKENNY	2339	1,226	25%	77%	19%	$31,054	-18.8%
270	DOVER	353	28,758	32%	57%	20%	$31,499	31.7%
216	DOW CHEMICAL	3089	42,861	22%	31%	14%	$69,761	39.0%
434	DRAVO	3274	738	21%	20%	14%	$29,042	19.8%
497	DRESS BARN	5621	7,100	41%	68%	26%	$19,662	16.6%
598	DRESSER INDUSTRIES	356	31,300	19%	52%	14%	$29,247	12.6%
174	DREW INDUSTRIES	3442	2,258	17%	58%	13%	$12,937	47.0%
1,152	DREYERS GRAND ICE CREAM	5143	3,500	26%	80%	20%	$54,179	-6.9%
746	DRS TECHNOLOGIES	3812	1,470	28%	86%	20%	$26,284	8.0%
1,024	DRUG EMPORIUM	5912	4,900	26%	327%	20%	$28,425	-1.4%
996	DSC COMMUNICATIONS	366	6,681	63%	39%	31%	$71,623	0.0%
1,287	DT INDUSTRIES	3829	3,100	20%	27%	14%	$16,480	-17.2%
127	DU PONT (E.I.) DE NEMOURS AND	2911	98,000	15%	37%	10%	$39,257	57.5%
458	DUCOMMUN	372	1,291	29%	43%	18%	$20,725	18.5%
1,524	DURA PHARMACEUTICALS	5122	644	432%	18%	54%	$125,720	-67.6%
1,295	DURAKON INDUSTRIES	3792	847	20%	46%	16%	$32,406	-18.2%
204	DYCOM INDUSTRIES	1731	2,864	12%	80%	10%	$7,425	41.3%
539	DYERSBURG	2257	3,850	14%	24%	10%	$9,872	15.3%
826	DYNAMICS RESEARCH	3577	1,455	12%	37%	10%	$9,848	5.8%
1,440	DYNEGY	1311	2,572	1%	11%	1%	$54,439	-37.8%
1,620	EA INDUSTRIES	357	474	22%	172%	21%	$34,825	-164.7%
923	EAGLE HARDWARE & GARDEN	5722	5,600	32%	67%	23%	$36,485	2.5%
856	EASTERN	3429	492	26%	38%	18%	$22,817	4.9%
398	EASTERN ENTERPRISES	4924	2,840	16%	24%	11%	$36,702	21.7%
134	EASTMAN CHEMICAL	3081	16,100	16%	32%	11%	$30,874	56.4%
668	EASTMAN KODAK	3861	97,500	72%	119%	34%	$53,607	10.4%
419	EATON	3714	49,000	26%	62%	18%	$24,665	20.5%
1,333	ECC INTERNATIONAL	3699	789	18%	29%	14%	$15,474	-21.2%
950	ECHLIN	3714	31,300	26%	62%	19%	$21,476	1.5%
1,594	ECHOSTAR COMMUNICATIONS	4841	1,930	66%	114%	44%	$99,900	-123.2%
638	ECOLAB	2841	10,210	110%	125%	43%	$66,337	11.2%
423	EDO	381	637	26%	77%	18%	$23,191	20.4%
1,592	EEX	1311	420	128%	14%	41%	$250,708	-120.0%
729	EG&G	3825	14,000	28%	81%	20%	$19,629	8.6%
1,423	EKCO GROUP	5023	1,018	34%	48%	22%	$49,752	-34.0%
281	ELCOR	2951	783	20%	28%	15%	$39,597	31.2%
1,085	ELECTROMAGNETIC SCIENCES	3663	1,200	47%	51%	29%	$36,946	-3.4%
95	ELXSI	5812	2,884	12%	24%	9%	$2,790	72.8%
120	EMC	3572	6,400	48%	33%	24%	$112,138	59.9%
295	EMERSON ELECTRIC	362	100,700	33%	41%	20%	$24,722	29.9%
504	EMPI	3842	527	254%	69%	54%	$71,611	16.5%
251	EMPIRE DISTRICT ELECTRIC	4911	626	17%	5%	6%	$21,499	33.4%
1,547	EMPIRE OF CAROLINA	394	530	33%	213%	25%	$42,188	-78.0%
1,434	EMULEX	3572	332	71%	102%	41%	$74,248	-36.9%
193	ENCORE WIRE	506	381	8%	25%	7%	$47,042	42.7%

INFORMATION PRODUCTIVITY

IP Rank	Company	SIC	EMPLOYEES	Information Management/ Cost of Goods	Information Management/ Net Assets	Information Management/ Revenue	Information Management/ Employee	Information Productivity
701	ENERGEN	4924	1,469	71%	52%	30%	$79,607	9.5%
1,462	ENERGY CONVERSION DEVICES	3692	345	81%	68%	49%	$55,866	-41.7%
669	ENERGYNORTH	4923	252	45%	48%	24%	$83,807	10.4%
1,320	ENESCO GROUP	5199	2,500	99%	123%	44%	$80,036	-20.1%
455	ENGELHARD	3341	2,800	11%	35%	8%	$76,191	18.6%
124	ENOVA	4911	3,665	32%	14%	11%	$61,898	58.5%
2	ENSCO INTERNATIONAL	1381	3,700	5%	1%	2%	$3,560	612.1%
1,481	ENVIRONMENTAL ELEMENTS	3822	131	17%	105%	14%	$55,116	-45.8%
1,157	EQUITABLE RESOURCES	4924	1,978	12%	22%	9%	$80,346	-7.2%
1,630	EQUITY OIL	1311	18	24%	6%	13%	$112,981	-199.7%
1,479	ESCO ELECTRONICS	3812	3,400	22%	36%	17%	$22,816	-45.4%
804	ESTERLINE TECHNOLOGIES	282	3,360	52%	83%	30%	$34,678	6.5%
739	ETHAN ALLEN INTERIORS	5021	6,417	52%	66%	29%	$24,346	8.3%
264	ETHYL	2869	1,500	25%	52%	16%	$100,901	32.3%
1,232	EVANS	5632	825	56%	173%	35%	$38,925	-12.1%
904	EVANS & SUTHERLAND COMPUTER	3571	831	89%	35%	41%	$69,251	3.0%
1,548	EVI WEATHERFORD	3533	7,200	19%	14%	13%	$15,039	-78.0%
1,441	EXABYTE	3572	1,299	33%	49%	25%	$62,692	-37.8%
1,369	EXAR	3825	347	77%	33%	36%	$100,335	-26.2%
837	EXCEL INDUSTRIES	3089	6,652	8%	38%	7%	$10,313	5.4%
1,438	EXECUTIVE TELECARD, LTD.	4813	145	60%	150%	34%	$74,885	-37.3%
1,301	EXECUTONE INFORMATION SYSTEMS	3661	700	63%	109%	38%	$65,219	-19.0%
1,638	EXPEDITORS INTERNAT'L OF WASHINGTON	4731	4,500	3%	13%	3%	$5,596	-225.0%
227	EXXON	1311	80,000	12%	18%	7%	$99,568	37.3%
1,095	E-Z-EM	2835	958	72%	54%	41%	$41,006	-3.8%
1,559	FAB INDUSTRIES	221	1,600	11%	11%	9%	$9,875	-87.5%
1,064	FABRI-CENTERS OF AMERICA	5719	17,100	73%	171%	39%	$20,686	-2.6%
468	FAIRCHILD	372	3,900	31%	57%	22%	$36,716	18.0%
1,251	FANSTEEL	3463	1,127	15%	29%	12%	$14,409	-13.7%
1,267	FARAH	2325	3,950	35%	82%	26%	$15,422	-15.4%
1,642	FARR	3564	1,319	24%	67%	17%	$16,058	-259.6%
1,460	FASTCOMM COMMUNICATION	3661	78	135%	82%	67%	$94,983	-41.1%
925	FDX	4513	126,000	45%	108%	27%	$25,155	2.4%
432	FEDDERS	3585	2,700	13%	25%	10%	$12,969	19.9%
1,449	FEDERAL SCREW WORKS	3452	491	7%	15%	5%	$10,291	-39.2%
373	FEDERAL SIGNAL	371	6,591	29%	63%	20%	$27,451	23.6%
1,414	FEDERAL-MOGUL	3714	13,300	22%	53%	16%	$20,816	-32.7%
1,065	FEDERATED DEPARTMENT STORES	5311	114,700	54%	101%	31%	$41,039	-2.6%
1,506	FEI	3674	940	49%	43%	30%	$57,156	-58.2%
46	FERRELLGAS PARTNERS,	5984	4,207	3%	16%	2%	$3,366	117.9%
1,097	FERRO	3479	6,851	23%	66%	17%	$33,046	-4.0%
785	FERROFLUIDICS	3679	261	41%	85%	28%	$59,543	6.9%
197	FINA	2911	2,873	3%	7%	2%	$33,310	42.4%
990	FINGERHUT	5961	9,500	135%	166%	53%	$109,466	0.2%
783	FIRST BRANDS	3089	4,800	39%	67%	24%	$63,492	6.9%
489	FLEETWOOD ENTERPRISES	379	18,000	18%	71%	14%	$22,416	16.9%
1,180	FLEMING	514	39,700	8%	112%	7%	$29,162	-8.4%
1,239	FLEXSTEEL INDUSTRIES	2512	2,400	23%	50%	18%	$16,196	-12.9%
392	FLORIDA ROCK INDUSTRIES	3273	2,448	13%	16%	9%	$16,397	22.4%
903	FLOW INTERNATIONAL	3569	990	57%	80%	31%	$51,167	3.1%
835	FLOWERS INDUSTRIES	205	7,300	70%	151%	38%	$64,078	5.5%
695	FLOWSERVE	3594	7,200	48%	79%	27%	$41,854	9.6%
1,109	FLUKE	382	2,525	102%	96%	45%	$72,519	-4.7%
526	FMC	281	16,805	26%	95%	18%	$40,959	15.6%
1,550	FOAMEX INTERNATIONAL	3086	6,414	8%	-159%	7%	$11,445	-79.0%
860	FOOD LION	5411	83,871	19%	110%	15%	$17,818	4.8%
1,034	FOODARAMA SUPERMARKETS	5411	4,000	34%	477%	25%	$38,356	-1.6%
1,243	FOODMAKER	5812	29,000	10%	154%	8%	$3,302	-13.2%
1,664	FORCENERGY INC	1311	275	21%	5%	6%	$47,121	-593.1%
345	FORD MOTOR	3711	363,892	14%	48%	9%	$36,402	25.8%
552	FORE SYSTEMS	3679	1,592	115%	37%	44%	$122,126	14.6%
1,634	FOREST OIL	1321	267	9%	7%	5%	$57,933	-210.0%
1,146	FORT JAMES	267	29,000	24%	61%	16%	$40,759	-6.7%
890	FORTUNE BRANDS	3429	24,920	58%	40%	29%	$53,173	3.6%
703	FOSSIL	3873	472	67%	93%	35%	$142,590	9.5%
1,100	FOSTER, (L.B.)	3312	563	11%	33%	9%	$40,339	-4.1%

Appendix C–Information Productivity Listing

IP Rank	Company	SIC	EMPLOYEES	Information Management/ Cost of Goods	Information Management/ Net Assets	Information Management/ Revenue	Information Management/ Employee	Information Productivity
450	FPL GROUP	4931	9,588	59%	25%	20%	$116,980	18.8%
319	FRANKLIN ELECTRIC	3621	2,388	25%	55%	17%	$19,730	27.4%
63	FREEPORT-MC MORAN COPPER & GOLD	1021	6,300	14%	11%	7%	$17,798	104.2%
1,424	FREQUENCY ELECTRONICS	3825	212	46%	16%	31%	$35,042	-34.2%
1,288	FRESH FOODS	2013	3,847	14%	40%	9%	$4,353	-17.2%
192	FRIEDMAN INDUSTRIES	3353	170	4%	19%	3%	$28,987	42.8%
1,455	FRISCH'S RESTAURANTS	5812	5,400	6%	13%	5%	$1,373	-40.3%
1,572	FRONTIER OIL	2911	291	3%	24%	2%	$27,471	-97.4%
1,510	FRUIT OF THE LOOM	2322	28,500	29%	56%	19%	$14,150	-59.4%
1,560	FSI INTERNATIONAL	3674	1,360	61%	41%	34%	$71,150	-87.9%
921	FULLER (H.B.)	2891	6,000	39%	97%	25%	$53,111	2.5%
693	FURNITURE BRANDS INTERNATIONAL	251	20,700	23%	74%	17%	$12,345	9.7%
1,154	FURON	282	3,315	35%	113%	23%	$30,065	-7.0%
205	FURR'S/BISHOP'S	5812	5,400	195%	-301%	61%	$20,499	41.2%
482	GALEY & LORD	2211	3,868	4%	16%	3%	$4,080	17.4%
1,230	GALILEO ELECTRO-OPTICS	382	229	60%	30%	33%	$55,156	-11.9%
85	GANNETT	2711	39,400	31%	25%	16%	$18,457	79.2%
1,261	GANTOS	5621	1,949	28%	142%	21%	$18,335	-14.7%
333	GAP	5651	81,000	41%	80%	24%	$18,887	26.4%
553	GARAN	2361	2,800	21%	24%	16%	$8,714	14.5%
219	GARDNER DENVER MACHINERY	3563	1,600	20%	41%	14%	$26,268	38.9%
494	GASONICS INTERNATIONAL	3674	487	79%	62%	38%	$92,935	16.7%
1,002	GATX	474	6,000	27%	27%	13%	$32,715	-0.2%
670	GAYLORD CONTAINER	2653	4,000	14%	105%	10%	$22,975	10.4%
232	GEN	3081	9,460	12%	125%	10%	$15,410	36.2%
766	GENENTECH	2834	3,242	1738%	38%	74%	$225,744	7.4%
760	GENERAL BINDING	3579	4,772	59%	111%	32%	$49,718	7.5%
1,172	GENERAL COMMUNICATION	4813	950	46%	34%	26%	$62,756	-8.0%
1,391	GENERAL DATACOMM INDUSTRIES	3661	1,727	125%	114%	55%	$67,607	-29.6%
86	GENERAL DYNAMICS	3731	29,000	10%	16%	8%	$10,564	79.1%
1,216	GENERAL HOUSEWARES	3421	540	56%	73%	33%	$54,651	-11.0%
1,355	GENERAL MICROWAVE	367	243	46%	48%	30%	$24,120	-24.1%
451	GENERAL MILLS	204	10,200	98%	688%	40%	$44,533	18.8%
258	GENERAL MOTORS	3711	608,000	12%	68%	9%	$22,549	32.5%
487	GENERAL NUTRITION	5499	13,834	37%	71%	22%	$19,145	17.0%
1,011	GENERAL SEMICONDUCTOR	3674	5,000	24%	40%	16%	$27,751	-0.7%
584	GENERAL SIGNAL	356	9,900	29%	58%	19%	$31,793	13.3%
915	GENESCO	5661	4,300	61%	301%	35%	$41,397	2.7%
1,509	GENEVA STEEL	3316	2,600	4%	16%	3%	$9,061	-59.0%
939	GENICOM	3577	1,749	28%	173%	20%	$40,189	1.8%
1,382	GENOME THERAPEUTICS	2834	211	298%	38%	86%	$82,508	-28.0%
987	GENOVESE DRUG STORES	5912	4,600	39%	250%	27%	$38,701	0.3%
416	GENUINE PARTS	5013	24,500	30%	66%	21%	$49,466	20.7%
1,345	GENUS	3559	301	63%	51%	36%	$103,004	-22.8%
1,218	GENZYME GENERAL DIVISION	2835	3,500	125%	24%	41%	$65,460	-11.2%
477	GEON	2821	2,000	5%	23%	4%	$28,199	17.8%
14	GEORGIA GULF	2812	1,041	6%	129%	5%	$42,214	244.2%
715	GEORGIA-PACIFIC	2452	46,500	13%	37%	10%	$27,442	9.1%
1,612	GEOTEK COMMUNICATIONS	3661	685	168%	155%	139%	$171,116	-142.9%
887	GERBER SCIENTIFIC	357	1,900	74%	57%	39%	$77,633	3.7%
1,668	GETCHELL GOLD	1041	437	6%	3%	7%	$11,354	-706.1%
56	GIANT CEMENT HOLDING	3241	435	11%	10%	7%	$18,212	109.3%
430	GIANT INDUSTRIES	2911	2,460	4%	13%	3%	$8,725	20.0%
496	GIBRALTAR STEEL	3316	1,450	11%	28%	9%	$31,379	16.6%
1,334	GIBSON GREETINGS	2771	2,100	146%	83%	48%	$29,978	-21.4%
351	GILLETTE	3634	44,000	120%	90%	41%	$88,461	25.4%
65	GLATFELTER (P.H.)	2621	3,076	9%	11%	6%	$12,244	102.3%
256	GLEASON	3566	2,656	31%	57%	20%	$27,592	32.6%
1,142	GLOBAL DIRECTMAIL	5045	2,792	26%	79%	19%	$75,980	-6.6%
574	GLOBAL INDUSTRIAL TECHNOLOGIES	3532	2,612	31%	46%	21%	$40,972	13.7%
1	GLOBAL MARINE	138	2,500	3%	3%	2%	$7,940	697.7%
744	GOODRICH B.F.	3728	16,838	29%	41%	19%	$35,600	8.1%
857	GOODYEAR TIRE & RUBBER	3011	95,472	19%	54%	14%	$20,744	4.8%
1,405	GOODY'S FAMILY CLOTHING	5651	8,800	30%	141%	22%	$27,321	-31.3%
1,173	GOTTSCHALKS	5311	5,661	44%	157%	30%	$23,392	-8.1%
44	GRACE, (W.R.) &	2821	6,300	43%	96%	26%	$50,107	120.8%

IP Rank	Company	SIC	EMPLOYEES	Information Management/ Cost of Goods	Information Management/ Net Assets	Information Management/ Revenue	Information Management/ Employee	Information Productivity
480	GRACO	3594	2,086	75%	110%	36%	$70,476	17.5%
326	GRADCO SYSTEMS	3579	122	19%	56%	14%	$132,412	26.7%
1,490	GRAHAM-FIELD HEALTH PRODUCTS	3841	2,236	39%	30%	27%	$31,194	-49.4%
566	GRAINGER (W.W.)	5063	15,299	43%	73%	26%	$69,167	14.0%
636	GRANITE CONSTRUCTION	1622	3,500	9%	31%	8%	$21,273	11.2%
998	GREAT ATLANTIC & PACIFIC TEA	5411	79,980	40%	315%	27%	$32,870	-0.1%
911	GREEN MOUNTAIN POWER	4911	369	161%	52%	38%	$184,304	2.8%
1,138	GREENBRIER	3743	2,533	11%	26%	8%	$13,293	-6.5%
440	GREIF BROS.	3412	4,500	14%	18%	11%	$15,543	19.5%
1,636	GREY WOLF	1381	3,000	5%	5%	4%	$2,701	-216.4%
1,219	GREYHOUND LINES	4111	11,700	110%	200%	44%	$28,037	-11.3%
688	GRIFFON	2431	5,000	26%	67%	19%	$30,066	9.9%
644	GTE	4813	114,000	49%	42%	19%	$38,071	11.0%
1,574	GTI	3677	6,700	39%	38%	27%	$3,703	-98.5%
870	GUEST SUPPLY	2844	880	23%	73%	17%	$33,502	4.5%
565	GUIDANT	3841	5,100	207%	110%	47%	$103,444	14.0%
633	GUILFORD MILLS	2258	6,571	13%	25%	10%	$13,448	11.4%
1,531	GUILFORD PHARMACEUTICALS	2834	140	163%	19%	91%	$123,674	-69.2%
498	H.J. HEINZ	203	44,700	37%	78%	22%	$45,368	16.6%
361	HALLWOOD GROUP	2221	994	21%	141%	13%	$14,828	24.6%
941	HA-LO INDUSTRIES	5199	4,000	36%	115%	24%	$42,874	1.7%
1,091	HANCOCK FABRICS	5949	6,700	80%	150%	42%	$23,193	-3.7%
1,183	HANDLEMAN	3652	3,500	26%	80%	20%	$61,417	-8.5%
910	HANNAFORD BROS.	5411	22,400	26%	100%	19%	$25,994	2.9%
1,352	HANOVER DIRECT	5961	3,100	55%	376%	36%	$70,934	-23.7%
1,023	HARCOURT GENERAL	5311	20,110	65%	101%	33%	$52,622	-1.4%
410	HARDINGE	3541	1,510	32%	29%	20%	$30,665	21.0%
1,596	HARKEN ENERGY	1311	106	126%	5%	44%	$66,181	-124.4%
935	HARLAND JOHN H.	275	5,328	59%	86%	30%	$28,727	1.9%
141	HARLEY-DAVIDSON	3751	5,700	28%	42%	18%	$52,408	53.9%
848	HARMAN INTERNATIONAL INDUSTRIES.	3651	8,384	34%	75%	22%	$36,378	5.1%
709	HARMON INDUSTRIES	3669	1,510	27%	56%	19%	$26,063	9.3%
749	HARNISCHFEGER INDUSTRIES	3532	17,700	21%	54%	15%	$24,994	8.0%
780	HARRIS	357	29,000	40%	65%	25%	$32,590	7.0%
160	HARSCO	3441	14,600	20%	30%	14%	$15,084	50.0%
981	HARTMARX	2311	8,100	28%	83%	21%	$16,224	0.4%
1,175	HASBRO INC	394	12,000	110%	80%	44%	$105,122	-8.2%
1,220	HASTINGS MANUFACTURING	3592	440	43%	261%	29%	$26,199	-11.4%
1,238	HATHAWAY	3825	380	68%	107%	40%	$41,047	-12.9%
960	HAVERTY FURNITURE	5712	3,112	86%	128%	42%	$65,157	1.2%
1,241	HAWAIIAN AIRLINES	4512	2,551	48%	155%	27%	$45,468	-13.0%
1,447	HAYES LEMMERZ INTERNATIONAL	3714	8,095	7%	37%	5%	$8,782	-38.8%
1,296	HEALTH-CHEM	2295	206	41%	187%	28%	$50,150	-18.5%
1,641	HEARTLAND WIRELESS COMMUNICATIONS	4841	790	147%	35%	64%	$29,993	-244.1%
1,666	HECLA MINING	1081	1,202	7%	6%	6%	$7,190	-646.7%
185	HEICO	3724	480	39%	24%	23%	$28,228	44.4%
732	HEIN-WERNER	3569	568	58%	111%	34%	$37,569	8.5%
1,675	HELMERICH & PAYNE	1311	3,627	4%	1%	2%	$2,675	-2163.9%
90	HERCULES	2819	6,221	28%	39%	16%	$49,361	76.8%
411	HERSHEY FOODS	206	16,200	52%	109%	28%	$75,022	20.9%
407	HEWLETT-PACKARD	3571	121,900	39%	66%	24%	$81,407	21.1%
741	HEXCEL	2679	5,597	18%	56%	13%	$20,908	8.2%
551	HILLENBRAND INDUSTRIES	2599	9,800	49%	55%	26%	$45,226	14.6%
1,252	HILLS STORES	5311	14,632	31%	165%	23%	$25,774	-13.9%
1,400	HIRSCH INTERNATIONAL	3571	450	40%	62%	25%	$92,995	-30.5%
1,394	HMI INDUSTRIES	3469	836	45%	100%	31%	$30,620	-30.1%
10	HMT TECHNOLOGY	3572	2,248	12%	14%	6%	$12,578	293.9%
165	HOLLY	2911	572	2%	15%	2%	$24,520	48.1%
1,567	HOLOGIC	3844	339	80%	34%	36%	$104,693	-91.5%
352	HOLOPHANE	3646	1,708	40%	70%	23%	$28,004	25.4%
467	HOME DEPOT	5211	124,400	28%	64%	20%	$38,569	18.1%
932	HOMEBASE	5399	9,100	15%	79%	13%	$31,447	1.9%
1,631	HOMESTAKE MINING	1041	1,585	7%	5%	5%	$23,493	-199.9%
403	HON INDUSTRIES	2522	9,400	33%	83%	22%	$32,138	21.5%
605	HONEYWELL	3822	57,500	36%	76%	23%	$31,499	12.3%
665	HORMEL FOODS	201	11,000	25%	75%	18%	$53,476	10.4%

Appendix C–Information Productivity Listing

IP Rank	Company	SIC	EMPLOYEES	Information Management/ Cost of Goods	Information Management/ Net Assets	Information Management/ Revenue	Information Management/ Employee	Information Productivity
894	HOUGHTON MIFFLIN	2731	2,550	115%	101%	41%	$115,299	3.4%
1,350	HOVNANIAN ENTERPRISES	1531	1,150	13%	47%	11%	$76,065	-23.5%
1,398	HOWELL	1382	60	2%	11%	2%	$51,868	-30.4%
1,552	HS RESOURCES	1311	260	9%	3%	4%	$27,299	-79.4%
218	HUBBELL	3643	8,801	23%	26%	15%	$23,642	38.9%
1,179	HUFFY	3751	6,770	17%	85%	14%	$12,732	-8.4%
821	HUGHES SUPPLY	5074	6,000	21%	87%	16%	$53,431	5.9%
736	HUNT	3579	1,200	49%	97%	29%	$49,647	8.3%
698	HUNTCO	3316	688	6%	11%	5%	$22,425	9.6%
395	HUTCHINSON TECHNOLOGY	3572	7,181	23%	32%	15%	$9,748	22.0%
99	IBP	2011	38,000	1%	13%	1%	$4,344	69.4%
490	ICN PHARMACEUTICALS	2834	15,744	86%	43%	36%	$18,671	16.9%
1,354	IDENTIX	3577	143	44%	64%	29%	$115,836	-23.8%
244	IDEX	3594	3,800	35%	56%	20%	$30,691	34.3%
312	IHOP	5812	2,600	27%	20%	14%	$11,003	27.7%
873	IKON OFFICE SOLUTIONS	5113	41,000	44%	94%	28%	$43,867	4.2%
794	IKOS SYSTEMS	3674	219	299%	87%	59%	$142,861	6.7%
156	ILLINOIS TOOL WORKS	3714	25,700	28%	35%	18%	$35,375	50.8%
1,583	IMAGYN MEDICAL TECHNOLOGIES INC	3842	600	190%	-272%	84%	$87,011	-104.1%
1,551	IMATRON	3844	195	54%	47%	44%	$72,618	-79.4%
1,077	IMC GLOBAL	287	8,949	10%	11%	7%	$22,065	-3.0%
402	IMCO RECYCLING	339	1,586	7%	12%	6%	$11,303	21.5%
945	IMMUCOR	2835	141	138%	41%	49%	$120,964	1.6%
1,385	IMMUNEX	2834	886	2132%	80%	99%	$198,843	-28.6%
1,409	IMO INDUSTRIES	3714	2,100	34%	611%	23%	$26,667	-31.9%
1,372	IMP	3674	228	46%	104%	29%	$59,240	-26.6%
1,134	INACOM	5045	4,200	9%	111%	8%	$77,971	-6.3%
1,364	INDUSTRIAL ACOUSTICS	3444	740	22%	31%	18%	$20,942	-25.3%
441	INGERSOLL-RAND	356	46,600	21%	45%	15%	$23,074	19.4%
940	INGLES MARKETS	5411	11,888	24%	140%	18%	$24,219	1.7%
580	INLAND STEEL INDUSTRIES	3312	14,318	5%	25%	4%	$14,202	13.6%
29	INNOVEX	3679	893	20%	16%	11%	$12,693	152.1%
198	INSILCO	3443	5,418	27%	-362%	18%	$18,917	42.2%
1,158	INSITUFORM TECHNOLOGIES	1623	1,420	34%	49%	22%	$45,119	-7.4%
1,151	INSTEEL INDUSTRIES	3315	1,137	6%	18%	5%	$12,133	-6.8%
968	INSTRON	382	1,087	64%	86%	35%	$47,682	0.9%
1,501	INTEGRATED CIRCUIT SYSTEMS	3613	177	57%	44%	30%	$150,174	-54.6%
1,192	INTEGRATED DEVICE TECHNOLOGY	3674	4,979	95%	39%	38%	$48,049	-9.4%
1,470	INTEGRATED PROCESS EQUIPMENT	3559	965	81%	46%	43%	$68,358	-43.5%
58	INTEL	367	63,700	58%	26%	20%	$81,320	107.3%
1,538	INTELLICALL	3661	166	16%	75%	14%	$62,886	-71.4%
1,507	INTERDIGITAL COMMUNICATIONS	4813	205	141%	62%	58%	$164,251	-58.5%
958	INTERFACE	2273	7,300	38%	81%	24%	$39,095	1.2%
1,430	INTERFACE SYSTEMS	357	220	25%	85%	20%	$68,622	-35.6%
1,307	INTERGRAPH	357	7,700	75%	106%	42%	$57,348	-19.3%
183	INTERLAKE	2542	2,491	19%	-57%	14%	$29,632	44.9%
1,128	INTERMAGNETICS GENERAL	3845	537	32%	29%	22%	$36,836	-6.1%
73	INTERMET	3321	6,520	5%	20%	4%	$4,897	90.8%
401	INTERNATIONAL BUSINESS MACHINES	357	269,465	53%	99%	28%	$86,300	21.5%
341	INTERNATIONAL FLAVORS & FRAGRANCES	2844	4,640	44%	30%	22%	$68,042	25.9%
795	INTERNATIONAL GAME TECHNOLOGY	3699	2,600	37%	24%	19%	$52,132	6.7%
1,063	INTERNATIONAL MULTIFOODS	2038	6,807	15%	111%	13%	$47,227	-2.6%
1,201	INTERNATIONAL PAPER	262	82,000	16%	22%	12%	$28,435	-9.8%
882	INTERNATIONAL RECTIFIER	3674	4,385	43%	32%	25%	$32,126	3.8%
1,247	INTERNATIONAL SHIPHOLDING	449	960	10%	15%	7%	$30,491	-13.4%
443	INTERNATIONAL SPECIALTY PRODUCTS	2899	2,675	38%	21%	20%	$55,668	19.4%
1,492	INTERNATIONAL TECHNOLOGY	3823	4,595	10%	20%	9%	$11,319	-50.2%
962	INTERSTATE BAKERIES	2051	32,000	85%	258%	42%	$31,852	1.1%
1,143	INTERTAN	5063	4,400	73%	182%	41%	$47,510	-6.6%
238	INTIMATE BRANDS	5632	50,000	32%	147%	20%	$14,493	34.7%
602	INVACARE	3841	4,550	35%	60%	23%	$31,999	12.4%
557	IOMEGA	3572	4,816	30%	78%	20%	$71,255	14.4%
328	IONICS	3589	2,000	35%	22%	21%	$36,994	26.5%
79	IPALCO ENTERPRISES	4911	2,095	25%	10%	10%	$35,132	83.6%
1,613	ISOLYSER	3842	2,100	35%	25%	27%	$17,522	-144.2%
1,071	ITRON	3669	1,213	66%	57%	36%	$61,332	-2.8%

IP Rank	Company	SIC	EMPLOYEES	Information Management/ Cost of Goods	Information Management/ Net Assets	Information Management/ Revenue	Information Management/ Employee	Information Productivity
354	ITT INDUSTRIES	3714	58,000	16%	145%	12%	$18,544	25.3%
1,452	IVAX	2834	4,500	57%	55%	36%	$52,215	-39.9%
1,030	J & J SNACK FOODS	205	1,700	105%	88%	44%	$55,862	-1.5%
1,009	J&L SPECIALTY STEEL	3316	1,302	4%	7%	4%	$19,267	-0.7%
1,306	J. ALEXANDER'S	5812	1,700	13%	17%	8%	$2,969	-19.1%
1,402	J.B. HUNT TRANSPORT SERVICES	4213	11,780	4%	12%	3%	$3,702	-30.6%
107	JABIL CIRCUIT	3672	3,661	4%	24%	4%	$9,619	66.8%
1,153	JACLYN	3161	262	32%	108%	24%	$65,658	-6.9%
378	JACOBS ENGINEERING GROUP	162	9,570	10%	52%	8%	$17,952	23.2%
1,162	JACOBSON STORES	5311	4,600	49%	189%	32%	$29,523	-7.5%
1,649	JACOR COMMUNICATIONS	4832	4,300	4%	2%	3%	$3,165	-317.6%
112	JEFFERSON SMURFIT	2631	15,800	9%	-62%	7%	$15,983	63.2%
1,236	JG INDUSTRIES	5311	688	53%	222%	35%	$27,076	-12.4%
152	JLG INDUSTRIES	3531	2,686	15%	39%	11%	$17,537	51.5%
787	JOHNS MANVILLE	2631	8,300	19%	24%	13%	$24,668	6.9%
442	JOHNSON & JOHNSON	284	90,500	173%	94%	48%	$115,414	19.4%
614	JOHNSON CONTROLS	2531	72,300	11%	61%	9%	$13,989	12.2%
1,207	JOHNSON WORLDWIDE ASSOCIATES	3949	1,366	53%	83%	32%	$80,057	-10.2%
1,265	JOHNSTON INDUSTRIES	221	2,700	10%	39%	8%	$11,948	-15.3%
486	JONES APPAREL GROUP	2331	3,135	25%	47%	17%	$58,456	17.0%
1,623	JONES INTERCABLE	4841	3,513	30%	15%	13%	$10,802	-178.8%
674	JOSTENS	3911	6,500	89%	157%	40%	$43,632	10.2%
305	JUNO LIGHTING	3646	1,061	57%	24%	28%	$36,926	28.7%
40	JUST FOR FEET	5661	7,975	6%	5%	3%	$1,669	128.0%
790	JUSTIN INDUSTRIES	3251	4,222	42%	46%	26%	$27,534	6.9%
872	K2	3949	3,800	29%	65%	21%	$29,826	4.4%
603	KAISER ALUMINUM	3353	9,533	7%	64%	6%	$13,745	12.4%
885	KAMAN	5085	4,318	28%	81%	21%	$39,036	3.7%
1,245	KAUFMAN AND BROAD HOME	1521	2,040	16%	57%	13%	$130,070	-13.2%
1,601	KCS ENERGY	4924	229	9%	15%	6%	$104,348	-130.2%
1,124	KEITHLEY INSTRUMENTS	382	693	149%	191%	55%	$93,513	-5.7%
1,671	KELLEY OIL & GAS	1311	57	24%	-28%	11%	$108,848	-996.2%
466	KELLOGG	204	14,339	84%	191%	36%	$170,575	18.1%
988	KELLWOOD	2321	17,300	18%	62%	14%	$11,983	0.3%
144	KEMET	3675	11,300	16%	26%	11%	$6,228	53.3%
643	KENNAMETAL	3545	7,500	56%	74%	30%	$44,986	11.1%
1,093	KERR-MCGEE	1311	3,746	13%	10%	8%	$36,464	-3.8%
350	KEY ENERGY GROUP	1389	3,175	15%	21%	11%	$4,909	25.5%
1,324	KEY TRONIC	357	2,434	15%	46%	12%	$8,598	-20.4%
318	KEYSTONE CONSOLIDATED INDUSTRIES	3315	2,025	7%	143%	6%	$10,871	27.4%
800	KIMBALL INTERNATIONAL	2517	8,949	32%	51%	21%	$22,840	6.6%
563	KIMBERLY-CLARK	267	57,000	38%	69%	23%	$53,555	14.1%
1,484	KIMMINS	1623	980	18%	70%	14%	$14,960	-46.6%
758	KIRBY	4449	1,225	18%	21%	11%	$25,957	7.6%
946	KLA-TENCOR	382	3,600	68%	33%	30%	$83,332	1.6%
934	KNAPE & VOGT MANUFACTURING	3429	1,100	23%	40%	16%	$24,771	1.9%
641	KOHL'S	5311	32,200	33%	88%	22%	$20,931	11.1%
547	KOLLMORGEN	362	1,863	42%	187%	27%	$33,289	14.7%
705	KROGER	5411	212,000	25%	-407%	19%	$23,080	9.4%
1,163	KRUG INTERNATIONAL	251	556	10%	54%	9%	$10,925	-7.6%
589	KUHLMAN	361	4,194	18%	60%	13%	$22,196	13.0%
1,656	KULICKE AND SOFFA INDUSTRIES	3559	2,229	48%	58%	28%	$57,056	-441.9%
656	K-V PHARMACEUTICAL	2834	353	56%	62%	29%	$61,061	10.7%
140	LACLEDE GAS	4924	2,086	6%	7%	3%	$8,606	54.0%
1,521	LACLEDE STEEL	3312	1,475	5%	77%	4%	$8,602	-67.2%
1,346	LADD FURNITURE	2511	6,200	19%	66%	15%	$13,366	-22.9%
506	LAFARGE	3241	2,870	13%	13%	9%	$37,113	16.4%
734	LAM RESEARCH	3674	4,800	63%	65%	34%	$80,762	8.5%
924	LAMSON & SESSIONS	3646	1,044	21%	123%	16%	$42,838	2.4%
230	LANCASTER COLONY	2035	6,400	25%	43%	16%	$22,248	36.7%
1,670	LANDRY'S SEAFOOD RESTAURANTS	5812	8,200	7%	4%	4%	$1,281	-937.8%
863	LANDS' END	5961	8,400	71%	196%	38%	$53,557	4.6%
779	LANDSTAR SYSTEM	4213	2,050	18%	126%	14%	$68,735	7.0%
713	LAYNE CHRISTENSEN	1781	2,949	23%	49%	17%	$16,996	9.1%
653	LA-Z-BOY	2512	11,236	26%	51%	19%	$15,706	10.7%
861	LCI INTERNATIONAL	4813	3,900	40%	61%	24%	$103,127	4.7%

IP Rank	Company	SIC	EMPLOYEES	Information Management/ Cost of Goods	Information Management/ Net Assets	Information Management/ Revenue	Information Management/ Employee	Information Productivity
266	LEAR	2396	51,000	4%	23%	3%	$4,877	32.2%
737	LEARONAL	3471	950	27%	34%	19%	$51,469	8.3%
247	LEE ENTERPRISES	2711	6,100	64%	38%	28%	$21,409	34.1%
273	LEGGETT & PLATT	2515	26,000	17%	32%	12%	$14,420	31.6%
239	LENNAR	153	2,173	13%	19%	10%	$60,167	34.5%
1,004	LESCO	2873	1,157	47%	140%	30%	$84,203	-0.4%
162	LEVEL ONE COMMUNICATIONS	3674	559	118%	49%	43%	$114,444	49.0%
1,005	LEXMARK INTERNATIONAL GROUP	3575	7,985	35%	111%	23%	$71,743	-0.5%
96	LIBBEY	3229	4,120	17%	387%	11%	$10,793	71.9%
404	LIFE TECHNOLOGIES	2835	1,586	87%	64%	38%	$77,724	21.4%
1,537	LIFECORE BIOMEDICAL	3841	156	127%	25%	67%	$71,284	-71.1%
1,669	LIGAND PHARMACEUTICALS	2834	345	17%	27%	25%	$29,105	-756.2%
1,290	LILLIAN VERNON	5961	1,500	109%	105%	49%	$85,822	-17.7%
975	LILLY (ELI) AND	2834	31,100	205%	60%	43%	$112,217	0.6%
645	LILLY INDUSTRIES	2851	2,100	42%	97%	25%	$66,975	11.0%
619	LIMITED	5621	131,000	31%	65%	21%	$15,216	11.9%
720	LINDBERG	3398	975	18%	45%	13%	$13,370	9.0%
1,497	LIPOSOME	5122	280	631%	74%	135%	$178,220	-52.8%
377	LITTELFUSE	3613	2,845	41%	47%	22%	$20,946	23.2%
413	LITTON INDUSTRIES	3812	31,500	14%	45%	11%	$13,071	20.9%
76	LONE STAR INDUSTRIES	327	1,060	13%	11%	8%	$21,995	87.0%
111	LONE STAR TECHNOLOGIES	1389	2,044	3%	11%	3%	$8,907	63.8%
276	LONGVIEW FIBRE	267	3,900	10%	13%	7%	$15,833	31.4%
1,563	LOUIS DREYFUS NATURAL GAS	1311	400	36%	5%	9%	$49,866	-89.3%
1,603	LOUISIANA-PACIFIC	5211	12,500	7%	10%	6%	$11,453	-132.0%
681	LOWE'S	5211	58,504	24%	71%	18%	$29,199	10.1%
1,377	LSB INDUSTRIES	2873	1,685	26%	90%	20%	$38,655	-27.4%
813	LSI INDUSTRIES	3648	1,200	36%	65%	24%	$31,569	6.1%
843	LSI LOGIC	367	4,443	66%	26%	28%	$86,009	5.3%
1,397	LTV	331	15,500	4%	10%	4%	$10,410	-30.4%
1,047	LTX	382	950	48%	53%	28%	$65,224	-2.0%
246	LUBRIZOL	2869	4,291	32%	39%	20%	$74,013	34.2%
55	LUBY'S CAFETERIAS	5812	13,000	5%	9%	4%	$1,637	111.0%
1,425	LUKENS	3312	3,300	6%	21%	6%	$16,201	-34.5%
220	LYDALL	3823	1,225	26%	39%	17%	$34,461	38.9%
71	LYONDELL PETROCHEMICAL	2911	6,800	6%	25%	5%	$56,040	91.5%
6	M & F WORLDWIDE	2064	321	24%	11%	15%	$25,000	360.5%
385	M.D.C. HOLDINGS	152	1,200	9%	34%	8%	$64,449	22.7%
495	MACDERMID	289	1,179	76%	94%	35%	$88,402	16.7%
1,300	MAGNETEK	3612	13,800	17%	187%	14%	$11,785	-18.9%
864	MAIL-WELL	2677	7,523	17%	78%	13%	$15,110	4.6%
507	MALLINCKRODT	3841	7,871	63%	52%	30%	$66,953	16.4%
323	MANITOWOC	3536	3,086	23%	71%	16%	$24,563	26.9%
167	MAPCO	2911	6,508	3%	12%	2%	$13,802	47.6%
1,606	MARINE TRANSPORT	4424	700	11%	10%	8%	$19,052	-135.4%
1,073	MARITRANS	4449	587	43%	34%	22%	$54,936	-2.9%
823	MARK IV INDUSTRIES	5531	17,000	27%	52%	18%	$22,869	5.8%
1,104	MARQUETTE MEDICAL SYSTEMS	3845	3,150	71%	91%	37%	$57,722	-4.3%
1,037	MARSH SUPERMARKETS	5411	12,800	28%	263%	21%	$24,444	-1.6%
476	MARSHALL INDUSTRIES	5045	1,400	13%	39%	11%	$87,807	17.8%
82	MARTIN MARIETTA MATERIALS	142	5,000	13%	13%	8%	$14,918	82.2%
1,089	MASCO	2434	28,100	36%	38%	22%	$30,120	-3.7%
171	MASCOTECH	3714	9,000	12%	47%	10%	$15,060	47.3%
336	MASTEC	1623	7,850	17%	50%	12%	$10,562	26.1%
483	MATERIAL SCIENCES	347	1,269	24%	35%	16%	$43,848	17.3%
1,211	MATLACK SYSTEMS	4212	1,059	10%	32%	8%	$17,025	-10.8%
606	MATTEL	394	25,000	71%	88%	33%	$52,863	12.3%
1,242	MATTHEWS INTERNATIONAL	3364	1,500	56%	51%	29%	$34,915	-13.1%
799	MAVERICK TUBE	3321	1,079	6%	17%	5%	$11,980	6.6%
1,428	MAXWELL TECHNOLOGIES	3675	607	36%	77%	26%	$37,991	-35.4%
509	MAXXAM	3365	11,275	9%	124%	8%	$16,854	16.3%
992	MAXXIM MEDICAL	3841	3,958	27%	60%	19%	$21,135	0.1%
431	MAY DEPARTMENT STORES	5311	116,000	29%	56%	19%	$20,873	20.0%
18	MAYNARD OIL	1311	35	11%	2%	4%	$31,092	213.2%
773	MAYTAG	3631	22,685	24%	77%	17%	$26,848	7.2%
721	MCCORMICK &	209	7,500	41%	100%	25%	$54,848	8.8%

INFORMATION PRODUCTIVITY

IP Rank	Company	SIC	EMPLOYEES	Information Management/ Cost of Goods	Information Management/ Net Assets	Information Management/ Revenue	Information Management/ Employee	Information Productivity
1,420	MCDERMOTT INTERNATIONAL	3731	24,700	9%	27%	8%	$10,197	-33.7%
297	MCDONALD'S	5812	267,000	180%	37%	30%	$13,574	29.7%
383	MCGRAW-HILL	2731	15,690	69%	79%	32%	$64,910	22.8%
1,052	MCKESSON	5122	13,700	7%	67%	6%	$76,523	-2.1%
381	MCN ENERGY GROUP	4924	3,209	36%	34%	20%	$114,040	22.9%
223	MCWHORTER TECHNOLOGIES	2821	791	9%	29%	7%	$36,470	37.9%
615	MEAD	2759	16,500	15%	25%	11%	$35,601	12.1%
855	MEDIA GENERAL	2711	8,800	48%	48%	25%	$23,714	4.9%
1,495	MEDICIS PHARMACEUTICAL	2834	89	175%	25%	46%	$202,434	-51.0%
1,511	MEDIMMUNE	384	344	281%	105%	110%	$210,328	-59.8%
357	MEDTRONIC	384	13,719	195%	56%	43%	$82,730	25.0%
1,108	MEDUSA	3241	1,300	14%	19%	9%	$24,319	-4.6%
287	MEMC ELECTRONIC MATERIALS	3674	7,700	14%	13%	10%	$14,313	30.6%
1,526	MEMRY	3545	75	81%	95%	51%	$48,813	-68.0%
1,098	MEN'S WEARHOUSE	5611	6,000	52%	91%	31%	$31,220	-4.0%
1,663	MENTOR	384	1,612	153%	66%	46%	$63,546	-583.4%
947	MERCANTILE STORES	5311	34,200	35%	45%	23%	$5,745	1.5%
128	MERCK &	283	53,800	59%	38%	27%	$107,635	57.3%
380	MERIX	3672	1,572	16%	26%	12%	$12,174	23.0%
663	MERRILL	275	3,626	41%	88%	25%	$32,425	10.5%
1,259	MESA AIR GROUP	4512	4,800	31%	47%	21%	$24,269	-14.4%
21	MESABA HOLDINGS	4512	2,634	8%	23%	6%	$5,923	188.4%
1,019	MESTEK	3585	2,596	25%	50%	18%	$21,741	-1.1%
335	METHODE ELECTRONICS	367	3,650	22%	27%	15%	$13,541	26.2%
147	MET-PRO	3564	387	31%	29%	19%	$29,462	52.9%
1,503	METROCALL	4812	2,950	216%	49%	52%	$46,408	-56.1%
1,006	MEYER (FRED)	5311	85,000	38%	131%	26%	$23,207	-0.6%
952	MICHAEL FOODS	5144	3,870	10%	28%	8%	$18,062	1.5%
1,212	MICHAELS STORES	5999	17,900	42%	105%	28%	$21,728	-10.9%
348	MICREL	3674	546	70%	44%	30%	$51,744	25.5%
684	MICRO LINEAR	3674	252	98%	39%	38%	$88,735	10.0%
1,349	MICROAGE	5045	4,400	5%	86%	5%	$54,772	-23.4%
514	MICROCHIP TECHNOLOGY	3674	2,153	71%	30%	27%	$47,508	16.1%
671	MICROS SYSTEMS	3578	1,534	72%	99%	35%	$52,539	10.3%
315	MICROSEMI	3674	2,503	20%	71%	14%	$11,343	27.6%
1,518	MIDWEST GRAIN PRODUCTS	2046	411	5%	9%	5%	$23,447	-64.8%
730	MIKASA	3229	3,460	66%	68%	35%	$42,106	8.6%
764	MILLIPORE	3826	4,754	105%	130%	39%	$60,560	7.5%
973	MILTOPE GROUP	3571	260	26%	53%	19%	$34,482	0.6%
943	MINE SAFETY APPLIANCES	3842	4,200	45%	55%	27%	$31,945	1.7%
488	MINERALS TECHNOLOGIES	2819	2,250	26%	21%	17%	$57,902	16.9%
284	MINNESOTA MINING & MANUFACTURING	2891	75,639	50%	54%	25%	$49,412	31.0%
1,674	MISSISSIPPI CHEMICAL	2873	1,700	20%	18%	13%	$45,163	-1353.6%
269	MOBIL	1311	42,700	12%	28%	8%	$115,283	31.8%
320	MODINE MANUFACTURING	3443	8,375	25%	45%	17%	$21,880	27.4%
879	MOHAWK INDUSTRIES	2273	12,600	22%	85%	16%	$23,826	4.0%
1,469	MONARCH MACHINE TOOL	3541	537	17%	35%	14%	$25,124	-42.5%
538	MONDAVI, (ROBERT)	2084	890	61%	40%	29%	$77,091	15.3%
735	MONSANTO	2819	21,900	74%	75%	34%	$109,980	8.3%
274	MONTANA POWER	4911	2,903	23%	10%	11%	$35,993	31.5%
971	MOOG	3812	3,657	34%	84%	22%	$27,956	0.7%
1,411	MOORE MEDICAL	5122	352	15%	146%	12%	$91,793	-32.1%
1,358	MORGAN PRODUCTS LTD.	5031	1,593	16%	96%	13%	$32,995	-24.3%
275	MORTON INTERNATIONAL	2891	10,500	24%	29%	16%	$37,781	31.5%
1,508	MOTIVEPOWER INDUSTRIES	3743	2,351	13%	25%	11%	$13,843	-58.9%
628	MOTOROLA	366	150,000	26%	41%	18%	$34,506	11.6%
1,651	MRV COMMUNICATIONS	3674	438	44%	27%	25%	$73,748	-333.5%
951	MTS SYSTEMS	3823	1,981	55%	72%	31%	$46,771	1.5%
150	MUELLER INDUSTRIES	3351	3,378	9%	16%	7%	$20,968	51.7%
1,341	MULTIGRAPHICS	355	651	37%	492%	26%	$46,428	-22.7%
1,375	MURPHY OIL	2911	1,338	4%	6%	3%	$44,686	-27.2%
1,331	MUSICLAND STORES	5735	15,400	47%	703%	31%	$33,774	-21.1%
867	MYERS INDUSTRIES	3089	2,083	32%	42%	21%	$35,587	4.6%
93	MYLAN LABORATORIES	283	1,946	52%	18%	26%	$66,412	73.8%
805	MYR GROUP	1623	350	8%	83%	7%	$79,532	6.5%
1,362	NABI	2836	2,122	27%	58%	20%	$20,157	-25.0%

IP Rank	Company	SIC	EMPLOYEES	Information Management/ Cost of Goods	Information Management/ Net Assets	Information Management/ Revenue	Information Management/ Employee	Information Productivity
1,074	NABISCO	2052	53,000	52%	59%	29%	$46,238	-2.9%
91	NABORS INDUSTRIES	1381	10,632	10%	11%	8%	$6,540	75.8%
515	NACCO INDUSTRIES	3537	13,400	15%	64%	12%	$21,396	16.0%
369	NALCO CHEMICAL	2899	6,905	108%	83%	39%	$79,911	24.2%
1,240	NAPCO SECURITY SYSTEMS	3669	1,000	28%	33%	20%	$9,657	-13.0%
1,010	NASH-FINCH	5141	12,200	13%	173%	11%	$31,860	-0.7%
1,453	NASHUA	5044	1,811	37%	98%	26%	$34,771	-40.0%
756	NATIONAL BEVERAGE	2086	1,200	38%	202%	26%	$85,034	7.6%
593	NATIONAL FUEL GAS	4923	2,524	57%	32%	24%	$98,041	12.9%
639	NATIONAL GAS & OIL	1311	131	24%	21%	15%	$68,843	11.1%
583	NATIONAL INSTRUMENTS	3577	1,465	292%	90%	58%	$95,118	13.4%
807	NATIONAL SEMICONDUCTOR	3674	12,400	62%	50%	31%	$40,913	6.4%
748	NATIONAL SERVICE INDUSTRIES	364	16,000	53%	87%	31%	$32,097	8.0%
213	NATIONAL STEEL	3312	9,417	6%	21%	5%	$15,227	40.1%
387	NATIONAL-STANDARD	3315	1,406	11%	-120%	9%	$16,302	22.6%
761	NATURE'S SUNSHINE PRODUCTS	2834	994	424%	306%	71%	$187,076	7.5%
290	NAUTICA ENTERPRISES	231	1,700	59%	56%	30%	$89,477	30.3%
554	NAVISTAR INTERNATIONAL	3713	16,168	10%	53%	8%	$32,089	14.5%
675	NBI	3231	212	46%	1864%	31%	$13,046	10.2%
777	NBTY	283	3,655	83%	86%	39%	$41,767	7.1%
1,456	NCH	2899	10,458	78%	100%	40%	$28,553	-40.7%
267	NCI BUILDING SYSTEMS	3448	2,472	17%	39%	13%	$20,444	32.1%
815	NEIMAN MARCUS GROUP	5632	11,300	36%	98%	23%	$41,812	6.1%
1,279	NETWORK COMPUTING DEVICES	357	352	70%	84%	42%	$158,741	-16.3%
1,315	NEW BRUNSWICK SCIENTIFIC	3821	412	63%	54%	37%	$41,093	-19.7%
592	NEW CENTURY ENERGIES	4911	3,352	19%	13%	9%	$56,419	13.0%
884	NEW YORK TIMES	2711	13,100	78%	57%	36%	$73,927	3.7%
280	NEWELL	3231	24,600	23%	25%	15%	$18,070	31.3%
15	NEWFIELD EXPLORATION	1311	86	50%	4%	6%	$130,260	238.9%
891	NEWMONT GOLD	1041	6,760	23%	10%	13%	$24,564	3.5%
7	NEWPARK RESOURCES	4953	1,097	4%	2%	2%	$3,874	355.1%
985	NEWPORT	3829	775	73%	77%	37%	$62,188	0.4%
1,474	NEXSTAR PHARMACEUTICALS	2834	558	1486%	121%	108%	$171,078	-44.0%
1,639	NEXTEL COMMUNICATIONS	4812	6,400	187%	17%	107%	$109,439	-226.0%
359	NICOR	4932	3,300	32%	44%	18%	$95,430	24.9%
370	NIKE	3149	21,800	43%	68%	25%	$95,832	24.1%
417	NIMBUS CD INTERNATIONAL	3652	816	19%	28%	12%	$17,863	20.7%
791	NINE WEST GROUP	5139	16,600	55%	130%	31%	$32,503	6.8%
329	NIPSCO INDUSTRIES	4911	5,984	42%	30%	20%	$82,734	26.5%
303	NL INDUSTRIES	2816	2,600	26%	-80%	18%	$56,801	28.8%
26	NN BALL & ROLLER	3562	444	9%	10%	6%	$11,240	168.8%
176	NOBLE AFFILIATES	1311	563	11%	7%	6%	$83,359	46.0%
137	NOBLE DRILLING	1381	2,781	17%	6%	10%	$17,850	55.3%
555	NORDSON	355	4,024	114%	115%	44%	$71,095	14.5%
853	NORDSTROM	5651	41,000	42%	84%	27%	$31,134	5.0%
342	NORFOLK SOUTHERN	4011	25,817	123%	30%	34%	$59,186	25.9%
769	NORSTAN	5065	2,167	35%	115%	24%	$41,828	7.4%
868	NORTEK	3585	9,262	28%	153%	20%	$26,122	4.5%
3	NORTH PITTSBURG SYSTEMS	481	276	9%	4%	4%	$7,541	468.7%
110	NORTHERN STATES POWER	4931	7,455	16%	6%	6%	$22,964	64.4%
686	NORTHROP GRUMMAN	3721	52,000	19%	55%	14%	$24,967	9.9%
367	NORTHWEST AIRLINES	4512	49,000	43%	168%	19%	$39,457	24.2%
471	NORTHWEST NATURAL GAS	4925	1,337	55%	20%	21%	$58,568	18.0%
517	NOVAMETRIX MEDICAL SYSTEMS	384	189	116%	84%	46%	$66,039	15.9%
621	NOVELLUS SYSTEMS	3674	1,776	73%	43%	30%	$109,998	11.8%
1,575	NS GROUP	3312	1,948	8%	20%	6%	$14,932	-99.1%
1,632	NTL	4841	4,135	77%	48%	47%	$40,380	-207.1%
47	NUCOR	331	6,900	4%	7%	4%	$20,126	117.8%
1,568	NUEVO ENERGY	1311	59	19%	5%	7%	$417,404	-93.4%
1,468	NU-KOTE HOLDING	5112	2,300	29%	159%	22%	$27,418	-42.4%
1,204	OAK INDUSTRIES	3678	3,373	36%	36%	21%	$20,274	-10.0%
208	OAK TECHNOLOGY	5065	430	50%	21%	25%	$114,067	40.8%
1,378	OAKLEY	3851	930	146%	70%	41%	$101,000	-27.8%
523	OAKWOOD HOMES	2451	7,078	38%	56%	24%	$36,518	15.6%
1,308	OCCIDENTAL PETROLEUM	281	12,380	17%	23%	11%	$74,653	-19.3%
210	OCEAN ENERGY	1311	377	39%	11%	8%	$52,659	40.4%

INFORMATION PRODUCTIVITY

IP Rank	Company	SIC	EMPLOYEES	Information Management/ Cost of Goods	Information Management/ Net Assets	Information Management/ Revenue	Information Management/ Employee	Information Productivity
753	OFFICE DEPOT	5399	35,000	24%	95%	18%	$33,760	7.8%
499	OGDEN	4953	28,400	8%	22%	6%	$3,607	16.6%
158	OGLEBAY NORTON	4432	908	13%	14%	9%	$13,932	50.1%
1,473	OHM	4953	2,800	11%	28%	9%	$15,357	-44.0%
1,058	OIL-DRI OF AMERICA	2842	665	36%	46%	23%	$53,236	-2.4%
961	OILGEAR	3594	1,092	42%	84%	27%	$23,301	1.1%
254	OLIN	2899	9,800	18%	40%	13%	$32,928	33.0%
184	OM GROUP	2869	758	12%	17%	9%	$67,654	44.7%
1,191	ONE PRICE CLOTHING STORES	5621	4,300	56%	249%	36%	$24,355	-9.3%
637	ONEIDA LTD.	3914	4,910	38%	89%	24%	$20,868	11.2%
1,059	OPTICAL COATING LABORATORY	3827	1,515	44%	55%	26%	$35,453	-2.4%
1,224	ORBITAL SCIENCES	3761	4,000	30%	33%	21%	$31,143	-11.6%
1,431	OREGON STEEL MILLS	3312	2,380	7%	13%	6%	$18,223	-35.8%
1,129	O'REILLY AUTOMOTIVE	5531	3,945	56%	51%	31%	$26,495	-6.1%
1,585	ORIOLE HOMES	1521	184	21%	28%	17%	$80,100	-109.0%
12	ORYX ENERGY	1381	1,046	18%	-486%	5%	$55,866	265.9%
1,189	OSHMAN'S SPORTING GOODS	5941	3,360	53%	257%	34%	$33,240	-8.7%
647	OSMONICS	3561	1,433	54%	47%	30%	$33,865	11.0%
1,178	O'SULLIVAN INDUSTRIES HOLDINGS	2511	2,000	25%	37%	18%	$28,126	-8.3%
39	OUTBACK STEAKHOUSE	5812	34,600	6%	10%	4%	$1,396	128.2%
1,593	OVERSEAS SHIPHOLDING GROUP	4412	2,000	15%	6%	10%	$21,410	-121.4%
1,130	OWENS & MINOR	5047	3,090	8%	94%	8%	$72,691	-6.1%
920	OWENS CORNING	3296	24,000	21%	-875%	15%	$29,613	2.5%
260	OWENS-ILLINOIS	3221	32,400	8%	22%	6%	$7,497	32.5%
957	OXFORD INDUSTRIES	2321	8,413	18%	73%	15%	$12,229	1.3%
229	PACCAR	5013	19,000	11%	35%	9%	$28,350	37.0%
89	PACIFI	4911	10,087	11%	7%	6%	$25,372	77.9%
1,451	PAGEMART WIRELESS	4812	2,249	156%	-1100%	54%	$63,241	-39.6%
1,367	PAGING NETWORK	4812	6,001	118%	-156%	37%	$54,921	-25.9%
446	PALL	3599	8,500	118%	53%	41%	$52,068	19.3%
1,269	PALM HARBOR HOMES	1521	4,700	21%	74%	16%	$21,278	-15.7%
1,616	PALOMAR MEDICAL TECHNOLOGIES	3845	352	96%	149%	78%	$73,949	-157.3%
57	PANAMSAT	3663	450	85%	3%	11%	$128,634	108.3%
478	PAPA JOHN'S INTERNATIONAL	5812	14,219	56%	64%	28%	$10,421	17.8%
919	PAR TECHNOLOGY	357	880	31%	39%	23%	$29,915	2.5%
170	PARK ELECTROCHEMICAL	3672	2,600	14%	25%	11%	$15,464	47.3%
1,368	PARKER DRILLING	138	4,313	12%	7%	8%	$6,117	-25.9%
286	PARKER HANNIFIN	3593	34,927	16%	31%	12%	$13,007	30.8%
298	PARK-OHIO HOLDINGS	3714	2,659	12%	33%	10%	$16,367	29.5%
1,038	PARLEX	367	573	18%	40%	14%	$13,253	-1.7%
255	PATRICK INDUSTRIES	5031	1,596	6%	33%	5%	$13,855	32.6%
926	PATTERSON DENTAL	5047	2,913	44%	109%	28%	$64,278	2.4%
51	PATTERSON ENERGY	1381	1,725	7%	7%	5%	$4,982	113.9%
662	PAXAR	3999	4,786	43%	55%	25%	$28,432	10.5%
1,388	PAYLESS CASHWAYS	5251	12,800	33%	229%	24%	$37,669	-28.9%
1,026	PENFORD	2087	533	27%	43%	18%	$66,320	-1.4%
1,165	PENN TRAFFIC	5399	20,500	27%	-637%	20%	$26,846	-7.6%
1,123	PENN VIRGINIA	131	59	178%	5%	25%	$130,593	-5.6%
852	PENNEY (J.C.)	5311	260,000	32%	86%	22%	$23,311	5.0%
1,316	PENNZOIL	3714	10,214	27%	39%	16%	$38,540	-19.8%
579	PENTAIR	356	10,433	31%	59%	21%	$33,884	13.6%
1,647	PEOPLE'S CHOICE TV	4841	357	143%	30%	83%	$56,316	-289.5%
743	PEP BOYS—MANNY, MOE & JACK	5531	24,203	29%	48%	20%	$17,292	8.2%
699	PEPSICO	2086	142,000	96%	161%	40%	$30,276	9.6%
1,545	PEPSI-COLA PUERTO RICO BOTTLING	2086	568	66%	58%	40%	$80,601	-74.9%
1,619	PERCLOSE	3841	198	247%	34%	203%	$84,893	-164.5%
770	PERFORMANCE FOOD GROUP	5812	2,800	13%	105%	11%	$46,927	7.3%
726	PERKIN-ELMER	3826	5,685	80%	125%	38%	$77,355	8.8%
1,516	PERRIGO	2834	4,122	24%	33%	16%	$30,568	-61.3%
1,263	PETCO ANIMAL SUPPLIES	5999	9,400	32%	74%	23%	$19,082	-15.0%
1,199	PETROLEUM HEAT & POWER	5983	2,211	28%	-92%	19%	$46,306	-9.7%
1,086	PETROLEUM HELICOPTERS	4522	1,851	7%	14%	6%	$6,739	-3.4%
1,205	PETSMART	5999	18,800	31%	101%	23%	$21,543	-10.1%
360	PFIZER	283	49,200	335%	89%	54%	$130,689	24.7%
454	PG&E	4911	23,500	30%	19%	15%	$79,489	18.7%
1,499	PHARMACEUTICAL RESOURCES	283	335	46%	31%	35%	$53,486	-54.2%

IP Rank	Company	SIC	EMPLOYEES	Information Management/ Cost of Goods	Information Management/ Net Assets	Information Management/ Revenue	Information Management/ Employee	Information Productivity
942	PHARMACIA & UPJOHN	283	30,000	245%	64%	56%	$120,580	1.7%
922	PHARMERICA	5122	7,496	60%	37%	33%	$28,612	2.5%
16	PHELPS DODGE	1021	15,869	5%	5%	3%	$8,282	223.0%
282	PHILIP MORRIS	2111	152,000	60%	107%	28%	$100,781	31.2%
62	PHILLIPS PETROLEUM	2911	17,100	5%	12%	4%	$31,721	105.2%
1,195	PHILLIPS-VAN HEUSEN	232	11,850	45%	158%	30%	$32,398	-9.5%
723	PHYSIO-CONTROL INTERNATIONAL	3845	840	79%	150%	38%	$74,159	8.8%
1,448	PICCADILLY CAFETERIAS	5812	8,200	8%	17%	4%	$1,567	-39.0%
1,110	PICTURETEL	4813	1,544	92%	84%	45%	$136,993	-4.7%
500	PIEDMONT NATURAL GAS	4924	1,904	33%	31%	18%	$60,942	16.6%
816	PIER 1 IMPORTS	5712	12,571	50%	88%	29%	$24,857	6.0%
1,237	PILGRIM'S PRIDE	2015	9,700	5%	31%	4%	$4,521	-12.8%
806	PILLOWTEX	2392	14,800	11%	30%	9%	$5,928	6.5%
586	PIONEER HI-BRED INTERNATIONAL	0181	4,994	100%	62%	38%	$130,117	13.2%
1,662	PIONEER NATURAL RESOURCES	1311	1,321	11%	7%	13%	$64,458	-561.6%
838	PIONEER-STANDARD ELECTRONICS	5065	2,333	17%	78%	13%	$95,568	5.4%
324	PITNEY BOWES	3579	29,901	111%	61%	36%	$48,366	26.7%
493	PITTSTON	4731	33,000	16%	50%	10%	$11,766	16.7%
1,013	PITTSTON BRINK'S GROUP	4513	22,400	21%	40%	14%	$7,961	-0.8%
242	PITTSTON MINERALS GROUP	1221	2,055	5%	-243%	5%	$13,986	34.5%
277	PLAINS RESOURCES	5172	230	1%	8%	1%	$36,784	31.4%
524	PLANAR SYSTEMS	3679	575	37%	25%	23%	$35,608	15.6%
154	PLANTRONICS	481	1,817	61%	222%	27%	$35,808	51.2%
750	PLAYBOY ENTERPRISES	2721	684	16%	56%	12%	$51,525	7.9%
505	PLAYTEX PRODUCTS	2676	1,640	107%	-68%	39%	$120,185	16.5%
472	PLEXUS	3672	2,168	5%	27%	4%	$6,261	18.0%
17	PLUM CREEK TIMBER	243	2,400	11%	10%	6%	$18,949	218.6%
1,304	PMC - SIERRA	3674	297	86%	65%	33%	$156,136	-19.0%
60	POGO PRODUCING	1311	137	29%	17%	9%	$145,417	106.3%
283	POLARIS INDUSTRIES	3799	2,900	19%	109%	14%	$52,126	31.0%
1,298	POLAROID	3861	10,011	70%	129%	36%	$75,598	-18.8%
1,042	POOL ENERGY SERVICES	1381	6,584	17%	24%	13%	$8,134	-1.8%
1,557	POPE & TALBOT	2436	2,300	5%	10%	4%	$7,378	-86.5%
1,477	PORTA SYSTEMS	366	457	54%	-159%	35%	$51,324	-44.5%
784	PORTEC	5084	212	31%	42%	21%	$30,735	6.9%
972	POTLATCH	267	6,700	8%	10%	6%	$15,057	0.7%
453	POWELL INDUSTRIES	3613	1,163	21%	42%	16%	$26,965	18.7%
186	PPG INDUSTRIES	3211	31,900	29%	48%	17%	$39,988	44.1%
427	PRAXAIR	2813	25,388	29%	31%	17%	$29,878	20.2%
181	PRECISION CASTPARTS	336	10,367	12%	19%	9%	$10,493	45.4%
768	PREMARK INTERNATIONAL	3556	17,200	48%	72%	29%	$39,538	7.4%
1,111	PREMISYS COMMUNICATIONS	3661	238	106%	31%	37%	$126,115	-4.7%
1,610	PRESLEY	1521	358	13%	67%	12%	$91,651	-138.8%
1,558	PRICELLULAR	4812	800	89%	20%	31%	$59,714	-87.3%
199	PRIDE INTERNATIONAL	1389	8,400	16%	15%	11%	$7,257	42.1%
1,268	PRIMEDIA	2731	6,300	235%	183%	56%	$110,270	-15.6%
409	PROCTER & GAMBLE	2841	106,000	52%	85%	28%	$95,065	21.1%
1,115	PROFFITT'S	5311	38,000	36%	80%	24%	$20,175	-5.0%
201	PUBLIC SERVICE OF NEW MEXICO	4911	2,789	16%	7%	6%	$19,393	41.8%
22	PUBLIC SERVICE OF NORTH CAROLINA	4924	1,125	3%	3%	2%	$4,537	182.6%
101	PUBLIC SERVICE ENTERPRISE	4911	10,092	15%	5%	5%	$25,726	68.6%
226	PUERTO RICAN CEMENT	3241	1,015	22%	12%	13%	$18,727	37.5%
576	PUGET SOUND ENERGY	4911	3,050	40%	16%	17%	$97,241	13.6%
1,103	PULASKI FURNITURE	2511	1,800	20%	46%	15%	$12,351	-4.3%
391	PULITZER PUBLISHING	2711	3,500	85%	68%	33%	$55,835	22.5%
461	PULTE	1521	4,300	12%	28%	10%	$54,065	18.4%
1,476	QMS	3577	734	52%	165%	36%	$67,287	-44.4%
1,040	QUAKER CHEMICAL	2899	871	66%	100%	36%	$99,003	-1.8%
1,028	QUAKER OATS	2043	14,123	79%	225%	39%	$141,178	-1.4%
982	QUAKER STATE	2992	5,254	39%	98%	26%	$54,316	0.4%
1,159	QUALCOMM	3669	9,000	44%	27%	28%	$50,112	-7.5%
1,658	QUALITY DINING	5812	8,200	13%	12%	7%	$1,772	-478.9%
121	QUANEX	3312	3,771	7%	23%	6%	$14,019	59.4%
1,050	QUANTUM	3572	6,219	12%	55%	10%	$79,145	-2.1%
1,217	QUICKTURN DESIGN SYSTEMS	3674	388	261%	72%	58%	$165,669	-11.2%
696	QUIKSILVER	2321	766	47%	68%	28%	$96,141	9.6%

INFORMATION PRODUCTIVITY

IP Rank	Company	SIC	EMPLOYEES	Information Management/ Cost of Goods	Information Management/ Net Assets	Information Management/ Revenue	Information Management/ Employee	Information Productivity
1,523	R&B FALCON	1381	5,700	11%	7%	6%	$7,984	-67.3%
177	RADISYS	3823	511	42%	34%	24%	$55,891	46.0%
1,106	RAGAN (BRAD)	5014	1,730	50%	172%	33%	$48,224	-4.3%
1,101	RAILTEX	4011	900	32%	19%	18%	$28,450	-4.1%
414	RALSTON-RALSTON PURINA GROUP	2047	30,162	60%	201%	31%	$61,325	20.7%
550	RAVEN INDUSTRIES	231	1,511	13%	25%	10%	$9,864	14.6%
625	RAYCHEM	3357	8,650	84%	76%	37%	$69,175	11.8%
1,336	RAYONIER	2611	2,500	5%	6%	3%	$14,674	-21.8%
168	RAYTECH	3499	1,360	18%	82%	13%	$21,367	47.6%
364	RAYTHEON	381	119,200	15%	22%	11%	$15,897	24.5%
334	READ-RITE	3572	23,107	14%	17%	9%	$4,448	26.2%
831	RECOTON	5065	4,100	56%	90%	33%	$39,080	5.6%
1,565	REDHOOK ALE BREWERY	2082	210	38%	10%	23%	$35,847	-89.3%
700	REEBOK INTERNATIONAL LTD.	3149	6,948	49%	163%	30%	$150,372	9.6%
203	REGAL-BELOIT	3594	4,810	18%	27%	12%	$13,315	41.4%
572	RELIANCE STEEL & ALUMINUM	3312	2,750	21%	52%	16%	$56,982	13.8%
1,625	REMINGTON OIL & GAS	1311	15	54%	13%	15%	$238,700	-183.4%
235	RENTERS CHOICE	5064	2,540	136%	26%	14%	$15,284	35.5%
995	REPUBLIC AUTOMOTIVE PARTS	5013	1,500	59%	128%	35%	$42,483	0.1%
1,291	RESOUND	3842	974	127%	170%	53%	$67,881	-17.7%
371	RESPIRONICS	3842	1,565	93%	47%	38%	$38,415	23.9%
31	REUTER MANUFACTURING	3544	149	23%	-47%	17%	$18,481	147.5%
1,039	REX STORES	5731	1,024	29%	87%	21%	$87,836	-1.7%
834	REXALL SUNDOWN	2834	820	119%	80%	44%	$120,459	5.6%
456	REYNOLDS AND REYNOLDS	2761	9,138	68%	104%	33%	$48,927	18.6%
1,148	REYNOLDS METALS	3353	25,500	8%	16%	6%	$15,330	-6.7%
1,044	RICHARDSON ELECTRONICS, LTD.	3671	728	33%	90%	23%	$86,584	-2.0%
776	RICHFOOD HOLDINGS	5142	5,151	8%	100%	7%	$50,794	7.1%
847	RITE AID	5912	83,000	29%	76%	21%	$25,729	5.1%
556	RIVAL	363	2,500	23%	48%	16%	$21,425	14.4%
1,090	RIVIANA FOODS	2044	2,751	31%	83%	22%	$37,871	-3.7%
1,182	RJR NABISCO HOLDINGS	2051	80,400	79%	52%	34%	$72,287	-8.5%
117	ROANOKE ELECTRIC STEEL	3441	1,161	9%	18%	7%	$23,701	61.0%
549	ROBBINS & MYERS	3443	3,000	38%	85%	23%	$31,334	14.6%
1,517	ROBERTS PHARMACEUTICAL	5122	498	141%	22%	56%	$133,059	-62.9%
83	ROBERTSON CECO	3441	1,500	13%	179%	10%	$19,062	79.9%
1,121	ROBINSON NUGENT	3678	773	27%	49%	19%	$21,504	-5.5%
811	ROBOTIC VISION SYSTEMS	3825	800	94%	84%	42%	$95,779	6.3%
272	ROCHESTER GAS AND ELECTRIC	4911	1,958	18%	5%	5%	$23,964	31.6%
689	ROCK-TENN	2631	8,415	24%	47%	17%	$23,371	9.8%
520	ROCKWELL INTERNATIONAL	381	45,000	32%	49%	20%	$33,895	15.8%
717	ROGERS	3674	993	31%	42%	21%	$34,940	9.0%
356	ROHM & HAAS	2821	11,592	36%	45%	21%	$70,669	25.1%
25	ROHN INDUSTRIES	3441	759	15%	19%	10%	$21,110	170.5%
1,528	ROHR	3728	4,600	4%	12%	3%	$6,543	-68.8%
980	RONSON	3999	135	41%	398%	27%	$48,739	0.5%
308	ROPER INDUSTRIES	3594	2,000	70%	52%	31%	$49,122	28.3%
146	ROWAN	1382	5,250	4%	3%	3%	$3,505	53.2%
740	ROWE FURNITURE	2512	1,650	26%	68%	19%	$16,682	8.2%
1,117	ROYAL APPLIANCE MFG.	3635	670	34%	127%	23%	$107,992	-5.1%
596	RPM	285	6,651	58%	84%	31%	$65,414	12.8%
825	RUBBERMAID	3089	12,618	29%	43%	20%	$34,188	5.8%
896	RUDDICK	5411	19,700	33%	146%	24%	$25,559	3.3%
115	RYAN'S FAMILY STEAK HOUSES	5812	18,000	7%	8%	5%	$1,465	62.1%
1,072	RYKOFF-SEXTON	203	8,500	23%	166%	18%	$64,613	-2.8%
1,099	RYLAND GROUP	152	2,229	19%	77%	15%	$97,752	-4.1%
974	SAFEGUARD SCIENTIFICS	5045	4,400	13%	89%	11%	$47,887	0.6%
1,626	SAFETY-KLEEN	4953	4,531	16%	21%	12%	$17,446	-188.8%
751	SAFEWAY	5411	147,000	32%	308%	23%	$33,537	7.9%
888	SAGA COMMUNICATIONS	4832	520	211%	81%	48%	$63,529	3.7%
1,323	SALANT	2321	3,800	24%	145%	19%	$21,342	-20.3%
1,193	SAMSONITE .	3161	7,800	55%	239%	31%	$29,854	-9.4%
1,339	SANDERSON FARMS	0251	6,155	4%	15%	4%	$3,061	-22.3%
36	SANMINA	3672	2,522	8%	16%	6%	$9,928	133.3%
1,589	SANTA FE ENERGY RESOURCES	1311	1,209	9%	5%	5%	$33,770	-115.1%
738	SARA LEE	201	141,000	51%	111%	30%	$39,311	8.3%

IP Rank	Company	SIC	EMPLOYEES	Information Management/ Cost of Goods	Information Management/ Net Assets	Information Management/ Revenue	Information Management/ Employee	Information Productivity
786	SBC COMMUNICATIONS	4813	118,340	77%	55%	25%	$54,769	6.9%
1,112	SCHEIN, HENRY	5047	5,000	38%	90%	26%	$71,739	-4.9%
327	SCHERER, (R.P.)	2899	3,600	27%	25%	16%	$28,094	26.5%
249	SCHERING-PLOUGH	283	22,700	318%	140%	52%	$143,379	33.5%
132	SCHLUMBERGER LIMITED	1381	63,500	19%	19%	12%	$19,409	56.5%
236	SCHNITZER STEEL INDUSTRIES	5093	1,183	7%	9%	5%	$16,949	35.1%
930	SCHOLASTIC	2731	6,570	86%	130%	41%	$61,439	2.1%
970	SCHULMAN, (A.)	3087	2,200	10%	19%	8%	$38,195	0.8%
822	SCHULTZ SAV-O STORES	514	1,680	16%	131%	14%	$38,245	5.9%
102	SCHWEITZER-MAUDUIT INTERNATIONAL	2141	2,465	12%	25%	8%	$4,088	68.5%
75	SCI SYSTEMS	3672	18,470	1%	11%	1%	$3,377	88.0%
1,457	SCIENTIFIC-ATLANTA	366	6,086	32%	50%	22%	$49,589	-40.8%
585	SCOTSMAN INDUSTRIES	3585	3,750	22%	50%	16%	$23,789	13.3%
1,215	SCOTT TECHNOLOGIES	3841	1,700	26%	94%	19%	$26,050	-11.0%
1,184	SCOTTS	287	2,383	57%	67%	32%	$109,764	-8.5%
1,092	SEABOARD	2015	12,031	11%	35%	9%	$11,878	-3.7%
23	SEACOR SMIT	4499	1,890	18%	6%	9%	$13,433	179.8%
302	SEAGATE TECHNOLOGY	3572	111,000	15%	32%	11%	$9,177	29.0%
1,614	SEAGULL ENERGY	1311	877	7%	3%	3%	$19,791	-146.8%
292	SEALED AIR	3086	4,400	35%	88%	21%	$38,631	30.1%
1,326	SEALRIGHT	2656	1,550	17%	36%	13%	$20,400	-20.8%
667	SEARS, ROEBUCK AND	5311	334,000	37%	142%	24%	$27,819	10.4%
963	SEAWAY FOOD TOWN	5411	5,051	33%	302%	24%	$29,497	1.1%
527	SEMITOOL	3559	1,363	70%	82%	34%	$45,230	15.6%
1,305	SEQUA	3728	11,000	20%	38%	15%	$23,219	-19.1%
1,125	SERVICE MERCHANDISE	5961	24,168	25%	195%	19%	$29,025	-5.7%
774	SHAW GROUP	4619	4,600	14%	29%	11%	$10,096	7.2%
1,082	SHAW INDUSTRIES	2273	29,500	23%	82%	17%	$19,658	-3.3%
658	SHELBY WILLIAMS INDUSTRIES	2531	1,703	20%	43%	15%	$15,153	10.6%
1,366	SHELDAHL	3672	1,129	23%	27%	17%	$16,532	-25.5%
742	SHERWIN-WILLIAMS	5231	25,000	59%	94%	32%	$61,596	8.2%
189	SHILOH INDUSTRIES	3312	1,590	11%	16%	8%	$16,195	43.3%
390	SHONEY'S	5812	33,000	11%	-180%	6%	$2,155	22.5%
209	SHOREWOOD PACKAGING	2657	2,700	14%	52%	10%	$15,134	40.6%
501	SIFCO INDUSTRIES	3724	770	19%	35%	14%	$18,509	16.6%
1,491	SIGMA DESIGNS	3571	71	54%	78%	40%	$190,806	-49.7%
475	SIGMA-ALDRICH	281	6,666	75%	35%	32%	$54,134	17.9%
1,605	SIGNAL APPAREL	2253	810	33%	-42%	30%	$20,607	-132.6%
1,566	SILICON VALLEY GROUP	3674	3,099	54%	35%	31%	$63,019	-89.9%
322	SILICONIX	3674	1,266	50%	64%	27%	$60,531	27.0%
187	SIMPSON INDUSTRIES	3714	2,355	4%	11%	3%	$5,858	44.0%
1,461	SIMULA	3728	1,000	39%	44%	27%	$24,143	-41.5%
1,463	SINCLAIR BROADCAST GROUP	4833	2,262	86%	20%	20%	$41,952	-41.7%
1,527	SKYTEL COMMUNICATIONS	4812	2,300	204%	65%	63%	$79,543	-68.4%
366	SKYWEST	4512	2,966	10%	15%	8%	$8,955	24.3%
1,328	SL INDUSTRIES	3621	1,800	42%	98%	27%	$16,938	-20.9%
263	SLI	3229	7,408	27%	25%	18%	$9,310	32.3%
858	SMART & FINAL	541	5,205	14%	84%	12%	$32,052	4.8%
1,615	SMART MODULAR TECHNOLOGIES	3577	636	10%	32%	8%	$74,707	-149.2%
109	SMITH (A.O.)	371	8,400	13%	27%	10%	$11,250	64.6%
617	SMITH INTERNATIONAL	3533	7,342	35%	50%	22%	$44,229	12.1%
767	SMITHFIELD FOODS	2013	17,500	6%	59%	6%	$10,481	7.4%
666	SNAP-ON	342	11,700	85%	72%	40%	$54,853	10.4%
655	SOFAMOR DANEK GROUP	3842	1,000	370%	82%	54%	$165,968	10.7%
754	SOLA INTERNATIONAL	3851	7,800	66%	57%	32%	$21,665	7.8%
207	SONAT	4923	2,110	6%	9%	5%	$75,159	41.1%
125	SONIC	5812	198	21%	16%	10%	$87,340	58.2%
473	SONOCO PRODUCTS	265	19,000	15%	33%	11%	$15,743	17.9%
1,168	SOUND ADVICE	5731	633	44%	284%	30%	$71,205	-7.7%
521	SOUTHDOWN	3241	2,400	12%	11%	8%	$21,315	15.7%
122	SOUTHERN	4911	30,756	14%	7%	7%	$24,248	59.4%
1,588	SOUTHERN ENERGY HOMES	1521	2,371	7%	24%	6%	$7,248	-112.7%
66	SOUTHERN PERU COPPER	3331	4,800	17%	7%	9%	$15,080	99.1%
1,118	SOUTHERN UNION	4924	1,595	31%	31%	18%	$64,959	-5.3%
691	SOUTHLAND	5411	30,323	40%	-234%	27%	$61,862	9.7%
1,120	SOUTHWEST WATER	4941	535	22%	33%	16%	$19,194	-5.4%

IP Rank	Company	SIC	EMPLOYEES	Information Management/ Cost of Goods	Information Management/ Net Assets	Information Management/ Revenue	Information Management/ Employee	Information Productivity
841	SOUTHWESTERN ENERGY	4923	705	82%	25%	25%	$74,775	5.4%
1,249	SPAGHETTI WAREHOUSE	5812	2,250	255%	96%	65%	$22,938	-13.5%
1,450	SPARTAN MOTORS	3711	620	12%	32%	11%	$32,986	-39.2%
164	SPARTECH	3081	2,125	8%	26%	6%	$15,756	48.3%
145	SPECIALTY EQUIPMENT	3585	2,565	23%	-88%	16%	$27,893	53.3%
649	SPECTRUM CONTROL	3677	763	35%	46%	22%	$15,684	10.9%
1,133	SPIEGEL	5699	12,400	60%	204%	37%	$85,042	-6.2%
1,404	SPORT SUPPLY GROUP	5091	395	54%	74%	33%	$66,492	-31.2%
1,033	SPRINGS INDUSTRIES	2392	19,500	16%	37%	13%	$13,302	-1.5%
405	SPRINT	4813	51,000	44%	42%	22%	$62,971	21.2%
570	SPS TECHNOLOGIES	3452	3,696	16%	33%	12%	$14,634	13.9%
1,318	SPX	3714	4,593	24%	246%	18%	$27,794	-20.0%
672	ST. JUDE MEDICAL	384	3,772	166%	45%	45%	$117,100	10.3%
67	ST. MARY LAND & EXPLORATION	1382	103	28%	7%	12%	$67,023	97.3%
388	STAAR SURGICAL	3851	269	296%	55%	54%	$85,459	22.6%
559	STANDARD COMMERCIAL	2141	2,187	6%	56%	5%	$34,451	14.2%
1,186	STANDARD MOTOR PRODUCTS	3694	4,400	44%	90%	29%	$45,980	-8.7%
1,536	STANDARD PACIFIC	1521	427	8%	12%	7%	$72,323	-70.5%
1,007	STANDARD PRODUCTS	3714	10,350	12%	40%	10%	$10,327	-0.6%
728	STANDARD REGISTER	2761	6,440	39%	50%	24%	$34,965	8.7%
492	STANDEX INTERNATIONAL	3589	4,800	35%	95%	23%	$26,681	16.8%
1,045	STANLEY WORKS	3546	18,377	36%	86%	23%	$32,032	-2.0%
718	STAPLES	5943	16,213	24%	96%	18%	$57,375	9.0%
719	STARBUCKS	2095	25,000	83%	62%	37%	$15,030	9.0%
1,502	STARMET	3312	235	33%	23%	24%	$29,141	-55.7%
828	STARRETT L.S.	3545	2,740	32%	29%	21%	$17,201	5.7%
1,322	STARTER	2253	1,000	48%	138%	33%	$117,947	-20.2%
543	STEPAN	284	1,292	13%	41%	10%	$41,490	15.0%
464	STEWART & STEVENSON SERVICES	3621	3,665	9%	18%	8%	$20,533	18.2%
1,648	STILLWATER MINING	1499	675	3%	1%	3%	$2,840	-294.9%
1,389	STONE CONTAINER	265	24,600	13%	85%	10%	$5,756	-29.3%
944	STONE ENERGY	1311	90	462%	3%	7%	$56,559	1.6%
397	STORAGE COMPUTER	3572	138	68%	73%	33%	$90,907	21.8%
1,185	STRATUS COMPUTER	3571	2,487	86%	43%	37%	$95,793	-8.6%
437	STRYKER	3841	5,691	105%	61%	40%	$71,707	19.6%
1,194	SUN	2911	10,900	7%	38%	5%	$49,822	-9.5%
97	SUN ENERGY PARTNERS,	1311	1,046	23%	4%	7%	$41,899	70.8%
569	SUN MICROSYSTEMS	3571	21,500	70%	107%	35%	$142,697	13.9%
1,422	SUNBEAM	3631	7,500	20%	33%	15%	$19,688	-33.8%
314	SUNDSTRAND	3728	10,400	31%	58%	19%	$30,966	27.6%
1,273	SUNGLASS HUT INTERNATIONAL	5995	8,843	47%	110%	29%	$22,248	-16.0%
1,226	SUNRISE MEDICAL	384	4,254	42%	59%	26%	$39,898	-11.6%
1,657	SUNSHINE MINING & REFINING	1044	315	20%	9%	28%	$18,572	-469.1%
1,498	SUPERIOR INDUSTRIES INTERNATIONAL	3714	4,500	5%	8%	4%	$4,436	-54.1%
759	SUPERIOR SURGICAL MFG.	2389	1,700	35%	43%	23%	$17,345	7.5%
363	SUPREME INDUSTRIES	3713	1,900	11%	43%	9%	$9,816	24.6%
1,202	SWANK	2387	1,280	72%	244%	41%	$41,794	-10.0%
20	SWIFT ENERGY	1311	194	67%	4%	11%	$31,676	198.4%
513	SWIFT TRANSPORTATION	4731	7,800	20%	32%	12%	$10,171	16.1%
228	SWISHER INTERNATIONAL GROUP	210	1,340	53%	107%	26%	$43,458	37.1%
353	SYBRON INTERNATIONAL	5047	6,300	58%	60%	27%	$30,825	25.4%
724	SYMBOL TECHNOLOGIES	3577	3,200	64%	52%	32%	$74,163	8.8%
632	SYMMETRICOM	3661	708	70%	57%	35%	$61,249	11.4%
1,360	SYMS	5611	2,300	36%	34%	23%	$34,987	-24.5%
118	SYNALLOY	3498	663	10%	21%	8%	$16,601	60.9%
978	SYNCOR INTERNATIONAL	2834	2,281	22%	75%	17%	$27,468	0.5%
938	SYNOPSYS	3825	1,961	1163%	92%	68%	$149,881	1.8%
712	SYSCO	5149	32,000	18%	134%	14%	$63,179	9.1%
1,027	TAB PRODUCTS	2542	1,075	61%	128%	35%	$51,448	-1.4%
817	TALBOTS	5632	8,300	43%	66%	27%	$36,184	6.0%
1,031	TANDY	5731	44,000	44%	127%	29%	$35,200	-1.5%
1,210	TANDYCRAFTS	2499	3,700	51%	94%	32%	$20,868	-10.7%
757	TASTY BAKING	2051	1,060	44%	101%	27%	$35,110	7.6%
271	TCA CABLE TV	4841	1,654	101%	28%	25%	$46,907	31.6%
1,289	TCBY ENTERPRISES	2024	440	86%	57%	42%	$76,575	-17.7%
590	TECH DATA	5045	5,075	5%	46%	5%	$59,790	13.0%

Appendix C–Information Productivity Listing

IP Rank	Company	SIC	EMPLOYEES	Information Management/ Cost of Goods	Information Management/ Net Assets	Information Management/ Revenue	Information Management/ Employee	Information Productivity
316	TECHNITROL	3677	14,400	34%	56%	22%	$5,276	27.6%
900	TECH-SYM	3663	2,459	45%	47%	28%	$33,862	3.2%
1,546	TECUMSEH PRODUCTS	3585	17,100	7%	10%	6%	$6,029	-77.6%
716	TEKTRONIX	3825	8,392	65%	89%	35%	$76,238	9.1%
1,673	TELE-COMMUNICATION INTERNATIONAL	4841	27	9%	1%	7%	$444,832	-1075.4%
465	TELEFLEX	3714	11,700	32%	50%	21%	$19,645	18.2%
1,022	TELXON	3571	1,550	63%	107%	36%	$96,644	-1.3%
690	TENNANT	3589	2,019	61%	90%	33%	$57,040	9.7%
607	TERADYNE	3679	6,300	50%	39%	27%	$59,460	12.3%
575	TEREX	3531	2,950	10%	-1074%	8%	$24,478	13.7%
479	TERRA INDUSTRIES	5191	4,435	17%	33%	13%	$77,220	17.6%
30	TESORO PETROLEUM	2911	1,100	2%	5%	1%	$14,549	147.5%
307	TETRA TECHNOLOGIES	2819	1,290	28%	27%	18%	$29,653	28.4%
139	TEXACO INC .	1311	29,313	5%	14%	4%	$57,012	54.3%
279	TEXAS INDUSTRIES	3449	3,400	10%	15%	7%	$22,137	31.3%
310	TEXAS INSTRUMENTS	367	44,140	34%	49%	21%	$42,422	28.0%
1,535	TEXFI INDUSTRIES	2221	1,500	8%	-213%	7%	$6,601	-70.5%
600	TEXTRON	3721	64,000	26%	41%	15%	$24,860	12.5%
1,486	THERMADYNE HOLDINGS	3545	3,563	37%	-60%	21%	$31,477	-47.0%
424	THERMEDICS	3812	1,876	73%	31%	36%	$55,038	20.3%
259	THERMO CARDIOSYSTEMS	3842	420	99%	15%	38%	$62,121	32.5%
94	THERMO ECOTEK	4911	275	17%	11%	9%	$53,527	72.9%
803	THERMO ELECTRON	3823	22,400	59%	39%	32%	$48,388	6.5%
438	THERMO INSTRUMENT SYSTEMS	382	9,398	69%	50%	34%	$58,616	19.5%
1,113	THERMO POWER	3585	486	21%	23%	17%	$37,842	-4.9%
1,421	THERMOLASE	2844	454	84%	26%	56%	$54,823	-33.7%
965	THERMOSPECTRA	3823	1,400	75%	52%	38%	$54,928	1.1%
597	THERMOTREX	3845	1,712	62%	30%	37%	$52,711	12.7%
707	THOMAS & BETTS	3679	16,400	30%	43%	20%	$26,182	9.3%
931	THOMAS INDUSTRIES	3646	3,200	34%	74%	23%	$37,350	2.0%
697	TIFFANY &	5944	4,360	97%	107%	42%	$97,286	9.6%
1,412	TII INDUSTRIES	3613	985	30%	31%	20%	$8,703	-32.5%
1,032	TIMBERLAND	3143	5,100	47%	118%	29%	$37,936	-1.5%
1,357	TIME WARNER	2721	67,900	68%	36%	33%	$50,024	-24.3%
240	TIMES MIRROR	2711	21,567	83%	92%	38%	$60,145	34.5%
394	TIMKEN	3562	20,994	18%	34%	13%	$16,619	22.2%
1,285	TITAN	366	1,200	26%	58%	19%	$23,719	-17.0%
368	TITAN INTERNATIONAL	3499	4,200	9%	18%	7%	$11,050	24.2%
1,439	TJ INTERNATIONAL	2411	3,592	23%	22%	15%	$29,444	-37.7%
537	TJX	5331	59,000	22%	102%	17%	$20,280	15.3%
1,067	TNP ENTERPRISES	4911	811	34%	32%	17%	$104,846	-2.7%
163	TOLL BROTHERS	1521	1,346	12%	23%	9%	$61,180	48.4%
469	TOOTSIE ROLL INDUSTRIES	2064	1,750	53%	29%	26%	$50,893	18.0%
1,532	TOP SOURCE TECHNOLOGIES	3714	62	63%	77%	41%	$74,889	-69.3%
1,164	TOPPS	5092	500	43%	105%	29%	$115,710	-7.6%
881	TORO	352	3,911	48%	135%	30%	$77,959	3.9%
793	TOSCO	1311	26,200	2%	14%	2%	$11,104	6.8%
206	TOWER AUTOMOTIVE	3714	8,750	6%	12%	5%	$7,262	41.1%
969	TOYS R US	5945	68,000	29%	51%	20%	$32,175	0.8%
839	TRACTOR SUPPLY	5261	2,700	27%	93%	20%	$41,739	5.4%
1,312	TRAK AUTO	5531	2,500	28%	91%	21%	$21,224	-19.4%
1,264	TRANS WORLD AIRLINES	4512	22,321	212%	396%	43%	$48,726	-15.1%
28	TRANSOCEAN OFFSHORE	1381	3,500	6%	2%	4%	$7,100	154.8%
966	TRANSTECHNOLOGY	3545	1,614	32%	41%	20%	$23,180	1.0%
13	TRANSTEXAS GAS	1311	2,500	44%	-43%	12%	$14,533	256.3%
1,522	TRC	382	675	5%	9%	5%	$5,307	-67.3%
169	TREDEGAR INDUSTRIES	3089	2,500	12%	24%	9%	$19,748	47.4%
1,475	TRESCOM INTERNATIONAL	4813	330	31%	64%	23%	$120,006	-44.2%
525	TRIANGLE PACIFIC	2426	5,404	18%	45%	13%	$14,443	15.6%
1,166	TRIARC	2086	2,000	48%	828%	29%	$41,604	-7.7%
172	TRIBUNE	2711	11,600	50%	38%	24%	$54,701	47.1%
1,137	TRIGEN ENERGY	4961	674	21%	20%	13%	$45,713	-6.5%
905	TRION	3564	501	45%	77%	28%	$34,160	3.0%
1,049	TRIQUINT SEMICONDUCTOR	3674	371	74%	27%	37%	$64,659	-2.1%
827	TRW	3679	79,700	14%	54%	11%	$15,793	5.7%
1,390	TUBOSCOPE	1389	4,598	19%	20%	12%	$12,409	-29.5%

INFORMATION PRODUCTIVITY

IP Rank	Company	SIC	EMPLOYEES	Information Management/ Cost of Goods	Information Management/ Net Assets	Information Management/ Revenue	Information Management/ Employee	Information Productivity
1,257	TULTEX	2253	6,708	21%	50%	16%	$14,693	-14.3%
1,533	TURNER	154	3,000	1%	21%	1%	$4,915	-70.3%
917	TWIN DISC	356	1,081	22%	39%	16%	$26,515	2.6%
1,380	TYCO INTERNATIONAL LTD	3669	75,400	28%	50%	18%	$23,421	-27.9%
677	TYSON FOODS	2015	59,400	13%	40%	10%	$10,190	10.2%
1,408	U.S. BIOSCIENCE	2834	150	1281%	77%	119%	$204,524	-31.8%
1,464	U.S. CAN	3411	3,757	5%	37%	4%	$7,819	-41.8%
1,365	U.S. HOME	1521	1,641	14%	37%	12%	$94,485	-25.5%
711	U.S. INDUSTRIES	3262	18,000	33%	90%	22%	$27,840	9.2%
1,068	U.S. OFFICE PRODUCTS	5112	17,000	32%	66%	23%	$35,291	-2.7%
340	UCAR INTERNATIONAL	3624	5,563	20%	-87%	11%	$24,634	25.9%
1,127	UGI	1321	5,131	53%	57%	30%	$68,974	-6.0%
33	UNIFI	2282	7,000	3%	8%	3%	$6,824	140.3%
1,080	UNI-MARTS	5411	2,750	29%	226%	22%	$26,378	-3.1%
812	UNION CAMP	2652	19,000	15%	20%	10%	$23,549	6.3%
54	UNION CARBIDE	2865	11,813	11%	22%	8%	$42,533	111.0%
778	UNION PACIFIC	4011	65,600	188%	45%	37%	$60,341	7.0%
5	UNION PACIFIC RESOURCES GROUP	1311	1,907	10%	4%	4%	$38,732	399.3%
8	UNION TEXAS PETROLEUM HOLDINGS	1311	1,300	7%	5%	3%	$22,783	319.7%
1,416	UNISYS	357	32,600	56%	124%	31%	$58,048	-33.0%
135	UNIT	1311	695	11%	5%	6%	$8,463	56.3%
1,174	UNIT INSTRUMENTS	3823	403	52%	40%	32%	$41,042	-8.2%
325	UNITED CAPITAL	331	319	32%	41%	17%	$24,964	26.7%
1,244	UNITED FOODS	203	2,080	22%	62%	17%	$16,156	-13.2%
1,233	UNITED INDUSTRIAL	3812	1,800	27%	48%	19%	$23,200	-12.2%
1,629	UNITED MERIDIAN	1311	380	15%	3%	6%	$37,103	-199.2%
862	UNITED STATES CELLULAR	4812	4,600	169%	20%	45%	$80,745	4.7%
1,379	UNITED STATES FILTER	3589	18,500	34%	47%	24%	$39,489	-27.8%
762	UNITED STATES SURGICAL	3841	5,776	135%	49%	45%	$83,651	7.5%
991	UNITED STATIONERS	5044	5,500	17%	231%	14%	$59,380	0.2%
796	UNITED TECHNOLOGIES	3724	180,100	23%	78%	17%	$22,326	6.7%
88	UNITED TELEVISION	4833	635	177%	20%	31%	$88,620	78.3%
399	UNITED VIDEO SATELLITE GROUP	4841	1,500	61%	145%	31%	$90,938	21.6%
664	UNIVERSAL	5159	25,000	10%	72%	9%	$11,424	10.4%
445	UNIVERSAL FOODS	2087	4,127	33%	45%	20%	$40,436	19.3%
485	UNIVERSAL FOREST PRODUCTS	2426	3,200	7%	55%	6%	$21,871	17.0%
1,281	UNO RESTAURANT	5812	6,389	10%	16%	7%	$1,995	-16.8%
609	UNOCAL	2911	8,394	6%	8%	4%	$21,314	12.3%
1,161	USA DETERGENTS	2841	592	38%	176%	27%	$96,391	-7.5%
1,471	USA NETWORKS	4833	4,750	54%	12%	29%	$41,795	-43.7%
463	USA WASTE SERVICES	4953	17,700	22%	12%	12%	$16,922	18.3%
52	UST	2131	4,677	171%	111%	28%	$85,220	113.8%
459	USX-MARATHON GROUP	1311	20,310	3%	9%	2%	$15,705	18.5%
788	V.F.	2325	62,800	34%	60%	22%	$18,085	6.9%
59	VALASSIS COMMUNICATIONS	2759	1,170	15%	-23%	10%	$53,025	106.5%
1,407	VALERO REFNG & MARKETING	2911	1,855	2%	7%	2%	$41,173	-31.6%
801	VALLEN	5047	982	28%	58%	20%	$53,820	6.5%
648	VALMONT INDUSTRIES	3441	3,751	26%	60%	18%	$25,806	11.0%
428	VALSPAR	285	3,200	29%	69%	20%	$60,841	20.2%
994	VALUE CITY DEPARTMENT STORES	5311	12,300	59%	140%	36%	$28,673	0.1%
1,088	VANGUARD CELLULAR SYSTEMS	4812	2,000	236%	679%	48%	$83,566	-3.5%
986	VARCO INTERNATIONAL	3533	2,437	38%	46%	23%	$49,726	0.3%
425	VARIAN ASSOCIATES	3679	6,500	43%	86%	26%	$59,256	20.3%
502	VARLEN	3743	3,177	21%	48%	15%	$23,815	16.5%
11	VASTAR RESOURCES	1311	1,063	19%	20%	6%	$56,390	283.1%
1,177	VENATOR GROUP	5331	75,000	36%	149%	25%	$22,737	-8.3%
1,519	VERITAS DGC	1382	3,500	4%	6%	3%	$3,743	-65.3%
1,512	VETERINARY CENTERS OF AMERICA	074	2,178	12%	11%	9%	$8,422	-60.0%
1,494	VI RESTAURANTS	5812	12,400	9%	20%	7%	$1,966	-50.8%
43	VINTAGE PETROLEUM	1311	580	11%	5%	5%	$34,152	124.3%
840	VIRCO MFG.	2531	2,390	32%	80%	22%	$20,203	5.4%
989	VISHAY INTERTECHNOLOGY	3676	17,400	18%	16%	13%	$8,714	0.3%
481	VITAL SIGNS	3841	1,037	72%	27%	30%	$37,885	17.4%
1,617	VITESSE SEMICONDUCTOR	3674	443	84%	18%	32%	$72,659	-159.3%
1,271	VLSI TECHNOLOGY	3674	2,500	69%	44%	31%	$79,191	-15.9%
1,181	VWR SCIENTIFIC PRODUCTS	5049	2,217	20%	69%	15%	$77,518	-8.4%

Appendix C–Information Productivity Listing

IP Rank	Company	SIC	EMPLOYEES	Information Management/ Cost of Goods	Information Management/ Net Assets	Information Management/ Revenue	Information Management/ Employee	Information Productivity
775	WABASH NATIONAL	3537	4,320	3%	9%	2%	$4,724	7.2%
1,513	WAHLCO ENVIRONMENTAL SYSTEMS	3822	425	36%	-1211%	30%	$38,089	-60.2%
1,313	WALBRO	3714	5,028	16%	49%	12%	$14,572	-19.5%
400	WALLACE COMPUTER SERVICES	276	4,610	29%	31%	18%	$36,101	21.6%
676	WAL-MART STORES	5311	825,000	21%	96%	16%	$22,934	10.2%
1,488	WANG LABORATORIES,INC	3571	9,300	36%	60%	24%	$32,710	-48.5%
1,332	WARNACO GROUP	2341	20,000	32%	36%	20%	$12,712	-21.1%
531	WARNER-LAMBERT	283	40,000	179%	150%	52%	$100,558	15.5%
299	WASHINGTON WATER POWER	4911	1,751	13%	9%	8%	$51,386	29.4%
1,459	WASTE MANAGEMENT	4953	58,900	18%	22%	11%	$16,007	-40.9%
1,126	WATERS	5049	2,640	145%	297%	50%	$93,098	-5.9%
820	WATKINS-JOHNSON	3674	1,520	54%	60%	33%	$63,205	5.9%
771	WATSCO	5075	2,000	22%	57%	17%	$50,281	7.3%
1,149	WATTS INDUSTRIES	3491	3,900	37%	43%	23%	$36,312	-6.7%
69	WAUSAU-MOSINEE PAPER	262	1,890	7%	11%	6%	$16,814	93.6%
660	WAXMAN INDUSTRIES	507	770	43%	-119%	28%	$46,362	10.6%
1,534	WEIRTON STEEL	3316	4,873	3%	21%	3%	$6,908	-70.5%
893	WELLMAN	2824	3,100	10%	14%	8%	$26,446	3.5%
687	WENDY'S INTERNATIONAL	5812	47,000	56%	47%	28%	$11,282	9.9%
1,667	WESCO FINANCIAL	5051	250	21%	1%	9%	$41,845	-657.6%
511	WEST	3069	4,800	25%	27%	16%	$14,146	16.3%
802	WEST MARINE	5551	3,095	32%	62%	22%	$30,994	6.5%
1,433	WESTELL TECHNOLOGIES	3661	795	94%	71%	57%	$60,886	-36.0%
1,571	WESTERN GAS RESOURCES	1311	920	2%	6%	2%	$31,631	-95.1%
77	WESTINGHOUSE AIR BRAKE	3743	3,400	15%	-56%	10%	$27,536	86.2%
406	WESTPOINT STEVENS	2392	16,100	17%	-44%	12%	$12,276	21.2%
1,132	WESTVACO	262	13,370	11%	11%	8%	$17,282	-6.2%
24	WESTWOOD ONE	4832	635	4%	5%	3%	$9,261	178.2%
447	WEYERHAEUSER	0811	35,800	10%	19%	8%	$22,996	19.3%
1,018	WHIRLPOOL	3631	61,000	26%	73%	19%	$31,508	-1.1%
824	WHITMAN	2086	6,391	38%	71%	23%	$43,367	5.8%
1,573	WHITTAKER	3812	500	73%	93%	40%	$72,605	-98.2%
1,084	WHOLE FOODS MARKET	5411	11,000	22%	79%	15%	$13,512	-3.4%
1,607	WHX	331	4,581	7%	10%	6%	$12,632	-136.0%
126	WILLAMETTE INDUSTRIES	267	13,800	9%	12%	6%	$16,690	57.7%
119	WILLIAMS	492	15,000	36%	18%	17%	$51,290	60.2%
830	WILLIAMS-SONOMA	5719	12,300	57%	174%	34%	$25,639	5.7%
1,293	WINDMERE-DURABLE HOLDINGS	3634	12,260	27%	24%	20%	$3,660	-17.9%
869	WINN-DIXIE STORES	5411	136,000	30%	213%	22%	$21,710	4.5%
1,515	WINNEBAGO INDUSTRIES	3711	2,830	12%	44%	10%	$16,319	-60.5%
1,611	WINSTAR COMMUNICATIONS	4813	2,100	158%	841%	135%	$70,840	-142.3%
1,645	WIRELESS ONE	4841	503	174%	48%	109%	$35,236	-276.3%
49	WISCONSIN CENTRAL TRANSPORTATION	4731	2,345	18%	11%	11%	$15,478	116.2%
1,442	WISER OIL	1311	143	24%	9%	13%	$65,744	-37.9%
1,395	WITCO	2843	5,970	18%	37%	13%	$41,120	-30.2%
1,284	WLR FOODS	2015	8,500	11%	58%	10%	$10,941	-17.0%
613	WMS INDUSTRIES	3999	1,047	32%	28%	22%	$24,808	12.2%
1,144	WOLOHAN LUMBER	5211	1,482	25%	76%	19%	$53,659	-6.6%
130	WOLVERINE TUBE	3366	3,467	4%	11%	3%	$6,820	57.0%
679	WOLVERINE WORLD WIDE	3143	6,696	30%	46%	21%	$17,350	10.2%
214	WORLD	4522	801	16%	-108%	13%	$42,663	39.7%
997	WORLD COLOR PRESS	2721	15,000	13%	34%	10%	$13,090	0.0%
1,584	WORLDCOM	4813	20,300	37%	11%	20%	$74,246	-105.0%
640	WORLDTEX	2241	1,227	10%	20%	8%	$14,110	11.1%
646	WORTHINGTON FOODS	2034	569	51%	62%	29%	$56,317	11.0%
108	WORTHINGTON INDUSTRIES	344	12,000	8%	16%	6%	$10,050	66.4%
880	WTD INDUSTRIES	2436	1,150	5%	65%	4%	$9,554	3.9%
304	WYMAN-GORDON	3724	3,650	10%	33%	8%	$13,441	28.7%
714	XICOR	3674	738	55%	70%	31%	$51,833	9.1%
1,156	YORK INTERNATIONAL	3585	20,270	18%	64%	14%	$23,240	-7.1%
954	ZALE	5944	10,000	79%	97%	40%	$47,310	1.4%
1,577	ZAPATA	2077	1,100	10%	6%	8%	$7,668	-100.4%
123	ZEBRA TECHNOLOGIES	3577	745	48%	28%	23%	$59,938	58.6%
35	ZEIGLER COAL HOLDING	1222	2,022	3%	16%	3%	$8,531	133.3%
682	ZEMEX	3399	574	16%	14%	12%	$19,735	10.1%
1,579	ZENITH ELECTRONICS	3651	11,400	17%	157%	16%	$13,145	-101.4%

INFORMATION PRODUCTIVITY

IP Rank	Company	SIC	EMPLOYEES	Information Management/ Cost of Goods	Information Management/ Net Assets	Information Management/ Revenue	Information Management/ Employee	Information Productivity
1,467	ZILA	5122	138	135%	103%	63%	$180,842	-42.1%
1,303	ZOLTEK	3624	1,710	21%	10%	14%	$7,101	-19.0%

Appendix D

List of High Productivity Firms

Industry	Company	Information Productivity
Adhesive and sealants	MORTON INTERNATIONAL	31.5%
Adhesive and sealants	MINNESOTA MINING & MANUFACTURING	31.0%
Air and gas compressors	GARDNER DENVER MACHINERY	38.9%
Air transportation, nonscheduled	WORLD	39.7%
Air transportation, scheduled	MESABA HOLDINGS	188.4%
Air transportation, scheduled	ASA HOLDINGS	79.4%
Air transportation, scheduled	SKYWEST	24.3%
Air transportation, scheduled	NORTHWEST AIRLINES	24.2%
Air-conditionning and warm air heating equipment	SPECIALTY EQUIPMENT	53.3%
Aircraft engines and engine parts	HEICO	44.4%
Aircraft engines and engine parts	CURTISS-WRIGHT	34.5%
Aircraft engines and engine parts	WYMAN-GORDON	28.7%
Aircraft parts and auxiliary equipment	COLTEC INDUSTRIES INC	74.8%
Aircraft parts and auxiliary equipment	ALLIEDSIGNAL	41.4%
Aircraft parts and auxiliary equipment	SUNDSTRAND	27.6%
Alkalies and chlorine	GEORGIA GULF	244.2%
Aluminium sheet, plate and foil	FRIEDMAN INDUSTRIES	42.8%
Arrangement of transportation of freight and cargo	WISCONSIN CENTRAL TRANSPORTATION	116.2%
Asphalt paving mixtures and blocks	ELCOR	31.2%
Automotive trimmings, apparel findings	COLLINS & AIKMAN	125.9%
Automotive trimmings, apparel findings	LEAR	32.2%
Ball and roller bearings	NN BALL & ROLLER	168.8%
Ball and roller bearings	TIMKEN	22.2%
Beverages	COCA-COLA	42.0%
Biological products	BIOGEN	23.1%
Bituminous coal and lignite surface mining	PITTSTON MINERALS GROUP	34.5%
Bituminous coal underground mining	ZEIGLER COAL HOLDING	133.3%
Books : publishing or publishing and printing	MCGRAW-HILL	22.8%
Broadwoven fabric mills, manmade fiber	HALLWOOD GROUP	24.6%
Cable and other pay television services	BET HOLDINGS	92.8%
Cable and other pay television services	TCA CABLE TV	31.6%
Cable and other pay television services	UNITED VIDEO SATELLITE GROUP	21.6%
Candy and other confectionery products	M & F WORLDWIDE	360.5%
Canned specialities	CAMPBELL SOUP	29.3%
Carbon and graphite products	CARBIDE/GRAPHITE GROUP	90.4%
Carbon and graphite products	UCAR INTERNATIONAL	25.9%
Carbon black	CABOT	32.2%
Cement, hydraulic	GIANT CEMENT HOLDING	109.3%
Cement, hydraulic	PUERTO RICAN CEMENT	37.5%
Ceramic wall and floor tile	ARMSTRONG WORLD INDUSTRIES	27.3%
Chemicals and allied products	ARCO CHEMICAL	38.6%
Chemicals and chemical preparations	OLIN	33.0%
Chemicals and chemical preparations	SCHERER, (R.P.)	26.5%
Chemicals and chemical preparations	NALCO CHEMICAL	24.2%
Chewing and smoking tobacco and snuffv	UST	113.8%
Cigarettes	PHILIP MORRIS	31.2%
Citrus fruits	CONSOLIDATED-TOMOKA LAND	117.1%
Citrus fruits	ALICO	32.4%
Cold-rolled steel sheet, strip	ARMCO	68.7%
Commercial printing, lithographic	CONSOLIDATED GRAPHICS	26.4%
Commercial printing, not elsewhere classified	VALASSIS COMMUNICATIONS	106.5%
Commercial, industrial and lighting fixtures	JUNO LIGHTING	28.7%
Commercial, industrial and lighting fixtures	HOLOPHANE	25.4%
Communications equipment	CABLE DESIGN TECHNOLOGIES	23.5%
Communications services	AMERITECH	43.2%
Computer and computer software stores	COMPUSA	35.9%
Computer peripheral equipment	ZEBRA TECHNOLOGIES	58.6%
Computer peripheral equipment	ADAPTEC INC	36.3%
Computer storage devices	HMT TECHNOLOGY	293.9%
Computer storage devices	AMPEX	85.1%
Computer storage devices	APPLIED MAGNETICS	61.1%
Computer storage devices	EMC	59.9%
Computer storage devices	SEAGATE TECHNOLOGY	29.0%
Computer storage devices	READ-RITE	26.2%
Computer storage devices	HUTCHINSON TECHNOLOGY	22.0%
Computer storage devices	STORAGE COMPUTER	21.8%

Appendix D–List of High Productivity Firms

Industry	Company	Information Productivity
Concrete, gypsum and plaster products	LONE STAR INDUSTRIES	87.0%
Construction machinery and equipment	JLG INDUSTRIES	51.5%
Construction machinery and equipment	CATERPILLAR	45.6%
Construction, mining and materials machinery	DOVER	31.7%
Converted paper and paperboard products	WILLAMETTE INDUSTRIES	57.7%
Converted paper and paperboard products	LONGVIEW FIBRE	31.4%
Converted paper and paperboard products	BEMIS	30.9%
Copper foundries	WOLVERINE TUBE	57.0%
Copper ores	PHELPS DODGE	223.0%
Copper ores	FREEPORT-MC MORAN COPPER & GOLD	104.2%
Crude petroleum and natural gas	UNIMAR	2811.2%
Crude petroleum and natural gas	UNION PACIFIC RESOURCES GROUP	399.3%
Crude petroleum and natural gas	UNION TEXAS PETROLEUM HOLDINGS	319.7%
Crude petroleum and natural gas	VASTAR RESOURCES	283.1%
Crude petroleum and natural gas	TRANSTEXAS GAS	256.3%
Crude petroleum and natural gas	NEWFIELD EXPLORATION	238.9%
Crude petroleum and natural gas	MAYNARD OIL	213.2%
Crude petroleum and natural gas	SWIFT ENERGY	198.4%
Crude petroleum and natural gas	VINTAGE PETROLEUM	124.3%
Crude petroleum and natural gas	POGO PRODUCING	106.3%
Crude petroleum and natural gas	CHEVRON	83.2%
Crude petroleum and natural gas	SUN ENERGY PARTNERS,	70.8%
Crude petroleum and natural gas	UNIT	56.3%
Crude petroleum and natural gas	TEXACO INC .	54.3%
Crude petroleum and natural gas	NOBLE AFFILIATES	46.0%
Crude petroleum and natural gas	OCEAN ENERGY	40.4%
Crude petroleum and natural gas	EXXON	37.3%
Crude petroleum and natural gas	MOBIL	31.8%
Crude petroleum and natural gas	CROSS TIMBERS OIL	24.9%
Crushed and broken stone, including riprap	MARTIN MARIETTA MATERIALS	82.2%
Crushed and broken stone	VULCAN MATERIALS	42.5%
Current-carrying wiring devices	HUBBELL	38.9%
Cyclic organic crudes and intermediates and dyes	UNION CARBIDE	111.0%
Deep sea transportation of passengers	CARNIVAL	132.4%
Drawing and insulating of nonferrous wire	AMPHENOL	27.5%
Drawing and insulating of nonferrous wire	CARLISLE	25.8%
Drilling oil and gas wells	ENSCO INTERNATIONAL	612.1%
Drilling oil and gas wells	ORYX ENERGY	265.9%
Drilling oil and gas wells	TRANSOCEAN OFFSHORE	154.8%
Drilling oil and gas wells	PATTERSON ENERGY	113.9%
Drilling oil and gas wells	ATWOOD OCEANICS	91.5%
Drilling oil and gas wells	NABORS INDUSTRIES	75.8%
Drilling oil and gas wells	SCHLUMBERGER LIMITED	56.5%
Drilling oil and gas wells	NOBLE DRILLING	55.3%
Drugs	MYLAN LABORATORIES	73.8%
Drugs	MERCK &	57.3%
Drugs	SCHERING-PLOUGH	33.5%
Drugs	PFIZER	24.7%
Eating places	OUTBACK STEAKHOUSE	128.2%
Eating places	LUBY'S CAFETERIAS	111.0%
Eating places	BENIHANA	83.5%
Eating places	ELXSI	72.8%
Eating places	RYAN'S FAMILY STEAK HOUSES	62.1%
Eating places	SONIC	58.2%
Eating places	FURR'S/BISHOP'S	41.2%
Eating places	APPLEBEE'S INTERNATIONAL	30.0%
Eating places	MCDONALD'S	29.7%
Eating places	IHOP	27.7%
Eating places	APPLE SOUTH	26.0%
Eating places	SHONEY'S	22.5%
Eating places	CONSOLIDATED PRODUCTS	22.3%
Electric and other services combined	SIG	79.1%
Electric and other services combined	NORTHERN STATES POWER	64.4%
Electric and other services combined	WPS RESOURCES	34.8%
Electric housewares and fans	GILLETTE	25.4%
Electric services	BLACK HILLS	132.9%

Industry	Company	Information Productivity
Electric services	AES	114.0%
Electric services	IPALCO ENTERPRISES	83.6%
Electric services	PACIFI	77.9%
Electric services	THERMO ECOTEK	72.9%
Electric services	PUBLIC SERVICE ENTERPRISE	68.6%
Electric services	CMS ENERGY	67.0%
Electric services	SOUTHERN	59.4%
Electric services	ENOVA	58.5%
Electric services	PUBLIC SERVICE OF NEW MEXICO	41.8%
Electric services	EMPIRE DISTRICT ELECTRIC	33.4%
Electric services	ROCHESTER GAS AND ELECTRIC	31.6%
Electric services	MONTANA POWER	31.5%
Electric services	WASHINGTON WATER POWER	29.4%
Electric services	BALTIMORE GAS AND ELECTRIC	27.7%
Electric services	NIPSCO INDUSTRIES	26.5%
Electric services	DPL	26.5%
Electrical appliances, television and radio	RENTERS CHOICE	35.5%
Electrical goods wholesale	ENCORE WIRE	42.7%
Electrical industrial apparatus	EMERSON ELECTRIC	29.9%
Electrical work	DYCOM INDUSTRIES	41.3%
Electronic capacitors	AVX	63.1%
Electronic capacitors	KEMET	53.3%
Electronic coils, transformers and other inductors	TECHNITROL	27.6%
Electronic components and accessories	INTEL	107.3%
Electronic components and accessories	BELDEN	57.3%
Electronic components and accessories	PHOTRONICS	43.8%
Electronic components and accessories	TEXAS INSTRUMENTS	28.0%
Electronic components and accessories	DII GROUP	27.7%
Electronic components and accessories	METHODE ELECTRONICS	26.2%
Electronic components	INNOVEX	152.1%
Electronic components	ALTRON	69.8%
Electronic computers	DELL COMPUTER	51.6%
Electronic connectors	AMP	23.7%
Electronic parts and equipment	OAK TECHNOLOGY	40.8%
Fabricated metal products	RAYTECH	47.6%
Fabricated metal products	TITAN INTERNATIONAL	24.2%
Fabricated pipe and pipe fittings	SYNALLOY	60.9%
Fabricated plate work (boiler shops)	CHART INDUSTRIES	50.1%
Fabricated plate work (boiler shops)	INSILCO	42.2%
Fabricated plate work (boiler shops)	MODINE MANUFACTURING	27.4%
Fabricated structural metal	ROHN INDUSTRIES	170.5%
Fabricated structural metal	ROBERTSON CECO	79.9%
Fabricated structural metal	ROANOKE ELECTRIC STEEL	61.0%
Fabricated structural metal	HARSCO	50.0%
Fabricated structural metal products	WORTHINGTON INDUSTRIES	66.4%
Family clothing stores	GAP	26.4%
Farm and garden machinery and equipment	ALLIED PRODUCTS	51.1%
Farm machinery and equipment	DEERE &	37.7%
Farm machinery and equipment	AGCO	33.2%
Farm machinery and equipment	CASE	28.2%
Fiber cans, tubes, drums	CARAUSTAR INDUSTRIES	49.2%
Flat glass	PPG INDUSTRIES	44.1%
Fluid power cylinders and actuators	PARKER HANNIFIN	30.8%
Fluid power pumps and motors	REGAL-BELOIT	41.4%
Fluid power pumps and motors	IDEX	34.3%
Fluid power pumps and motors	ROPER INDUSTRIES	28.3%
Folding paperboard boxes	SHOREWOOD PACKAGING	40.6%
Footwear, except rubber	NIKE	24.1%
Freight transportation on the great-lakes	OGLEBAY NORTON	50.1%
Gas and other services combined	NICOR	24.9%
Gas production and distribution	WILLIAMS	60.2%
General building contractors-residential buildings	CENTEX	411.0%
General building contractors-residential buildings	M.D.C. HOLDINGS	22.7%
General contractors- residential buildings	D.R. HORTON	26.0%
General contractors-single-family houses	NEWHALL LAND & FARMING	307.1%
General contractors-single-family houses	TOLL BROTHERS	48.4%

Appendix D–List of High Productivity Firms

Industry	Company	Information Productivity
General industrial machinery and equipment	CLARCOR	24.4%
Glass containers	OWENS-ILLINOIS	32.5%
Glass products, made of purchased glass	NEWELL	31.3%
Gray and ductile iron foundries	INTERMET	90.8%
Guided missile and space vehicle propulsion units	ALLIANT TECHSYSTEMS	30.2%
Guided missile and space vehicle propulsion units	CORDANT TECHNOLOGIES	24.6%
Hand and edge tools	DANAHER	33.5%
Hardware wholesale	ACE HARDWARE	42.9%
Heavy construction	JACOBS ENGINEERING GROUP	23.2%
Industrial and commercial fans and blowers	MET-PRO	52.9%
Industrial gases	AIR PRODUCTS AND CHEMICALS	22.9%
Industrial inorganic chemicals	CHEMFIRST	31.8%
Industrial inorganic chemicals	HERCULES	76.8%
Industrial inorganic chemicals	GREAT LAKES CHEMICAL	42.4%
Industrial inorganic chemicals	CYTEC INDUSTRIES	40.4%
Industrial inorganic chemicals	TETRA TECHNOLOGIES	28.4%
Industrial inorganic chemicals	CALGON CARBON	23.5%
Industrial instruments for measurement, display	RADISYS	46.0%
Industrial instruments for measurement, display	LYDALL	38.9%
Industrial organic chemicals	OM GROUP	44.7%
Industrial organic chemicals	LUBRIZOL	34.2%
Industrial organic chemicals	ETHYL	32.3%
Industrial trucks, tractors, trailers and stackers	CASCADE	23.3%
Inorganic pigments	NL INDUSTRIES	28.8%
Internal combustion engines	BRIGGS & STRATTON	45.4%
Iron ores	CLEVELAND-CLIFFS INC	212.2%
Liquefied petroleum gas dealers	FERRELLGAS PARTNERS,	117.9%
Lumber, plywood, millwork, and wood panels	PATRICK INDUSTRIES	32.6%
Malt beverages	ANHEUSER-BUSCH	38.9%
Manmade organic fibers	ALBEMARLE	44.9%
Mattresses, foundations and convertible beds	LEGGETT & PLATT	31.6%
Meat packing plants	IBP	69.4%
Medical, dental, and hospital equipment	SYBRON INTERNATIONAL	25.4%
Medical, dental, and hospital equipment	BAXTER INTERNATIONAL	21.8%
Men's and boys' suits, coats and overcoats	NAUTICA ENTERPRISES	30.3%
Men's footwear, except athletic	WELLCO ENTERPRISES	33.4%
Metal doors, sash, frames, molding and trim	DREW INDUSTRIES	47.0%
Millwork, veneer, plywood and structural wood	PLUM CREEK TIMBER	218.6%
Miscellaneous structural metal work	TEXAS INDUSTRIES	31.3%
Molded, extruded and mechanical rubber goods	COOPER TIRE & RUBBER	53.6%
Motor vehicle parts and accessories	BREED TECHNOLOGIES	54.8%
Motor vehicle parts and accessories	ILLINOIS TOOL WORKS	50.8%
Motor vehicle parts and accessories	MASCOTECH	47.3%
Motor vehicle parts and accessories	SIMPSON INDUSTRIES	44.0%
Motor vehicle parts and accessories	TOWER AUTOMOTIVE	41.1%
Motor vehicle parts and accessories	PARK-OHIO HOLDINGS	29.5%
Motor vehicle parts and accessories	DANA	29.3%
Motor vehicle parts and accessories	ITT INDUSTRIES	25.3%
Motor vehicle supplies and new parts wholesale	TBC	51.5%
Motor vehicle supplies and new parts wholesale	PACCAR	37.0%
Motor vehicles and motor vehicle equipment	SMITH (A.O.)	64.6%
Motor vehicles and motor vehicle equipment	FEDERAL SIGNAL	23.6%
Motor vehicles and passenger car bodies	CHRYSLER	40.3%
Motor vehicles and passenger car bodies	GENERAL MOTORS	32.5%
Motor vehicles and passenger car bodies	FORD MOTOR	25.8%
Motorcycles, bicycles and parts	HARLEY-DAVIDSON	53.9%
Motors and generators	AMETEK	52.5%
Motors and generators	FRANKLIN ELECTRIC	27.4%
Motors and generators	BALDOR ELECTRIC	26.5%
Natural gas distribution	PUBLIC SERVICE OF NORTH CAROLINA	182.6%
Natural gas distribution	CONNECTICUT ENERGY	141.1%
Natural gas distribution	AGL RESOURCES	55.8%
Natural gas distribution	LACLEDE GAS	54.0%
Natural gas distribution	COLONIAL GAS	25.1%
Natural gas distribution	MCN ENERGY GROUP	22.9%
Natural gas distribution	EASTERN ENTERPRISES	21.7%

Industry	Company	Information Productivity
Natural gas liquids	ENRON OIL & GAS	118.6%
Natural gas transmission	COASTAL	37.8%
Natural gas transmission and distribution	AQUILA GAS PIPELINE	56.4%
Natural gas transmission and distribution	SONAT	41.1%
Newspapers publishing or publishing and printing	GANNETT	79.2%
Newspapers publishing or publishing and printing	TRIBUNE	47.1%
Newspapers publishing or publishing and printing	TIMES MIRROR	34.5%
Newspapers publishing or publishing and printing	LEE ENTERPRISES	34.1%
Newspapers publishing or publishing and printing	PULITZER PUBLISHING	22.5%
Nondurable goods, not elsewhere classified	DEPARTMENT 56	53.8%
Nonferrous foundries (castings)	PRECISION CASTPARTS	45.4%
Office and store fixtures, parttions, shelving	INTERLAKE	44.9%
Office machines	PITNEY BOWES	26.7%
Office machines	GRADCO SYSTEMS	26.7%
Oil and gas field exploration services	ST. MARY LAND & EXPLORATION	97.3%
Oil and gas field exploration services	COMSTOCK RESOURCES	56.6%
Oil and gas field exploration services	ROWAN	53.2%
Oil and gas field services, not elsewhere classified	LONE STAR TECHNOLOGIES	63.8%
Oil and gas field services, not elsewhere classified	PRIDE INTERNATIONAL	42.1%
Oil and gas field services, not elsewhere classified	KEY ENERGY GROUP	25.5%
Oil and gas fields services	GLOBAL MARINE	697.7%
Operative builders	LENNAR	34.5%
Ophtalmic goods	STAAR SURGICAL	22.6%
Orthopedic, prosthetic and surgical	THERMO CARDIOSYSTEMS	32.5%
Orthopedic, prosthetic and surgical	RESPIRONICS	23.9%
Overhead traveling cranes, hoists and monorail	MANITOWOC	26.9%
Packaging paper and plastics film	CONSOLIDATED PAPERS	165.7%
Packaging paper and plastics film	ARTRA GROUP	30.6%
Paper mills	GLATFELTER (P.H.)	102.3%
Paper mills	WAUSAU-MOSINEE PAPER	93.6%
Paper mills	BOWATER	35.7%
Paperboard mills	JEFFERSON SMURFIT	63.2%
Perfumes, cosmetics and other toilet preparations	INTERNATIONAL FLAVORS & FRAGRANCES	25.9%
Petroleum and petroleum products wholesalers	ADAMS RESOURCES & ENERGY	112.5%
Petroleum and petroleum products wholesalers	PLAINS RESOURCES	31.4%
Petroleum refining	TESORO PETROLEUM	147.5%
Petroleum refining	PHILLIPS PETROLEUM	105.2%
Petroleum refining	LYONDELL PETROCHEMICAL	91.5%
Petroleum refining	AMOCO	68.4%
Petroleum refining	ATLANTIC RICHFIELD	67.6%
Petroleum refining	DU PONT (E.I.) DE NEMOURS AND	57.5%
Petroleum refining	HOLLY	48.1%
Petroleum refining	MAPCO	47.6%
Petroleum refining	FINA	42.4%
Pharmaceutical preparations	AMGEN	50.2%
Pharmaceutical preparations	ABBOTT LABORATORIES	45.8%
Pharmaceutical preparations	BIOMATRIX	39.0%
Pharmaceutical preparations	BRISTOL-MYERS SQUIBB	30.0%
Pickled fruits and vegetables, vegetable sauces	LANCASTER COLONY	36.7%
Plastic materials, synthetic resins	BORDEN CHEMICALS & PLASTICS	137.0%
Plastic materials, synthetic resins	GRACE, (W.R.) &	120.8%
Plastic materials, synthetic resins	MCWHORTER TECHNOLOGIES	37.9%
Plastic materials, synthetic resins	ROHM & HAAS	25.1%
Plastic products	TREDEGAR INDUSTRIES	47.4%
Plastic products	DOW CHEMICAL	39.0%
Plastics foam products	SEALED AIR	30.1%
Prefabricated metal buildings and components	NCI BUILDING SYSTEMS	32.1%
Pressed and blown glass and glassware	LIBBEY	71.9%
Pressed and blown glass and glassware	SLI	32.3%
Primary production of aluminium	ALUMINUM OF AMERICA	34.2%
Primary smelting and refining of copper	SOUTHERN PERU COPPER	99.1%
Printed circuit boards	SANMINA	133.3%
Printed circuit boards	SCI SYSTEMS	88.0%
Printed circuit boards	JABIL CIRCUIT	66.8%
Printed circuit boards	PARK ELECTROCHEMICAL	47.3%
Printed circuit boards	ATMEL	32.6%

Appendix D—List of High Productivity Firms

Industry	Company	Information Productivity
Printed circuit boards	MERIX	23.0%
Pulp mills	BUCKEYE TECHNOLOGIES INC	105.4%
Radio and television broadcasting equipment	PANAMSAT	108.3%
Radio broadcasting stations	WESTWOOD ONE	178.2%
Radio broadcasting stations	CLEAR CHANNEL COMMUNICATIONS	52.2%
Railroad equipment	WESTINGHOUSE AIR BRAKE	86.2%
Railroad equipment	TRINITY INDUSTRIES	38.5%
Railroads, line-haul operating	CSX	32.4%
Railroads, line-haul operating	NORFOLK SOUTHERN	25.9%
Ready-mixed concrete	FLORIDA ROCK INDUSTRIES	22.4%
Reconstituted wood products	ABT BUILDING PRODUCTS	25.6%
Refined petroleum pipelines	BUCKEYE PARTNERS,	62.9%
Refuse systems	NEWPARK RESOURCES	355.1%
Rolling, drawing and extruding of copper	CHASE INDUSTRIES	124.4%
Rolling, drawing and extruding of copper	MUELLER INDUSTRIES	51.7%
Scrap and waste materials wholesale	SCHNITZER STEEL INDUSTRIES	35.1%
Search, detection, navigation, guidance, aeronautical	RAYTHEON	24.5%
Semiconductors and related devices	MICRON TECHNOLOGY	95.0%
Semiconductors and related devices	ALTERA	68.0%
Semiconductors and related devices	LEVEL ONE COMMUNICATIONS	49.0%
Semiconductors and related devices	APPLIED MATERIALS	42.5%
Semiconductors and related devices	ANALOG DEVICES	34.4%
Semiconductors and related devices	ELECTROGLAS	33.6%
Semiconductors and related devices	MEMC ELECTRONIC MATERIALS	30.6%
Semiconductors and related devices	MICROSEMI	27.6%
Semiconductors and related devices	SILICONIX	27.0%
Semiconductors and related devices	BURR-BROWN	25.6%
Semiconductors and related devices	MICREL	25.5%
Service industry machinery	IONICS	26.5%
Ship building and repairing	GENERAL DYNAMICS	79.1%
Ship building and repairing	AVONDALE INDUSTRIES	31.3%
Shoe stores	JUST FOR FEET	128.0%
Special dies and tools, dis sets, jigs and fixtures	REUTER MANUFACTURING	147.5%
Speed changers, industrial high-speed drives	GLEASON	32.6%
Steel wiredrawing and steel nails and spikes	KEYSTONE CONSOLIDATED INDUSTRIES	27.4%
Steel wiredrawing and steel nails and spikes	NATIONAL-STANDARD	22.6%
Steel works, blast furnaces	AK STEEL HOLDING	103.8%
Steel works, blast furnaces	QUANEX	59.4%
Steel works, blast furnaces	ALLEGHENY TELEDYNE	47.0%
Steel works, blast furnaces	SHILOH INDUSTRIES	43.3%
Steel works, blast furnaces	NATIONAL STEEL	40.1%
Steel works, blast furnaces	CARPENTER TECHNOLOGY	25.8%
Steel works, blast furnaces, rolling and finishing	NUCOR	117.8%
Steel works, blast furnaces, rolling and finishing	UNITED CAPITAL	26.7%
Storage batteries	C&D TECHNOLOGIES	22.8%
Surgical and medical instruments and apparatus	MERIDIAN DIAGNOSTICS	30.3%
Surgical and medical instruments and apparatus	ARROW INTERNATIONAL	29.8%
Surgical, medical and dental instruments	MEDTRONIC	25.0%
Switchgear and switchboard apparatus	LITTELFUSE	23.2%
Telephone and telegraph apparatus	ADTRAN	48.1%
Telephone communications	NORTH PITTSBURG SYSTEMS	468.7%
Telephone communications	PLANTRONICS	51.2%
Telephone communications	BELL ATLANTIC	26.1%
Television broadcasting	UNITED TELEVISION	78.3%
Television broadcasting	BHC COMMUNICATIONS	46.2%
Television broadcasting	CHRIS-CRAFT INDUSTRIES	28.4%
Tobacco products	SWISHER INTERNATIONAL GROUP	37.1%
Tobacco stemming and redrying	SCHWEITZER-MAUDUIT INTERNATIONAL	68.5%
Transportation equipment	POLARIS INDUSTRIES	31.0%
Truck and bus bodies	SUPREME INDUSTRIES	24.6%
Unsupported plastics film and sheet	EASTMAN CHEMICAL	56.4%
Unsupported plastics film and sheet	SPARTECH	48.3%
Unsupported plastics film and sheet	GEN	36.2%
Water supply	AQUARION	25.5%
Water transportation services	SEACOR SMIT	179.8%
Water, sewer, pipeline and communications	MASTEC	26.1%

Industry	Company	Information Productivity
Women's accessory and specialty stores	INTIMATE BRANDS	34.7%
Wood household furniture, except upholstered	BUSH INDUSTRIES	22.7%
Wood household furniture, except upholstered	CHROMCRAFT REVINGTON	22.5%
Yarn texturizing, throwing, twisting	UNIFI	140.3%

Appendix E

Information Productivity of Non-Industrial firms

HOW DO INDUSTRIAL AND NON-INDUSTRIAL FIRMS COMPARE?

Non-industrial firms (SIC 600 to SIC 990) account for 26% of the employment of listed U.S. corporations. An analysis of their Information Productivity will be the subject of a follow-on study. However, preliminary findings show that many of the characteristics that have been identified in this report will also apply to these information-intensive organizations.

The Information Productivity of non-industrial firms has been consistently higher than the Information Productivity of industrial firms:[109]

Much, if not most, of the explanation for the differences in Information Productivity is almost certainly attributable to the level and trend of interest costs. The elaborate calculations for estimating the tax- and interest-adjusted constant Information Productivity indicators for the Non-Industrial firms will have to wait until the next study is complete.

109 Based on a sample of 577 corporations from the November 1998 Worldscope Data base.

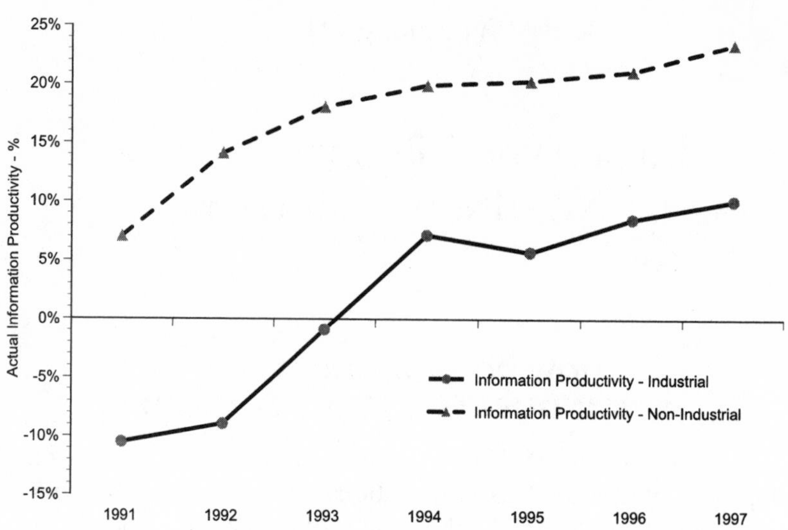

Figure E-1 - Non-industrial Firms Show Higher Information Productivity

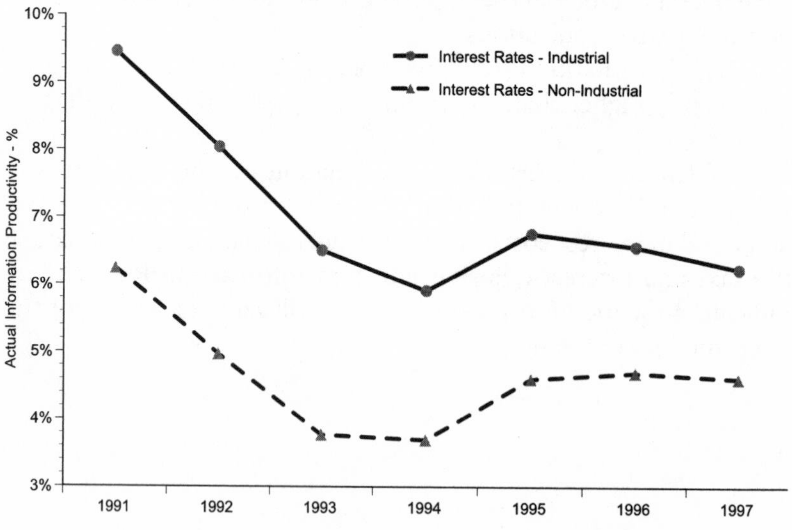

Figure E-2 - Non-Industrial Firms Also Show Declining Interest Costs

It is likely that the enormous leverage of interest rates on the profitability of banking and financial institutions will result in findings that are comparable to what we found with regard to industrial firms. It is improbable that after adjustment for interest and tax rates the 1991-1997 Information Productivity levels would show much improvement.